Artificial Intelligence

Ethical, social, and security impacts for the present and the future

Second edition

Artificial Intelligence

Ethical, social, and security impacts for the present and the future

Second edition

DR JULIE E. MEHAN

it gp ™

IT Governance Publishing

IT Governance Publishing Ltd
Unit 3, Clive Court
Bartholomew's Walk
Cambridgeshire Business Park
Ely, Cambridgeshire
CB7 4EA
United Kingdom
www.itgovernancepublishing.co.uk

First published in the United Kingdom in 2022 by IT Governance Publishing.

ISBN 978-1-78778-370-6

Second edition published in the United Kingdom in 2024 by IT Governance Publishing.

ISBN 978-1-78778-512-0

FOREWORD

"Throughout history, new technologies have disrupted society in different ways – some positively and some negatively – from steam-powered engines and electricity, to the Internet, and now again with artificial intelligence (AI); generative AI in particular in this instance. The creation of art, journalism, education, and the very truth itself have all been tested by the use of ChatGPT and other generative AIs."

Markkula Center for Applied Ethics

In the interests of full disclosure, I am a Professor of *Digital Ethics* at the University of Maryland and not a researcher or developer of Artificial Intelligence (AI). In addition to digital ethics, I've also taught courses in *Cyberterrorism, Information Technology,* and *Information Systems Management.* Although I possess no formal training in the mathematical and statistical underpinnings of AI, my longstanding engagement with digital ethics, and more recently the ethics of AI and its associated technologies, has given me a front-row seat to many of the efforts to assess and define the potential impact of AI on individuals, our society, and our ethical foundation.

Over the past few years, the topic of AI, or essentially algorithmic[1] systems, has played a greater role in my Digital Ethics classes. AI, I began to sense, is much more than just a simple tool powering our smartphones or allowing us to ask Alexa about the latest movie schedules. AI is a technology that is, in very subtle but unmistakable ways, exerting an ever-increasing influence over our lives – and in somewhat unpredictable ways. And the more we use it, the more AI is altering our lives and our environment.

And it is not just that humans are spending more and more time staring at a smartphone screen, their habits and routines are also being affected by the services offered by AI-power applications and tools. AI is changing the way our brains work, how we relate to other individuals, how we get and understand our news, how well we retain information or not, and even how we define what it is to be "human."

For a long time, artificial intelligence (AI) seemed like a problem that we would have to tackle tomorrow – until it wasn't! Unless you've had your head in the sand, you've likely been hearing a lot about artificial intelligence. It is a big deal right now. In late 2022, OpenAI released a generative AI[2] called ChatGPT and the AI playing field was

---

[1] An algorithm is a set of instructions for how a computing system should accomplish a particular task.

[2] Generative AI, also referred to as GenAI, allows users to input a variety of prompts to generate new content, such as text, images, videos, sounds, code, 3D designs, and other media. It 'learns' and is trained on documents and artifacts that already exist online. Generative AI evolves as it continues to train on more data. It operates on AI models and algorithms that are trained on large unlabeled data sets, which require complex math and lots of computing power to create. These data sets train the AI to predict outcomes in the same ways humans might act or create on their own.

irreversibly changed. Initially, most of the discussion about this new technology centered around how students would be using ChatGPT to write their homework assignments (which it does quite well, by the way), but more serious implications of the capabilities of generative AI have become apparent. And overall, we've realized that AI and the associated systems are evolving much more quickly than anticipated.

I wrote the first edition of this book on AI and ethics in 2022 – and already it requires updating to reflect the new developments in AI and ethics, particularly in terms of generative AI. While the first edition remains relevant, there is increased interest in AI ethics, and organizations operating in the AI space are starting to take AI ethics seriously, as indicated by the growing proportion of peer-reviewed AI ethics papers and proposed legislation.

Humans are insatiably curious. And they are now engaged in a quest to build an AI that can do everything a human can do – and throughout 2022 and 2023, new large-scale AI models were released almost every month. These capabilities, such as ChatGPT, Stable Diffusion, Whisper, and DALL-E 2[3] are able to perform an increasingly broad range of tasks, from text manipulation and analysis, to image generation, to unprecedentedly good speech recognition.

Along with the new changes in AI technologies, there is an increased interest in AI and digital ethics. Policy- and lawmakers are talking about AI and the need for better

---

[3] Stable Diffusion is an open-source machine learning model that can generate images from text, modify images based on text, or fill in details on low-resolution or low-detail images. Whisper is a multi-task model that is capable of speech recognition in many languages, voice translation, and language detection. DALL-E 2 is an AI system that creates realistic images and art from a description in natural language.

controls and ethical approaches more than ever before. Industry leaders who have effectively incorporated AI into their business models are seeing tangible cost and revenue benefits. And the general public is becoming more informed (and concerned) about AI and which elements they like or dislike.

It is certain that AI will continue to evolve and, as such, become more integrated into our daily lives. Given the increased deployment of powerful AI technologies and the potential for massive disruption, we should all think more critically about exactly HOW we want AI to be developed and deployed. We should also ask important questions about who is developing and deploying it to avoid AI being increasingly defined by the actions of a small set of private-sector actors, rather than a broader range of societal actors.

"AI and Ethics," published online by SpringerLink in November 2022, proposed this definition of AI ethics: *"AI ethics is a set of values, principles, and techniques that employ widely accepted standards of right and wrong to guide moral conduct in the development and use of AI technologies."*[4] This definition captures the true essence of the goals of this book on AI and ethics.

As AI continues to evolve and becomes increasingly integrated into our daily lives, it is crucial that we continue to examine its ethical and societal implications. For this reason, I've updated the book with a new chapter dedicated to looking at some of the most recent trends in AI and their ethical and societal implications, such as the ethics of using

---

[4] Rees, C. & Muller, B. (November 16, 2022). "All that glitters is not gold: trustworthy and ethical AI principles". Published online in the AI and Ethics Journal, SpringerLink. Available at *https://link.springer.com/article/10.1007/s43681-022-00232-x*.

generative AI, the treatment of increasingly sentient machines, the potential for bias, how AI could affect human decision-making capabilities, and how these new AI technologies may change the workforce. This chapter focuses on the moral imperative to address the challenges posed by the highly disruptive technologies evolving through AI.

So far, it seems as if 2024 and beyond will be the years when there is an international push for stronger legislation and more ethical approaches to the development and deployment of AI-based technologies. It is a good time to take a close look at some of these technologies and how they are/can be affecting our society and our application of digital ethics.

Unless stated otherwise, all figures are the author's own. Some figures have been created using the Creative Commons Organization:
https://creativecommons.org/.

x

ABOUT THE AUTHOR

Dr Julie E. Mehan is semi-retired, but still serves as a professor at the University of Maryland Global College (UMGC), where she teaches Digital Ethics, Cyberterrorism, and Information Systems in organizations. It was the students in her Digital Ethics and Computer Science classes that inspired this book.

Until her semi-retirement to Florida, she was the founder and president of JEMStone Strategies and a principal in a strategic consulting company in the state of Virginia.

Dr Mehan has been a career government service employee, a strategic consultant, and an entrepreneur – which either demonstrates her flexibility or her inability to hold on to a steady job! She has led business operations, as well as information technology governance and cybersecurity-related services, including designing and leading white-hat and black-hat penetration testing exercises, certification and accreditation, systems security engineering process improvement, and cybersecurity strategic planning and program management. During her professional years, she delivered cybersecurity and related privacy services to senior Department of Defense staff, Federal Government, and commercial clients working in Italy, Australia, Canada, Belgium, Germany, and the United States.

She has served on the President's Partnership for Critical Infrastructure Security, Task Force on Interdependency and Vulnerability Assessments. Dr Mehan was chair for the development of criteria for the International System Security Engineering Professional (ISSEP) certification, a voting board member for development of the International Systems

Security Professional Certification Scheme (ISSPCS), and Chair of the Systems Certification Working Group of the International Systems Security Engineers Association.

Dr Mehan graduated *summa cum laude* with a PhD from Capella University, with dual majors in Information Technology Management and Organizational Psychology. Her research was focused on success and failure criteria for Chief Information Security Officers (CISOs) in large government and commercial corporations, and development of a dynamic model of Chief Security Officer (CSO) leadership. She holds an MA with honors in International Relations Strategy and Law from Boston University, and a BS in History and Languages from the University of New York.

Dr Mehan was elected 2003 Woman of Distinction by the women of Greater Washington and has published numerous articles including *Framework for Reasoning About Security – A Comparison of the Concepts of Immunology and Security*; *System Dynamics, Criminal Behavior Theory and Computer-Enabled Crime*; *The Value of Information-Based Warfare to Affect Adversary Decision Cycles*; and *Information Operations in Kosovo: Mistakes, Missteps, and Missed Opportunities, released in Cyberwar 4.0*.

Dr Mehan is the author of several books published by ITGP: *Insider Threat* published in 2016; *Cyberwar, CyberTerror, CyberCrime, and CyberActivism*, 2nd Edition published in 2014; and *The Definitive Guide to the Certification & Accreditation Transformation* published in 2009. She is particularly proud of her past engagement as pro-bono President of Warrior to Cyber Warrior (W2CW), a non-profit company which was dedicated to providing cost-free cybersecurity career transition training to veterans and wounded warriors returning from the various military campaigns of recent years.

Dr Mehan is fluent in German, has conversational skills in French and Italian, and is working on learning Croatian and Irish.

She can be contacted at *je.mehan@outlook.com*.

ACKNOWLEDGEMENTS

This is not my first book, but I have to admit that the process of writing this book has been both more difficult and more gratifying than I could ever have imagined.

I have to begin by thanking my awesome partner, John. From reading the very first chapters to giving me advice on things to consider, he was as important to this book being written as I was. He was the one who had to put up with me and my frequent hour-long absences to the office – and he did so without strangling or shooting me and dropping me into the St. Johns River. Thank you so much.

Next, my sincere appreciation goes to John's oldest son, also John Deasy. As a computer scientist and physicist, he provided me with critical insight into the concepts around AI from the perspective of a scientist. Without some of these insights, this book would have been missing some key elements.

It was the students in my digital ethics course that inspired my interest in AI and its impact on the world we live in. Without them, the concepts for this book would never have evolved.

This section would definitely not be complete without acknowledging the superb support from the entire ITGP team. This includes Nicola Day, publications manager; Vicki Utting, managing executive; copy editor Susan Dobson; Jonathan Todd, senior copy editor at GRC International Group PLC; and Jo Ace, the book cover designer. Their assistance and patience during the process from start to publication has been exemplary.

Acknowledgements

I would also like to thank Chris Evans; Christopher Wright; and Adam Seamons, information security manager at GRC International Group PLC; for their helpful comments during the production of this book.

CONTENTS

Contents

Contents

Contents

FIGURES

Figures

TABLES

INTRODUCTION

Let's start by saying that this book is **not** a guide on how to develop AI. There are plenty of those – and plenty of YouTube videos providing introductions to machine learning (ML) and AI. Rather, the intent is to provide an understanding of AI's foundations and its actual and potential social and ethical implications – though by no means ALL of them, as we are still in the discovery phase. Although it is not technically-focused, this book can provide essential reading for engineers, developers, and statisticians in the AI field, as well as computer scientists, educators, students, and organizations with the goal of enhancing their understanding of how AI can and is changing the world we live in.

An important note: throughout this book, the term AI will be used as an overarching concept encompassing many of the areas and sub-areas of AI, ML, and deep learning (DL). So, readers, allow some latitude for a certain degree of inaccuracy in using the overarching AI acronym in reference to all of its permutations.

It is essential to begin at the outset to define and describe AI, all the while bearing in mind that there is no one single accepted definition. This is partly because intelligence itself is difficult to define. As Massachusetts Institute of Technology (MIT) Professor Max Tegmark pointed out, *"There's no agreement on what intelligence is even among intelligent intelligence researchers."*[5]

---

[5] Tegmark, M. 2017. *Life 3.0: Being Human in the Age of Artificial Intelligence*. London: Penguin Books.

In fact, few concepts are less clearly defined as AI. The term AI itself is polysemous – having multiple meanings and interpretations. In fact, it appears that there are as many perceptions and definitions of AI as there are proliferating applications. Although there are multiple definitions of AI, let's look at this really simple one: AI is intelligence exhibited by machines, where a machine can learn from information (data) and then use that learned knowledge to do something.

According to a 2017 Rand Study,

> *"algorithms and artificial intelligence (AI) agents (or, jointly, artificial agents) influence many aspects of our lives: the news articles we read, the movies we watch, the people we spend time with, our access to credit, and even the investment of our capital. We have empowered them to make decisions and take actions on our behalf in these and many other domains because of the efficiency and speed gains they afford."[6]*

AI faults in social media may have only a minor impact, such as pairing someone with an incompatible date. But a misbehaving AI used in defense, infrastructure, or finance could represent a potentially high and global risk. A "misbehaving" algorithm refers to an AI whose processing results lead to incorrect, prejudiced, or simply dangerous

---

[6] Osonde A. Osoba, and William Welser IV. (2017). *An Intelligence in Our Image: The Risks of Bias and Errors in Artificial Intelligence.* RAND Corporation.

consequences. The market's "Flash Crash" of 2010[7] is a painful example of just how vulnerable our reliance on AI can make us. The recent evolutions in AI, especially in generative AI, are showing us just how great the impact can be on our lives. Melvin Kranzberg[8] wrote as early as 1986 that *"Many of our technology-related problems arise because of the unforeseen consequences where apparently benign technologies are employed on a massive scale."* And this is becoming the case with generative AI. As with other technologies, a messy period of behavioral, societal, and legislative adaptation will certainly have to follow.

As an international community, we need to address the more existential concerns. For example, where will continued innovation in AI ultimately lead us? Will today's more narrow applications of AI make way for fully intelligent AI? Will the result be a continuous acceleration of innovation resulting in exponential growth in which super-intelligent AI will develop solutions for humanity's problems, or will future AI intentionally or unintentionally destroy humanity – or even more likely, be distorted and abused by humanity? These are the immediate and long-term concerns arising from the increased development and deployment of AI in so many facets of our society.

---

[7] On May 6, 2010, Wall Street experienced its worst stock plunge in several decades, wiping almost a trillion dollars in wealth out in a mere 20 minutes. Other so-called flash crashes have occurred since, and most were a result of a misbehaving algorithm.

[8] From the Six Laws of Technology, written in 1986 by Melvin Kranzberg, a professor of the History of Technology at Georgia Tech. Published in July 1986 in "Technology and Culture", Vol. 27, No. 3. Available at *https://www.jstor.org/stable/i356080*.

But there is a counter to this argument that runs central to this book, and it could not be better expressed than in the words of Kevin Kelly, founder of *Wired* magazine:

> *"But we haven't just been redefining what we mean by AI – we've been redefining what it means to be human. Over the past 60 years, as mechanical processes have replicated behaviors and talents that we once thought were unique to humans, we've had to change our minds about what sets us apart ... In the grandest irony of all, the greatest benefit of an everyday, utilitarian AI will not be increased productivity or an economics of abundance or a new way of doing science – although all those will happen. The greatest benefit of the arrival of artificial intelligence is that AIs will help define humanity. We need AIs to tell us who we are."*[9]

---

[9] Kelly, Kevin. (October 27, 2014). The Three Breakthroughs That Have Finally Unleashed AI on the World. *Wired* magazine online. Available at *www.wired.com/2014/10/future-of-artificial-intelligence/*.

CHAPTER 1: AI DEFINED AND COMMON DEPICTIONS OF AI – IS IT A BENEVOLENT FORCE FOR HUMANITY OR AN EXISTENTIAL THREAT?

> *"By far, the greatest danger of Artificial Intelligence is that people conclude too early that they understand it."*
> **Eliezer Yudkowsky**[10]

"OK! AI will destroy humans!"

This statement sums up some of the common (mis-) perceptions held by humans about AI. In truth, we are at no near-term (or even long-term) risk of being destroyed by intelligent machines.

Elon Musk, the noted tech tycoon, begs to differ, with his claim that *"AI is a fundamental risk for the existence of human civilization."*[11] Musk made this statement based on his observations that the development and deployment of AI is far outpacing our ability to manage it safely.

Narratives about AI play a key role in the communication and shaping of ideas about AI. Both fictional and non-fictional narratives have real-world effects. In many cases, public knowledge about the AI and its associated technology is limited. Perceptions and expectations are therefore usually

---

[10] Eliezer Shlomo Yudkowsky is an American artificial intelligence AI theorist and writer best known for popularizing the idea of friendly AI.

[11] Elon Musk at a gathering of U.S. governors in Rhode Island in 2017. Available at *www.cnbc.com/2017/07/16/musk-says-a-i-is-a-fundamental-risk-to-the-existence-of-human-civilization.html*.

informed by personal experiences using existing applications, by film and books, and by the voices of prominent individuals talking about the future. This informational disconnect between the popular narratives and the reality of the technology can have potentially significant negative consequences.

Narratives that are focused on utopian extremes could create unrealistic expectations that the technology is not yet able to meet. Other narratives focused on the fear of AI may overshadow some of the real challenges facing us today. With real challenges, such as wealth distribution, privacy, and the future of work facing us, it's important for public and legislative debate to be founded on a better understanding of AI. Bad regulation is another potential consequence resulting in misleading narratives and understanding, and influencing policymakers: they either respond to these narratives because these are the ones that resonate with the public, or because they are themselves influenced by them. AI may develop too slowly and not meet expectations, or it may evolve so fast that it is not aligned with legal, social, ethical, and cultural values.

A very brief history of AI – and perceptions of AI

Whether AI is a potential threat or not may be debatable, but before entering the debate, let's look at the history of AI. AI is not a new term. In fact, it was first introduced in 1956 by John McCarty, an assistant Professor at Dartmouth College, at the Dartmouth Summer Research Project. His definition of AI was the *"science and making of intelligent machines"* or getting machines to work and behave like humans.

But the concept of AI was not first conceived with the term in 1956. Although it is not surprising that AI grew rapidly post-computers, what *is* surprising is how many people thought about AI-like capabilities hundreds of years before there was even a word to describe what they were thinking about. In fact, something similar to AI can be found as far back as Greek mythology and Talos. Talos was a giant bronze automaton warrior said to have been made by Hephaestus to protect Europa, Zeus's consort, from pirates and invaders who might want to kidnap her.

Between the fifth and fourteenth centuries, or the "Dark Ages," there were a number of mathematicians, theologians, philosophers, professors, and authors who contemplated mechanical techniques, calculating machines, and numeral systems that ultimately led to the idea that mechanized "human" thought might be possible in non-human beings.

Although never realized, Leonardo da Vinci designed an automaton (a mechanical knight) in 1495.

Jonathan Swift's novel *Gulliver's Travels* from the 1700s talked about an apparatus it called *the engine*. This device's supposed purpose was to improve knowledge and mechanical operations to a point where even the least talented person would seem to be skilled – all with the assistance and knowledge of a non-human mind.

Inspired by engineering and evolution, Samuel Butler wrote an essay in 1863 entitled *Darwin Among the Machines* wherein he predicted that intelligent machines would come to dominate:

" *... the machines are gaining ground upon us; day by day we are becoming more subservient to them [...] that the time will come when the machines will hold the real supremacy over the world and its inhabitants is what no* *person of a truly philosophic mind can for a moment question. "*[12]

Fast forward to the 1900s, where concepts related to AI took off at full tilt and there was the first use of the term "robot." In 1921, Karel Čapek, a Czech playwright, published a play entitled *Rossum's Universal Robots* (English translation), which featured factory-made artificial people – the first known reference to the word.

One of the first examples in film was Maria, the "Maschinenmensch" or "machine-human," in the Fritz Lang directed German movie *Metropolis* made in 1927. Set in a dystopian future, the gynoid[13] Maria was designed to resurrect Hel, the deceased love of the inventor, Rotwang, but Maria evolved to seduce, corrupt, and destroy. In the end, her fate was to be destroyed by fire. Many claims have been made that this movie spawned the trend of futurism in the cinema. Even if we watch it today in its 2011 restoration, it is uncanny to see how many shadows of cinema yet to come it already contains.

---

[12] Dyson, George. (September 4, 2012). *Darwin among the Machines: The Evolution of Global Intelligence.* Basic Books, 2nd Edition.

[13] A gynoid is a female android or robot.

1: AI defined and common depictions of AI – Is it a benevolent force for humanity or an existential threat?

Figure 1-1: Gynoid Maria from the movie Metropolis[14]

In 1950, Alan Turing published *"Computing Machinery and Intelligence,"* which proposed the idea of The Imitation Game – this posed the question of whether machines could actually think. It later became known as *The Turing Test*, a way of measuring machine (artificial) intelligence. This test became an important component in the philosophy of AI, which addresses intelligence, consciousness, and ability in machines.

In his novel, *Dune,* published in 1965, Frank Herbert describes a society in which intelligent machines are so dangerous that they are banned by the commandment *"Thou shalt not make a machine in the likeness of a human mind."*[15]

---

[14] Review of the movie Metropolis (October 23, 2011). *The Independent.*

[15] Herbert, Frank. (1965) *Dune.* Penguin Random House Publishing.

Fast forward to 1969, and the "birth" of Shakey – the first general purpose mobile robot. Developed at the Stanford Research Institute (SRI) from 1966 to 1972, Shakey was the first mobile robot to reason about its actions. Its playground was a series of rooms with blocks and ramps. Although not a practical tool, it led to advances in AI techniques, including visual analysis, route finding, and object manipulation. The problems Shakey faced were simple and only required basic capability, but this led to the researchers developing a sophisticated software search algorithm called "A*" that would also work for more complex environments. Today, A* is used in applications, such as understanding written text, figuring out driving directions, and playing computer games.

1997 saw the development of Deep Blue by IBM, a chess-playing computer that became the first system to play chess against the reigning world champion, Gary Kasparov, and win. This was a huge milestone in the development of AI and the classic plot we've seen so often of man versus machine. Deep Blue was programmed to solve the complex, strategic problems presented in the game of chess, and it enabled researchers to explore and understand the limits of massively parallel processing. It gave developers insight into ways they could design a computer to tackle complex problems in other fields, using deep knowledge to analyze a higher number of possible solutions. The architecture used in Deep Blue has been applied to financial modeling, including marketplace trends and risk analysis; data mining – uncovering hidden relationships and patterns in large databases; and molecular dynamics, a valuable tool for helping to discover and develop new drugs.

From 2005 onwards, AI has shown enormous progress and increasing pervasiveness in our everyday lives. From the first rudimentary concepts of AI in 1956, today we have speech recognition, smart homes, autonomous vehicles (AVs), and so much more. What we are seeing here is a real compression of time in terms of AI development. But why? Blame it on the increase in data or "big data." Although we may not see this exact term, it hasn't disappeared. In fact, data has just got bigger. This increase in data has left us with a critical question: Now what? As in: We've got all this stuff (that's the technical term for it!) and it just keeps accumulating – so what do we do with it? AI has become the set of tools that can help an organization aggregate and analyze data more quickly and efficiently. Big data and AI are merging into a synergistic relationship, where AI is useless without data, and mastering today's ever-increasing amount of data is insurmountable without AI.

So, if we have really entered the age of AI, why doesn't our world look more like The Jetsons, with autonomous flying cars, jetpacks, and intelligent robotic housemaids? Oh, and in case you aren't old enough to be familiar with The Jetsons – well, it was a 1960s TV cartoon series that became the single most important piece of twentieth-century futurism. And though the series was "just a Saturday morning cartoon," it was based on very real expectations for the future.

In order to understand where AI is today and where it might be tomorrow, it's critical to know exactly what AI is, and, more importantly, what it is not.

What exactly is AI?

In many cases, AI has been perceived as robots doing some form of physical work or processing, but in reality, we are surrounded by AI doing things that we take for granted. We are using AI every time we do a Google search or look at our Facebook feeds, as we ask Alexa to order a pizza, or browse Netflix movie selections.

There is, however, no straightforward, agreed-upon definition of AI. It is perhaps best understood as a branch of computer science that endeavors to replicate or simulate human intelligence in a machine, so machines can efficiently – or even more efficiently – perform tasks that typically require human intelligence. Some programmable functions of AI systems include planning, learning, reasoning, problem solving, and decision-making.

In effect, AI is multidisciplinary, incorporating human social science, computing science, and systems neuroscience,[16] each of which has a number of sub-disciplines.[17]

---

[16] Systems neuroscience is about how neural circuits and brain networks support behavior and cognitive function.

[17] Tyagi, N. (2021, January 23) *6 Major Branches of Artificial Intelligence.* Available at *www.analyticssteps.com/blogs/6-major-branches-artificial-intelligence-ai*.

1: AI defined and common depictions of AI – Is it a benevolent force for humanity or an existential threat?

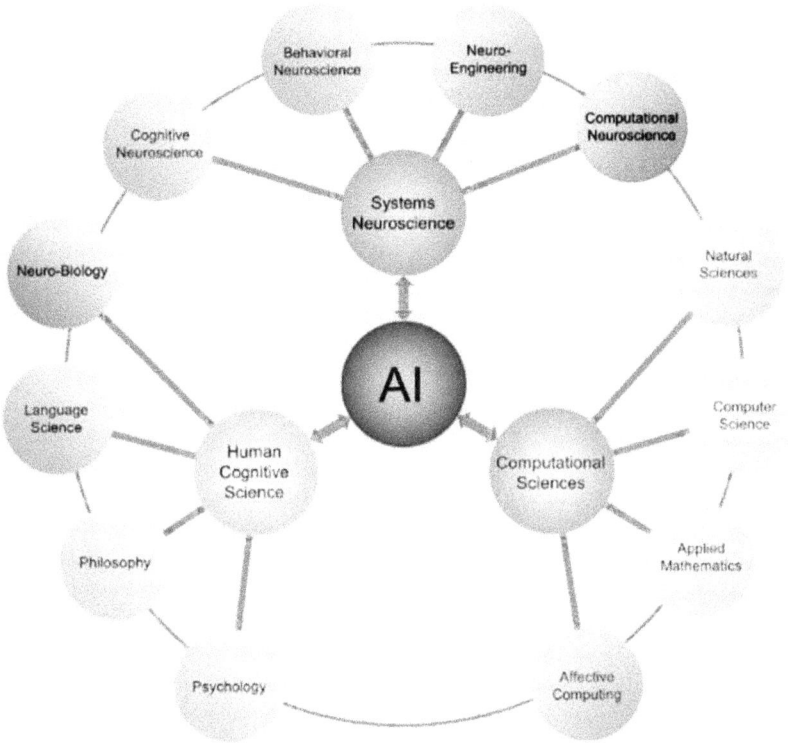

Figure 1-2: AI is multidisciplinary[18]

Computer scientists and programmers view AI as *"algorithms for making good predictions."* Unlike statisticians, they are not too interested in how we got the

[18] Extracted from Cichocki A, Kuleshov AP. Future Trends for Human-AI Collaboration: A Comprehensive Taxonomy of AI/AGI Using Multiple Intelligences and Learning Styles. 2020. Accessed August 11, 2021.

data or in models as representations of some underlying truth. For them, AI is black boxes making predictions.

Statisticians understand that it matters how data is collected, that samples can be biased, that rows of data need not be independent, that measurements can be censored, or truncated. In reality, the majority of AI is just applied statistics in disguise. Many techniques and algorithms used in AI are either fully borrowed from or heavily rely on the theory from statistics.

And then there's mathematics. The topics at the heart of mathematical analysis – continuity and differentiability – are also what is at the foundation of most AI/ML algorithms.

All AI systems – real and hypothetical – fall into one of three types:

1. **Artificial narrow intelligence (ANI)**, which has a narrow range of abilities;
2. **Artificial general intelligence (AGI)**, which is on par with human capabilities; or
3. **Artificial superintelligence (ASI)**, which is more capable than a human.

ANI is also known as "weak AI" and involves applying AI only to very specific and defined tasks, i.e. facial recognition, speech recognition/voice assistants. These capabilities may seem intelligent, however, they operate under a narrow set of constraints and limitations. Narrow AI doesn't mimic or replicate human intelligence, it merely simulates human behavior based on a narrow and specified range of parameters and contexts. Examples of narrow AI include:

1: AI defined and common depictions of AI – Is it a benevolent force for humanity or an existential threat?

- Siri by Apple, Alexa by Amazon, Cortana by Microsoft, and other virtual assistants;
- IBM's Watson;
- Image/facial recognition software;
- Disease mapping and prediction tools;
- Manufacturing and drone robots; and
- Email spam filters/social media monitoring tools for dangerous content.

AGI is also referred to as "strong" or "deep AI," or intelligence that can mimic human intelligence and/or behaviors, with the ability to learn and apply its intelligence to solve any problem. AGI can think, understand, and act in a way that is virtually indistinguishable from that of a human in any given situation. Although there has been considerable progress, AI researchers and scientists have not yet been able to achieve a fully-functional strong AI. To succeed would require making machines conscious, and programming a full set of cognitive abilities. Machines would have to take experiential learning to the next level, not just improving efficiency on singular tasks, but gaining the ability to apply the experiential knowledge to a wide and varying range of different problems. The physicist Stephen Hawking stated that there is the potential for strong AI to " ... *take off on its own and re-design itself at an ever-increasing rate. Humans, who are limited by slow biological evolution, could not compete, and would be superseded.* "[19]

---

[19] Until his death from the motor neuron disease amyotrophic lateral sclerosis (ALS), Stephen Hawking was one of Britain's most preeminent physicists and scientific thinkers. He made this statement in an interview with the BBC in 2014. Available at www.bbc.com/news/technology-30290540.

One of the most frightening examples of AGI is HAL (Heuristically programmed ALgorithmic computer) in *2001: A Space Odyssey*. HAL 9000, the sentient computer at the heart of *2001*, remains one of the most memorable "characters" in the film. Faced with the prospect of disconnection after an internal malfunction, HAL eventually turns on the Discovery 1 astronaut crew, killing one, before being manually shut down by the other crew member. HAL continues to represent a common fear of future AI, in which man-made technology could turn on its creators as it evolves in knowledge and consciousness.

ASI is still only a hypothetical capability. It is AI that doesn't just mimic or understand human intelligence and behavior; ASI represents the point machines become self-aware and may even surpass the capacity of human intelligence and ability. ASI means that AI has evolved to be so similar to a human's emotions and experiences that it doesn't just understand them, it even develops emotions, needs, beliefs, and desires of its own.

A possible example of ASI is the android Data who appeared in the TV show, *Star Trek: The Next Generation*. In one episode, "The Measure of a Man," Data becomes an object of study, threatened with his memory being removed and then being deactivated and disassembled in order to learn how to create more Data-like androids. The scientist argues that Data is purely a machine; Data claims that he will lose himself, as his identity consists of a complex set of responses to the things he has experienced and learned over time, making him unique. And if other androids were created, they would be different from him for precisely this reason. The possibility of new androids does not make him worry about his own identity; rather, it is the possibility that he will be reverted to something like a blank slate, which would then no longer be him. In the end, it came down to the question of "What is human"? Can humanity be defined by something like sentience, self-awareness, or the capacity for self-determination (autonomy), and how are these determined? It appears that these questions could not even be fully answered for humans, much less for Data, the android.

As AI continues to evolve, however, these may become the most salient questions.

Before we talk any further about AI, it's critical to understand that AI is an overarching term. People tend to think that AI, ML, and DL are the same things, since they have common applications. These distinctions are important – but this book will continue to us AI as the primary term that reaches across all of these subsets.

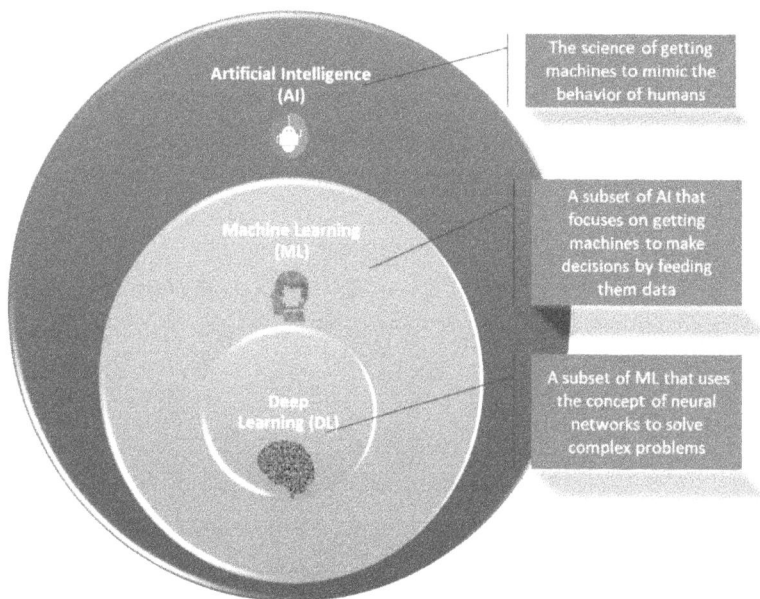

Figure 1-3: Definitions of AI, ML, and DL

Let's take a deeper look at each of these. A machine is said to have AI if it can interpret data, potentially learn from the data, and use that knowledge to achieve specific goals, or perform specific tasks. It is the process of making machines "smart," using algorithms[20] that allow computers to solve problems that used to be solved only by humans.

AI technologics are brilliant today at analyzing vast amounts of data to learn to complete a particular task or set of tasks – ML. The main goal of ML is to develop machines with the ability to learn entirely or almost entirely by themselves, without the need for anyone to perfect their algorithms. The

---

[20] The most concise and clear definition of an algorithm is a "list of instructions for solving a problem."

objective is to be so much like the human mind that these machines can independently improve their own processes and perform the tasks that have been entrusted to them with an ever-greater degree of precision. However, in order for ML to function, ideally, humans must supply the machine with information, either through files loaded with a multitude of data, or by enabling the machine to gather data through its own observations and to even interact with the world outside itself.

AI learning styles

AI has a variety of learning styles and approaches that enable its ability to solve problems or execute desired tasks. These learning styles fall mostly into the category of ML or DL.

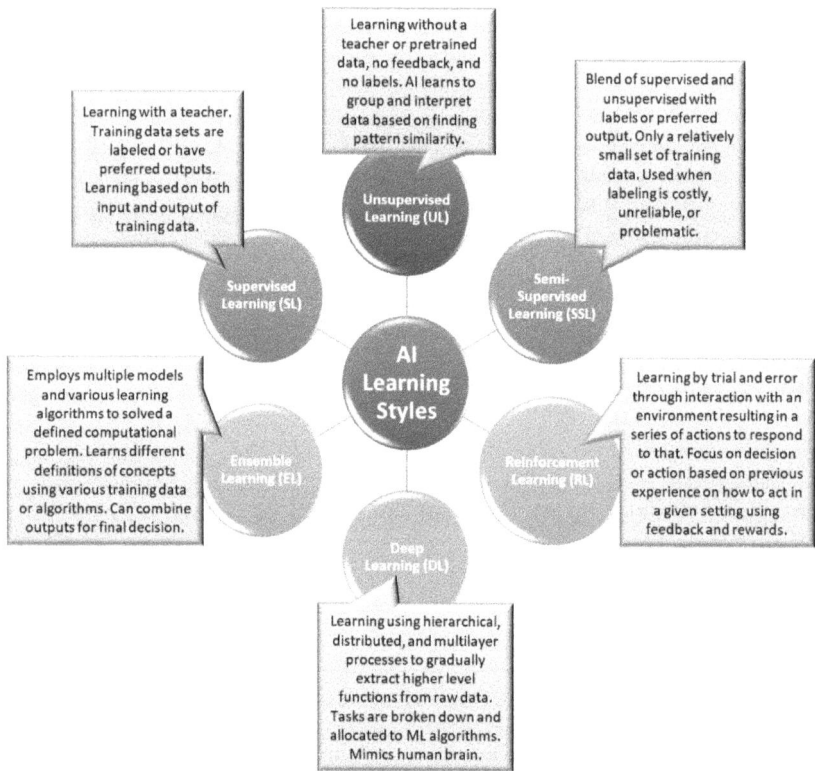

Learning without a teacher or pretrained data, no feedback, and no labels. AI learns to group and interpret data based on finding pattern similarity.

Blend of supervised and unsupervised with labels or preferred output. Only a relatively small set of training data. Used when labeling is costly, unreliable, or problematic.

Learning with a teacher. Training data sets are labeled or have preferred outputs. Learning based on both input and output of training data.

Unsupervised Learning (UL)

Semi-Supervised Learning (SSL)

Supervised Learning (SL)

AI Learning Styles

Employs multiple models and various learning algorithms to solved a defined computational problem. Learns different definitions of concepts using various training data or algorithms. Can combine outputs for final decision.

Ensemble Learning (EL)

Reinforcement Learning (RL)

Learning by trial and error through interaction with an environment resulting in a series of actions to respond to that. Focus on decision or action based on previous experience on how to act in a given setting using feedback and rewards.

Deep Learning (DL)

Learning using hierarchical, distributed, and multilayer processes to gradually extract higher level functions from raw data. Tasks are broken down and allocated to ML algorithms. Mimics human brain.

Figure 1-4: AI learning styles

ML

ML is the core to AI, because it has allowed the machines to advance in capability from relatively simple tasks to more complex ones. A lot of the present anticipation surrounding the possibility of AI is derived from the enormous promise of ML. ML encompasses supervised learning, unsupervised learning, and reinforcement learning.

*1: AI defined and common depictions of AI – Is it a
benevolent force for humanity or an existential threat?*

Supervised learning

Supervised learning feeds the machines with existing information so that they have specific, initial examples and can expand their knowledge over time. It is usually done by means of labels, meaning that when we program the machines, we pass them properly labeled elements so that later they can continue labeling new elements without the need for human intervention. For example, we can pass the machine pictures of a car, then we tell it that each of these pictures represents a car, and how we want it to be interpreted. Using these specific examples, the machine generates its own supply of knowledge so that it can continue to assign labels when it recognizes a car. Using this type of ML, however, the machines are not limited to being trained from images, but can use other data types. For example, if the machine is fed with sounds or handwriting data sets, it can learn to recognize voices or detect written patterns and associate them with a particular person. The capability evolves entirely from the initial data that is supplied to the machine.

Figure 1-5: Dog vs. not a dog

As humans, we consume a lot of information, but often don't notice these data points. When we see a photo of a dog,[21] for example, we instantly know what the animal is based on our prior experience. But the machine can only recognize an image as a dog if it has been fed the examples and told that these images represent a dog.

Unsupervised learning

In **unsupervised learning**, the developers do not provide the machine with any kind of previously labeled information about what it should recognize, so the machine does not have an existing knowledge base. Rather, it is provided with data regarding the characteristics of the thing it is meant to

---

[21] An actual photo of my dog, but not my guitar!

identify, and then has to learn to recognize those characteristics on its own. Essentially, this type of learning algorithm requires the machine to develop its own knowledge base from a limited data set.

This form of ML is actually closest to the way the human mind learns and develops. The machine learns to analyze groups using a method known as clustering. This is nothing more than grouping the elements according to a series of characteristics they have in common.

Figure 1-6: Dogs

In unsupervised learning, a data scientist provides the machine with, for example, a photo of a group of dogs, and it's the system's responsibility to analyze the data and conclude whether they really are dogs or something else, like a cat or a trombone.

Unsupervised learning problems can be classified into **clustering** and **association** problems.

Semi-supervised learning

Semi-supervised ML is a mixture of both supervised and unsupervised learning. It uses a small amount of labeled data and a larger amount of unlabeled data. This delivers the benefits of unsupervised and supervised learning, while sidestepping the issues associated with finding a large amount of labeled data. It means that AI can be trained to label data without having to apply as much labeled training data.

Reinforced learning

Using **reinforced learning**, systems or machines are designed to learn from acquired experiences. In these cases, when humans program the algorithm, they define what the final result should be without indicating the best way to achieve it. Consequently, the machine discovers itself how to achieve its goal. The machine is in charge of carrying out a series of tests in which it obtains success or failure, learning from its successes and discarding actions that led to failure. In short, it detects patterns of success that it repeats over and over again to become increasingly efficient. In simple words, the machine learns from its mistakes – much like humans do – without pre-programming and largely without human intervention.

Reinforcement learning is how most of us learn. Even our dogs. Nikita, my dog, is a Siberian Husky. Like other dogs, she doesn't understand any human language, but she picks up intonation and human body language with surprisingly good accuracy.

So, I can't really tell her what to do, but I can use treats to persuade her to do something. It could be anything as simple as sitting or shaking hands. If I can get Nikita to shake hands, she gets a treat. If she doesn't shake hands, she doesn't get her treat.

After a few of these interactions, Nikita realizes that all she needs to do is raise her paw at the "shake" command and she gets a treat.

In the case of reinforcement learning, the goal is to identify an appropriate action model that will maximize the total reward of the agent. The figure below depicts the typical action-reward feedback loop of a generic reinforced learning model.

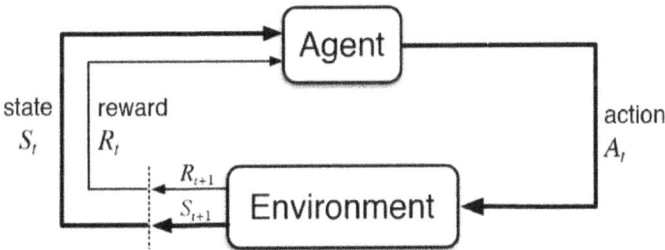

Figure 1-7: Feedback loop in reinforced learning

Just looking at the figure above might be a bit overwhelming, so let's take a quick look at the terminology and definitions:

- **Agent:** The AI system that undergoes the learning process. Also called the learner or decision maker. The algorithm is the agent.
- **Action:** The set of all possible moves an agent can make.
- **Environment:** The world through which the agent moves and receives feedback. The environment takes the agent's current state and action as inputs, and then outputs the reward and the next state.

- **State:** An immediate situation in which the agent finds itself. It can be a specific moment or position in the environment. It can also be a current as well as a future situation. In simple words, it's the agent's state in the environment.
- **Reward:** For every action made, the agent receives a reward from the environment. A reward could be positive or negative, depending on the action.

This can perhaps be better explained using the example of a computer game. Let's use Pac-Man. In the grid world of Pac-Man, the goal of the Agent (Pac-Man) is to devour the food on the grid, at the same time as avoiding any of the ghosts that might get in the way of getting the food. The grid world is the Environment where the Agent acts. The Agent is rewarded for getting the food and is punished if killed by a ghost. The State is the location of the Agent and the total cumulative Reward is the Agent winning the game.

Autonomous vehicles are also a good example of this type of learning algorithm. Their task is very clear: take passengers safely to their intended destination. As the cars make more and more journeys, they discover better routes by identifying shortcuts, roads with fewer traffic lights, etc. This allows them to optimize their journeys and, therefore, operate more efficiently.

Ensemble learning

Ensemble learning is a form of ML that merges several base models in order to produce one optimal predictive model. In ML, the AI equivalent of crowd wisdom can be attained through ensemble learning. The result obtained from ensemble learning, which combines a number of ML models, can be more accurate than any single AI model. Ensemble learning can work in two ways: using different algorithms (e.g. linear regression, support vector machine, regression decision tree, or neural network) with the same data set or by training the AI using different data sets with the same algorithm.

From ML, we progress to the next level – DL.

DL

DL is the next generation of ML inspired by the functionality of human brain cells, or neurons, which evolved into the concept of an artificial neural network. DL differentiates itself through the way it solves problems. ML requires a domain expert to identify most applied features, i.e. someone to tell the machine that a dog is a dog. On the other hand, DL understands features incrementally, thus eliminating the need for domain expertise. As a result, DL algorithms take much longer to train than ML algorithms, which only need a few seconds to a few hours. But the reverse is true during processing. DL algorithms take much less time to run than ML algorithms, whose time increases along with the size of the data.

Now that's a lot of words. So, let's break it down. It's basically a form of ML inspired by the human brain. In essence, the algorithms used in DL attempt to reach the same or similar conclusions as the human brain by analyzing data with a given logical structure. This requires a multi-layered structure of algorithms called neural networks, which are based on the structure of the human brain. We use our brains to identify patterns in our environment, and to classify different types of information. Neural networks can be taught to do the same thing. But it's a tricky prospect to ensure that a DL model doesn't draw incorrect conclusions – like other examples of AI, it still requires a lot of data and training to get the learning processes correct.

Deep is actually a real technical term – not just a reference to depth. It refers to the number of layers in a neural network. A typical neural network architecture is made up of several layers. The first layer is the input layer, which receives input x or data from which the neural network learns. The last layer is the output layer, and in between there are one or more hidden layers.

What does this look like? The figure below is a high-level graphical representation of a deep neural network.

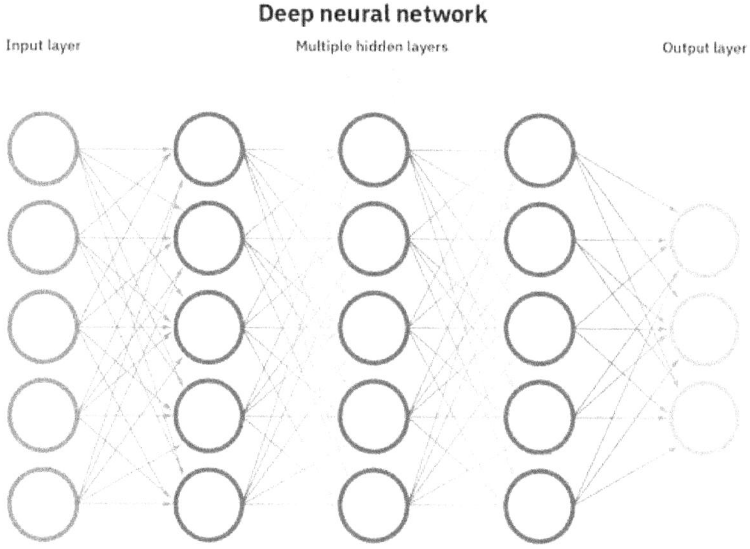

Deep neural network

| Input layer | Multiple hidden layers | Output layer |

Figure 1-8: Deep neural network representation

DL algorithms require a large amount of data to learn from, and the increase in data creation is one reason that DL capabilities have grown in recent years. If you want to know how much data was created every day in 2021, the current estimate stands at **2.5 quintillion data bytes daily**.[22]

The application of DL within a machine follows a relatively simple process. DL is what powers our self-driving cars, enables personal assistants, such as Alexa or Siri, or provides the foundation for the Google Translate app.

---

[22] Bulao, Jacquelyn. (May 19, 2021' updated March 14 2022) How Much Data is Created Every Day in 2021? *techjury*. Available at *https://techjury.net/blog/how-much-data-is-created-every-day/*.

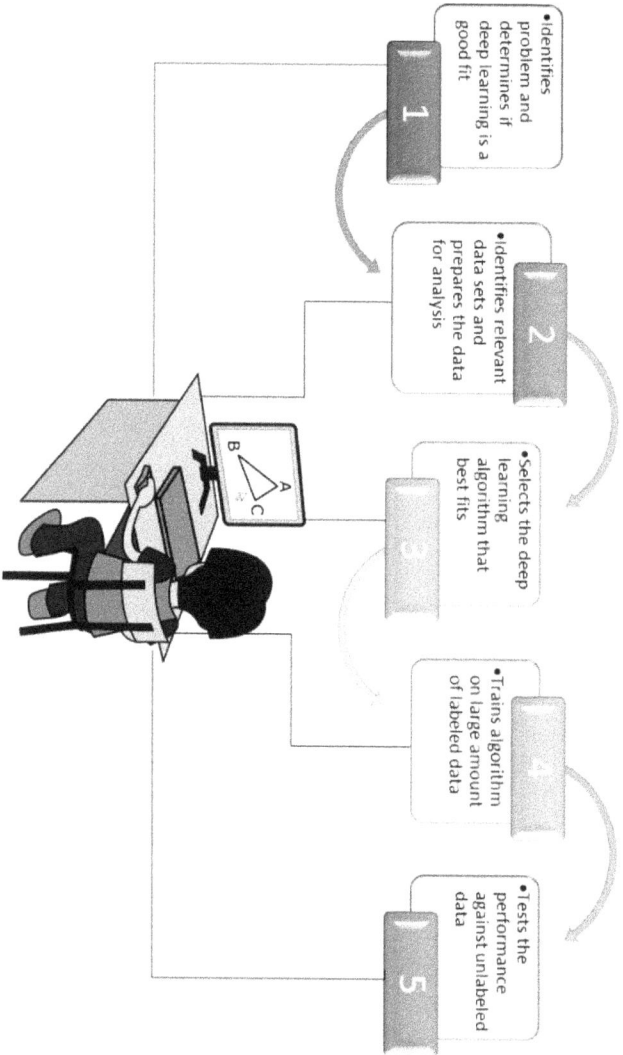

Figure 1-9: The DL process

1. • Identifies problem and determines if deep learning is a good fit
2. • Identifies relevant data sets and prepares the data for analysis
3. • Selects the deep learning algorithm that best fits
4. • Trains algorithm on large amount of labeled data
5. • Tests the performance against unlabeled data

DL does have limitations. The biggest limitation of DL models is that they learn only through observation, so they only know what was in the data on which they trained. If a user has a small amount of data or it comes from one specific source that is not necessarily representative of the broader functional area, the models will not learn in a way that is generalizable.

The issue of bias has also been recognized as a problem for DL models. If a model trains on data that contains biases, intentional or unintentional, the model will reproduce those biases in its predictions. This has been a frustrating challenge for DL programmers, since models learn to differentiate based on subtle variations in data elements. And often, the programmers are not aware of the factors it determines are important. As a consequence, a facial recognition model might make determinations about people's characteristics based on things, such as race or gender, even if that was not the intent of the programmer. More about bias in Chapter 5.

And finally, DL machines require an enormous amount of computing power. Multicore, high-performing graphics and other similar processors are required to ensure maximum efficiency and less time consumption. But these processors are expensive and use large amounts of energy.

AGI

One of the primary questions is when, or even if, DL can lead to the development of AGI, or the point at which it reaches human-level intelligence, engagement, and creativity.

Some scientists contend that because of the disruption of the COVID-19 pandemic ravaging the global economy, the race to realize AGI may have sped up significantly. *"Experts believe that there is a 25% chance of achieving human-like AI by 2030.*"[23] Other scientists, such as Rodney Brook, founder of iRobot and an MIT roboticist, think that full AGI will not be achieved before 2300.[24] If we believe some of the researchers in AI, it is only a matter of time until AGI becomes a part of the new normal.[25]

In fact, advances in robotic approaches and machine algorithms, paired with the recent data explosion and computing advancements, are serving as a fertile foundation for more human-level AI platforms.

If achieved, AGI would have the ability to think, comprehend, learn, and apply its intelligence to solve problems much like humans would in a similar situation. In essence, AGI would attain anthropomorphic abilities, such as sensory perception, enhanced motor skills, natural language understanding and processing, problem solving, social and emotional engagement. At the same time, however, there are a number of doomsayers, from prominent leaders to scientists, who contend that AGI could place civilization as we know it under serious threat.

---

[23] Cheishvili, A. (July 16, 2021). The Future of Artificial General Intelligence. *Forbes.* Available at *www.forbes.com/sites/forbestechcouncil/2021/07/16/the-future-of-artificial-general-intelligence/?sh=6f14b6e43ba9.*

[24] Berruti, F., Nel, P., and Whiteman, R. (April 29, 2020). An executive primer on artificial general intelligence. *McKinsey & Company.* Available at *www.mckinsey.com/business-functions/operations/our-insights/an-executive-primer-on-artificial-general-intelligence.*

[25] Cheishvili, A. (July 16, 2021). The Future of Artificial General Intelligence. *Forbes.* Available at *www.forbes.com/sites/forbestechcouncil/2021/07/16/the-future-of-artificial-general-intelligence/?sh=6f14b6e43ba9.*

1: AI defined and common depictions of AI – Is it a benevolent force for humanity or an existential threat?

A further subset is ASI, and this is where it becomes largely theoretical – and perhaps a bit scary. ASI refers to AI technology that not only matches, but can surpass the human mind. An ASI technology would be more capable than a human in every single way imaginable. Not only could ASI executive human-like tasks, but they would also even be capable of feeling emotion and having relationships. At this point, ASI remains hypothetical. The possibility and potential of having such powerful capability at our disposal may seem appealing, but it is an area full of unknown consequences. What impact it will have on humanity, our survival, our existence, is just pure speculation at this point.

In his book **Superintelligence**, Nick Bostrom describes the "The Unfinished Fable of Sparrows."

> *"The idea was basically that some sparrows wanted to control an owl as a pet. The idea seemed awesome to all except one of the skeptical sparrows who raised her concern as to how they can control an owl. This concern was dismissed for the time being in a 'we'll deal with that problem when it's a problem' matter."*[26]

At this point, ASI is something we will have to deal with in the future – but hopefully before it becomes a problem.

---

[26] What is Artificial Super Intelligence (ASI)? (July 2, 2020). *GeeksforGeeks*. Available at *www.geeksforgeeks.org/what-is-artificial-super-intelligence-asi/*.

1: AI defined and common depictions of AI – Is it a benevolent force for humanity or an existential threat?

In general, AI in all its forms might be considered a disruptive technology.[27] Since its early emergence in the mid-1950s to today, the subsets of AI – ML, DL, and AGI – have contributed to even larger disruptions, and have become even more widespread than we actually know.

Back to the original question

Is AI a benevolent force or even a possible existential threat? This question persists in science fiction, whether AI is seen as utopian, with an emphasis on all of the potential benefits, or dystopian, emphasizing the danger posed by errant AI.

This question has been asked at least since the 1950s when computer scientist, Alan Turing, first coined the term AI. The answer to this question lies not necessarily with the AI itself, but is perhaps more closely bound with the humans that design and use it.

In 1985, Professor James Moor wrote an essay on computer ethics, which he defined as:

" ... *the analysis of the nature and social impact of computer technology and the corresponding formulation and justification of policies for the ethical use of such technology.*"[28]

---

[27] According to Investopedia, a disruptive technology is " *... an innovation that significantly alters the way that consumers, industries, or businesses operate. A disruptive technology sweeps away the systems or habits it replaces because it has attributes that are recognizably superior.*" Examples include the automobile, television, GPS, and more recently cryptocurrency.

[28] Moor, James H. "What is Computer Ethics"? Available at *https://web.cs.ucdavis.edu/~rogaway/classes/188/spring06/papers/moo r.html*.

1: AI defined and common depictions of AI – Is it a benevolent force for humanity or an existential threat?

According to Moor, information technology professionals continually face new ethical questions because the continual emergence of new technology creates a *"vacuum of rules or policies"* (Moor, 1985). Technology professionals are left with little to no guidance on how to act in unexpected situations generated by these technologies. Moor contends that enhanced processing and new technologies are revolutionizing the world because the syntactic and semantic malleability of computer technology, and its enormous application, makes it a universal tool, therefore unlike any other tool known to man. The rapidity of the technological evolution presents technology professionals – and society – with new and unprecedented choices.

But like most developments in technology – or advances in any realm – AI offers both significant benefits but also risks.

To echo James Moor, our society has often spent significant time and money on developing new technologies, but minimal time and resources on understanding the ramifications of the innovation that is being introduced. Think about many of society's major innovations, such as industrial machinery, planes, trains, automobiles, cigarettes, and microwaves. We are amazing at creating things that have the ability to completely change the way we live. We are also very good at getting excited about implementing the new innovation, only to discover much later the unintended consequences.

In the mid-1800s, there was the Industrial Revolution, which resulted in significant changes in society and social norms. These changes included an increase and redistribution of wealth, the production of goods, and, at least for many, an improved standard of living. More people had access to healthier diets, better housing, and cheaper goods. In addition, access to education across societal and cultural barriers increased. Much of this was because of the transition of mundane, labor-intensive tasks performed by humans being performed by machines.

But this was not all positive – well, at least not immediately. The Industrial Revolution brought about massive movements of people from agrarian tasks in rural areas to urban areas where there was the promise of better wages. People living in such close proximity, fatigued by poor working conditions, and drinking unsafe water, presented the ideal conditions for outbreaks of infectious diseases. Many types of career paths closed, as there was less need for specialized craftsmen. Although new work opportunities were opening up, others were closing, causing massive shifts in the societal fabric. It was impossible to discern exactly the impact of these changes, and there was a time lag between the appearance of new technologies and policies to address these changes. But over time, new jobs were created. Industrialization reduced the emphasis on landownership as the chief source of personal wealth. The rising demand for manufactured goods meant that the average person could actually make a good living in cities as factory employees or as employees of the organizations that supported the factories, all of which paid a more living wage than farm-related jobs. This eventually gave rise to a burgeoning middle class.

1: AI defined and common depictions of AI – Is it a benevolent force for humanity or an existential threat?

Like the Industrial Revolution, AI represents a new revolution in technology,[29] one that could potentially facilitate a dramatic acceleration in scientific discovery and technological development. If not properly managed, however, the increased reliance on AI could also pave the way for unprecedented inequality, loss of privacy and certain civil liberties, excessive concentrations of power in certain societal sectors, and – like the Industrial Revolution – substantial shifts in our current society. This begs the question of how can we reap the benefits of AI while also mitigating its negative consequences?

In movies and books, AI is often depicted as an evil and scary-looking android-like machine carrying a weapon that has the will to rise up and annihilate us because it has become conscious of its superior intelligence and capability, and, consequently, is evil.

For some, the most important question is what will happen if the quest for strong AI succeeds, and an AI system becomes better than humans at all cognitive tasks? The creation of fully intelligent AI might become one of the most important events in human history. However, there are many who have expressed concern that it might also be the last event, unless we learn to align the policies regulating AI with our society before this occurs. Stephen Hawking, Elon Musk, Steve Wozniak, Bill Gates, and many other big names in science and technology, have publicly expressed concern

---

[29] Some are calling AI the "Fourth Industrial Revolution," following on from the third or digital revolution based on the merging of technologies that are eventually blurring the lines across the physical, digital, and biological domains. The Fourth Industrial Revolution may be based on the digital revolution, but speed, scope, and system impacts are the factors that make the Fourth Industrial Revolution distinctive.

about the potential risks posed by AI, and have been joined by a good number of leading AI researchers. These discussions present fascinating controversies where many of the world's leading experts disagree on such matters as to how AI might impact society; if/when human-level AI will be developed; whether this will lead to an intelligence explosion; and whether all of this is something to welcome or fear.

To avoid the policy vacuum that might emerge with the increasing and – perhaps unmanaged – growth of AI, it is critical to define the societal alignment of AI well in advance of designing "smarter-than-human" systems.

We need to prepare for a future where AI plays an increasingly important role, even if we are a long way from a machine that will exhibit broad intelligence that is equal to or exceeds that of humans. AI is neither inherently good or evil – it is a reflection of the fact that we humans are not very good at identifying and then centralizing the behaviors of multiple millions of human beings. AI will function in accordance with the fundamentals and principles of those creating and feeding data to the algorithms. A given algorithm could dramatically change the future for millions of people, and through AI small changes can become significantly magnified.

And this leads us to the exponential increase in the iterations of AI throughout society. But can we really call AI ubiquitous at this point in time? Chapter 2 begins to address that question.

CHAPTER 2: IS AI REALLY UBIQUITOUS – DOES IT OR WILL IT PERMEATE EVERYTHING WE DO?

> *"Artificial intelligence is going to have a bigger impact on the world than some of the most ubiquitous innovations in history.*
>
> *AI is one of the most important things humanity is working on. It is more profound than, I dunno, electricity or fire."*
>
> **Sundar Pichai**[30]

Today, we take AI in its many forms for granted. It is so embedded in our daily lives that we see it practically everywhere.

But is it really ubiquitous and what does that mean exactly?

Ubiquitous AI

First, let's look at the very definition of ubiquitous. According to Merriam-Webster's Dictionary, ubiquitous

---

[30] Sundar Pichai is the chief executive officer of Alphabet Inc. and its subsidiary Google.

means *"existing or being everywhere at the same time: constantly encountered; widespread."*[31]

Following this definition, AI is perhaps not yet completely ubiquitous – or everywhere – but its use is certainly increasing rapidly. It has become so common that – even if we're unaware of its existence – it may be performing background tasks on the floor of a retail outlet, managing your Internet searches, making recommendations on Netflix, guiding surgeons in the operating room of a hospital, making your smartphone smart, and so much more.

One might look at AI today as one might have looked at electricity in the past. Once unknown, electricity today has evolved into the commodity most of us now know and take for granted – standardized, affordable, and available, everywhere, and all the time. Kevin Kelly of *Wired* Magazine has the following to say: AI is more like a kind of

"Cheap, reliable, industrial-grade digital smartness running behind everything, and almost invisible except when it blinks off. This common utility will serve you as much IQ as you want but no more than you need. Like all utilities, AI will be supremely boring, even as it transforms the Internet, the global economy, and civilization."[32]

---

[31] Merriam-Webster. Available at *www.merriam-webster.com/dictionary/ubiquitous*.

[32] Kelly, Kevin. (October 27, 2014). The Three Breakthroughs That Have Finally Unleashed AI on the World. *Wired* Magazine online. Available at *www.wired.com/2014/10/future-of-artificial-intelligence/*.

2: Is AI really ubiquitous – Does it or will it permeate everything we do?

What is allowing AI to become almost a "common utility"?

Twenty years ago, I had to have surgery on my right hand, and I decided to buy a program that would translate speech to text so I could continue working. It was great, except that I spent hours upon hours trying to train the program to recognize my specific speech patterns and type out the right words on the computer.

I'd say something such as: "In reference to your recent order ... " and it would come out like this: "Referring to your youngest daughter ... " Well, needless to say, it was somewhat frustrating.

But today, I can just say, "Alexa, play Adele," and within a few seconds, there comes "Rolling in the Deep" from my speakers. I can say, "Find my phone," and my Alexa will call the number, and I am able to track down my missing cell phone somewhere in the cupboard or refrigerator.

So, how did this big change come about in such a short space of time? Why are algorithms that were basically developed in the mid-1950s to 1980s only now causing such a huge change in how we do business or relate to society?

Changes in technology

The answer is really quite simple: the technology has finally become powerful enough to enable the early promise of AI. Twenty years ago, computers were doing an "all right" job at processing, and supercomputers cost millions of dollars and took up massive amounts of space. Today, we have supercomputers in our smartphones.

There are a number of features that have enabled this massive change in processing capability, and thus the growth of AI.

2: Is AI really ubiquitous – Does it or will it permeate everything we do?

First, chips today can run trillions of calculations per second. But more recently, chips have acquired other advanced abilities, aside from just raw power. Because many AI "math problems" have a similar structure, some chips are being optimized to carry out those calculations more quickly.

An example of these are the 3rd generation Intel® Xeon® Scalable Processors[33] (code-named "Ice Lake"), which provide the foundation for Intel's data center platform, enabling organizations to capitalize on some of the most significant transformations today by leveraging the power of AI.

In addition, more memory is now being built into the processor itself, so there is less need to move data back and forth between the processor and memory chips, further speeding up the processes.

And not only is the hardware faster, sometimes augmented by specialized arrays of processors (e.g. GPUs), it is also accessible in the various cloud services. What once had to be run in specialized labs using supercomputers, can now be set up in the cloud at a much smaller cost and with less effort. Access to cloud processing has made access to the necessary hardware platforms to run AI simply much more available, enabling a proliferation of new efforts in AI development. And emerging open-source technologies, such as Hadoop, allow speedier development of scaled AI technologies applied to large and distributed data sets.

---

[33] According to Intel, the 3rd generation Intel Xeon is a balanced architecture that delivers built-in AI acceleration and advanced security capabilities, which allows you to place your workloads securely where they perform best. See
https://www.intel.com/content/www/us/en/products/details/processors/x eon/scalable.html.

Simply defined, Hadoop is an open-source software framework for storing data and running applications on clusters of commodity hardware. It provides massive storage for any kind of data, enormous processing power, and the ability to handle virtually limitless concurrent tasks or jobs.

Additionally, since Hadoop is open source and free, it is less costly. It also has significant fault tolerance, so that processing is protected against hardware failure – if one node fails, jobs are automatically redirected to other nodes to make sure the distributed computing can continue. Multiple copies of all data are stored automatically.

Massive increase in data

The term "big data" has now been around for a while. But what is big data? Simply put, the term "big data" refers to the collection of massive amounts of data from a multiplicity of sources, and our ability to organize, analyze, and use it to our advantage.

The amount of data that is generated is increasing at an exponential rate. On average, in less than two days, we create as much data as we did from the dawn of time until today.[34]

Massive capability for data collection combined with less expensive storage, perhaps in the cloud, paired with the awareness by all kinds of industry players that collecting every little bit of data might someday come in handy, has brought about a high demand for solutions that go beyond the simple statistical analysis of data, and promise new insights and intelligence through enhanced pattern

---

[34] Vuleta, Branka. (January 28, 2021). How Much Data is Created Every Day? [27 Staggering Stats]. *SeedScientific*. Available at *https://seedscientific.com/how-much-data-is-created-every-day/*.

recognition and analytical capability. The AI industry to big data is as the automobile industry is to the horse and cart.

Faster communication speeds

The use of fiber-optic cables and 3G, 4G, and now 5G wireless capability was critical for permitting very large quantities of data to move rapidly back and forth. In fact, none of the video streaming services we now enjoy would be possible without these rapid data movement capabilities.

Optical computing is so rapid because it uses laser-generated light, instead of the much slower electricity used in traditional digital electronics, to transmit information at mind-boggling speeds.

Deployment of 5G-enabled wireless is ever-increasing. AI and 5G are synergistic, working together in a hyperconnected world in which virtually everyone and everything are connected.

Improved algorithms

Simply defined, an algorithm is a set of instructions that are executed when triggered by a command or an event. At their foundation, algorithms are essentially mathematical instructions.

To make computers function, programmers created algorithms to tell the computer step-by-step how to do what the programmer wanted it to do. A program could be 20 or 20 million lines of very specific code. Once completed and triggered, the computer executes the program, following each step mechanically, to accomplish the end goal.

Rather than have a computer follow a specific set of pre-determined instructions, algorithms for AI are designed to allow computers to learn on their own; e.g. ML. And that is the main breakthrough between traditional computer programming and the algorithms that allows AI to *learn* to perform a task.

What makes people refer to AI as ubiquitous?

Now that we've taken a short look at how improved technologies have allowed AI to take a quantum leap forward in just a couple of decades, let's go back to the original question. **Is AI really ubiquitous?**

Well, there is virtually no major industry that hasn't been affected to some degree by modern AI – more specifically, "narrow AI," which performs objective functions using data-trained models and often falls into the categories of DL or ML. This statement is especially true in the last few years, as data collection and analysis have ramped up considerably thanks to a robust Internet of Things (IoT), improved connectivity, the proliferation of connected devices, and ever-speedier computer processing.

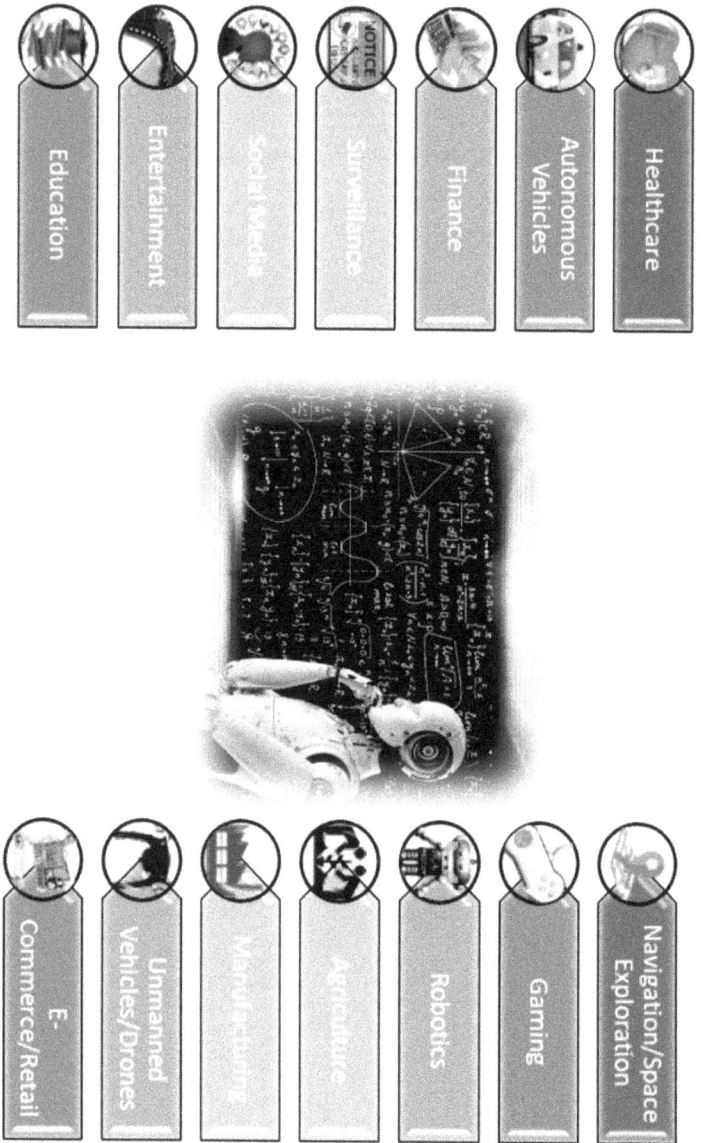

Figure 2-1: AI is integrated into many areas

Education
Entertainment
Social Media
Surveillance
Finance
Autonomous Vehicles
Healthcare

E-Commerce/Retail
Unmanned Vehicles/Drones
Manufacturing
Agriculture
Robotics
Gaming
Navigation/Space Exploration

2: Is AI really ubiquitous – Does it or will it permeate everything we do?

To further answer this question, we need to look at some, if not all, of the areas where AI and its use is proliferating. Looking at this rather limited list, it quickly becomes clear that AI is indeed highly integrated into much of the world around us – even if there remain areas where AI has not yet made its presence felt. Note that the list below is in no particular order in reference to the level or degree of AI implementation, nor do the descriptions below claim to fully and deeply address the degree of AI implementation in each area.

Healthcare

Using AI, diseases are more quickly and accurately diagnosed, development of new drugs is speedier and more streamlined, virtual nursing assistants monitor patients, and big data analysis helps to create a more personalized patient experience.

In healthcare, AI-based systems are always working in real time, which means the data is continuously being updated, thus improving both accuracy and relevance. As a result, doctors and practitioners are able to access thousands of diagnostic resources rapidly and efficiently. Although physicians are deeply educated in their field and make every effort to remain current with the newest advances in medical research, the use of AI facilitates immediate access to a larger pool of diagnostic information that can be augmented by their clinical knowledge.

AI-powered machines can act as roving healthcare companions for elderly people, delivering medications in their correct dosages, and reminding them about their daily schedules. Medical robots can be used to take a piece of intestine that has been cut open during a surgical procedure and stitch it back together with the same, or even better, precision as the surgeon themself.

The COVID-19 pandemic highlighted another area for the use of AI in healthcare – telemedicine. Social distancing and fears of transmission resulted in a proliferation of telehealth tools being implemented in the homes of patients to help detect, treat, and prevent high-risk situations, while also reducing hospital admissions. AI-based telehealth tools allow for various metrics to be taken, documented, and processed. The equipment can also notify an actual practitioner immediately if an individual manifests a high-risk variable. Early detection, faster diagnostics, and a timely treatment plan, can reduce time and resources for both the patient and healthcare provider, while ensuring more immediate care.

Self-driving or AVs

In recent times, almost every automotive company has broadcast a self-driving car development program. Developers of AVs claim they have the potential to save time, limit energy consumption, and dramatically reduce the millions of injuries and deaths attributed to road traffic accidents each year.

Companies, such as the former Argo AI, contributed to this development. According to Bryan Salesky, the founder and CEO of Argo AI, its " ... *mission is not to replace the personal freedom that driving provides, but rather to build technology to empower mobility products that offer choice.* "[35] So, although vehicles operating completely driverless may still be some time away, companies such as

---

[35] Previously available at *www.argo.ai/*.

Argo attempted to design software not to take away the freedom of driving from humans, but to make navigating the dangers of everyday driving less distracting – and well, less dangerous, using AI to provide enhanced 360° awareness.

Finance

AI is transforming the finance industry in a number of tangible ways: financial risk, fraud detection, financial advisory services, trading, remote onboarding, and personal financial management. According to a recent survey by Deloitte Insights, 70% of all financial services companies are using ML to predict cash flow events, fine-tune credit scores, and detect fraud.[36]

Today, we use a credit score, such as FICO, as a means of determining who is eligible for a mortgage or a loan and who is not. However, grouping people into "haves" and "have-nots" is not always efficient. Increasingly, data about an individual's loan repayment habits, rental and utility payment records, the number of existing credit cards, etc. can be used to customize the risk determination so that it makes more sense to the financial institution.

Banks and financial institutions take fraud very seriously. AI can use past spending behaviors on multiple types of transactions to identify odd behavior, such as using a card in another country just a few hours after it has been used elsewhere, or an attempt to withdraw an amount of cash that is unusual for that specific account.

---

[36] Digital Banking Maturity 2020. *Deloitte.* Available at https://www2.deloitte.com/ce/en/pages/financial-services/articles/digital-banking-maturity-2020.html.

2: Is AI really ubiquitous – Does it or will it permeate everything we do?

A recent report by PriceWaterhouseCoopers indicates a strong trend away from costly personal financial advisors to "robo-advisors," which can reduce their commissions paid on individual investments.[37] Robo-advisors act as low-cost alternatives to a personal financial advisor by reducing or even eliminating the human in the analysis, and making investment recommendation accessible to the average investor. They are based on ML models trained through the ingestion of a huge amount of historical market data, with the goal of developing a personalized, optimized, and diversified portfolio to maximize returns in alignment with the risk appetites of the customer.

The domain of trading and investments depends on the ability to predict the future reasonable accurately. AI is great at this because it can analyze a huge amount of data in a short timescale.

More and more institutions are transitioning to online banking, thus eliminating the need for a bricks-and-mortar presence. But this also means better ways to on-board new clients. Remote client on-boarding uses AI for fraud detection, replacing traditional knowledge-based authentication methods for customer due diligence, and saving account processing time and costs by digitizing the processes for customer verification. Personal financial management (PFM) is another one of the recent developments in the AI-based financial skill set. AI can be used to build algorithms that help consumers make better decisions about their money and how and where to spend it.

---

[37] Financial Services Technology 2020 and Beyond: Embracing disruption. *A Report by PriceWaterhouseCoopers*. Available at www.pwc.com/gx/en/financial-services/assets/pdf/technology2020-and-beyond.pdf.

2: Is AI really ubiquitous – Does it or will it permeate everything we do?

Surveillance

In a traditional sense, surveillance is simply defined as watching someone or something. In many nations, governments have invested heavily in setting up a robust surveillance infrastructure composed of millions of cameras – but with one to continuously monitor. Here's where AI comes in. AI can process every frame and present real-time analysis of data from numerous cameras or other surveillance devices. Locations are adopting sophisticated AI surveillance technologies to map, track, and control people to meet various policy aims – some legitimate, some raising privacy concerns, and some of which may fall into a gray area.

Retail surveillance is an area where the application of AI is growing. Major stores and shopping centers are now using AI for behavioral analysis of individuals in or in the vicinity of the store – not only for the obvious reason of shoplifting, but also to identify potential threats, such as shooters, and to send real-time warnings to emergency responders to help mitigate the threats to personnel and buildings.

Almost every European nation has implemented some form of facial recognition technology.

> *"Dutch police use it to match photos of suspects to a criminal database. The London Metropolitan Police uses live facial recognition to match faces to criminals in a database. The French government is a fan of using AI to track 'suspicious behavior.'"*[38]

---

[38] Heikkila, Melissa. The Rise of AI Surveillance. *Politico online.* Available at *www.politico.eu/article/the-rise-of-ai-surveillance-coronavirus-data-collection-tracking-facial-recognition-monitoring/*.

AI acts as a correlation engine that reads not only a location's sensor feeds for live audio (e.g. gunshots, 911 calls) and video (e.g. license plate readers, traffic cameras), but also historical police records searching for patterns and connections, and presenting either a real-time picture of events occurring, which require official attention, or reasonably accurate predictions of events that might occur.

China has taken surveillance to a new level. Its extensive surveillance network aids in the implementation of a social scoring system designed to keep residents compliant with government requirements and preferences. China has linked its surveillance network with sophisticated AI software that can not only recognize faces and, based on what an individual is "caught" doing, either give them social credits or promptly place social demerits in their account – demerits that may cost that citizen a job, an apartment, permission to start a family, or even bring in government enforcers to take the citizen's freedom.

Social networking and smart devices

This is perhaps where the everyday user most frequently encounters AI and AI-based applications. Using social media, smartphones, search engines, and online shopping platforms all involves AI algorithms designed to improve the user experience. Although smart devices and social media are not the same, they are inextricably linked through the use of AI.

Many of us are constantly interacting with some form of social media, whether it's Facebook, TikTok, Snapchat, or another variation. It might even be fair to say that many of us are addicted to our social media feeds and our smart devices.

2: Is AI really ubiquitous – Does it or will it permeate everything we do?

Social media relies on something called recommendation engines, which learn from an individual's past activity, and then interprets patterns in the data to predict a list of accounts or activities with which one could potentially interact.

AI is used to control smart devices, with the voice control feature of AI-enabled units, such as Alexa, Siri, and Google Assistant. Recent developments in smart devices have led to improvements in AI in terms of communicating with the cloud, learning human behavioral patterns, and automating smart devices according to user preferences. Smart devices are considered part of the IoT. Within the IoT, certain tasks can be performed automatically or by using smartphones to control our home appliances, secure our homes, etc. by limiting the need for human involvement. But, security and privacy are significant concerns for smart devices and the IoT, as every connected device leaves digital footprints of personal data that need to be safeguarded and secured.

Entertainment

The media and entertainment industries are primarily using the power of AI to make visual content more interactive and interesting – and addictive – to users. AI is helping to provide the audience with an immersive, data-intensive, and personalized automated experience, thus ensuring that their engagement will be more interesting and entertaining.

There are several applications of AI that are evolving in the entertainment industry.

Figure 2-2 is adapted from 6 Applications of AI in Entertainment Industry.[39]

---

[39] Adapted from Prajapati, S. (October 28, 2021). 6 Applications of AI in Entertainment Industry. *AnalyticSteps* blog. Available at *www.analyticssteps.com/blogs/6-applications-ai-entertainment-industry*.

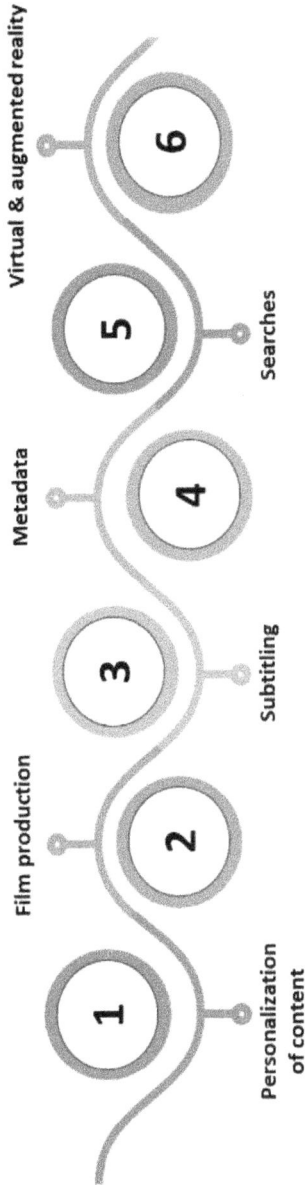

Figure 2-2: Use of AI in entertainment

2: Is AI really ubiquitous – Does it or will it permeate everything we do?

1. **Content personalization:** Users are increasingly expecting – no, demanding – entertainment choices tailored to their individual preferences. Entertainment providers, such as Netflix and YouTube, are using AI/ML algorithms to analyze individual user preferences and demographics to elevate user interest and keep them regularly involved. To this end, AI presents users with content that is consistent to their particular tastes, thus providing an extremely personalized encounter.

2. **Film production:** AI is also being used to create visual designs and film content much more rapidly. For example, *"IBM produced a horror movie trailer called Morgan using artificial intelligence. In order to come up with the list of spectacular moments for the trailer, the research team trained the AI system on scenes from 100 horror movies, which were later analyzed on the basis of their visual and audio effects. This led to the final product which was a 6-minute trailer created within 24 hours."*[40] Certainly much faster than the normal human-driven process. AI also offers a means to automate routine film-making tasks, such as breaking down scripts, storyboarding, generating shot-lists, creating schedules, and managing movie budgets.

3. **Subtitling:** International media companies need to make their content quickly available for consumption by audiences across the globe. To do so, they have to provide accurate multilingual subtitles for TV and film content. Using human translators to manually create

---

[40] Rose, S. (January 26, 2020). How AI is Transforming Media and Entertainment Industry? *Codeburst*. Available at https://codeburst.io/how-ai-is-transforming-media-and-entertainment-industry-e40b7f72e24d.

subtitles for shows and movies in dozens of languages can take hundreds or even thousands of hours. To overcome this limitation, media companies are leveraging AI-based technologies, such as natural language processing and generation.

4. **Metadata:** Countless bits of media content are being created every minute. *"With innumerable sections of content being produced every minute, incorporating these items and making them simple to search for watchers becomes a difficult task for entertainment company employees. That's due to the fact that this process needs watching videos and recognising objects, pictures, or places in the video to match and append tags."*[41] To perform this task on a large scale, media creators and distributors use AI-based tools to analyze the content of videos frame by frame, identifying objects, and adding appropriate tags.

5. **Searches:** With so much content online, finding a specific item can be difficult. Streaming platforms are using AI to optimize their search algorithms to assist users in finding relevant content. Search engine optimization (SEO) has benefits for both the users and the creators in the entertainment industry. Entertainment marketers and creators can use AI-driven SEO to build traffic to their content. Users find SEO useful for rapidly locating desired entertainment content.

6. **Virtual and augmented reality:** Augmented reality (AR) and virtual reality (VR) are making media and entertainment content more immersive and captivating

---

[41] Prajapati, S. (October 28, 2021). 6 Applications of AI in Entertainment Industry. *AnalyticSteps* blog. Available at *www.analyticssteps.com/blogs/6-applications-ai-entertainment-industry*.

for users. Integrating AI into VR/AR allows entertainment creators and marketers to drive innovation, develop new customer experiences, and find fresh ways of interacting with entertainment content.

Education

For most of 2020 and part of 2021, the COVID-19 pandemic radically changed the face of education, with many schools having to pivot rapidly from in-person to online education. As a result, educators began looking at AI tools to manage students and enhance the learning environment, especially in grades K-12.

AI-powered tools are being evaluated and implemented, such as AI-powered virtual teaching assistants that help teachers to grade homework and provide real-time feedback to students, or that can aid teachers in orchestrating and organizing social activity in the online classroom. The AI tools can provide more accurate performance assessments, virtual reality programs, voice- or gesture-based systems, or even robots that can help students with academic or social skills. Schools can use AI to offer a more personalized and tailored learning experience – thus conquering one of the primary limitations of our current standardized education model.

Navigation and GPS/space exploration

Does anyone recall the days of trying to drive with paper maps? There you are trying to unfold the map, fold it again, turn to the right page in an atlas, or try to read and follow printed directions – all the while navigating potentially unknown or confusing road signs. Whew!

2: Is AI really ubiquitous – Does it or will it permeate everything we do?

Along comes GPS navigation and Google Maps – and suddenly driving in new areas is no longer as threatening or frustrating. Traditional GPS has only limited AI, with no memory or analytical capabilities. But this is changing.

Today, most smartphone or in-vehicle navigation systems, such as Google Maps or Waze, can leverage data and the IoT to alert the driver to police speed control traps, traffic jams, and other travel disruptions, and readjust the route accordingly. But most current GPS navigation systems are not sufficiently complex to anticipate how a traffic situation might change during the travel time on any possible route. For example, the European road network alone has, theoretically, about a hundred quadrillion possible routes.[42] This requires more dynamic routing, which is increasingly becoming a reality as a result of the enormous amount of road and traffic data being generated and fed into AI engines.

AI navigation is a critical foundation to the creation and use of autonomous vehicles. Pierluigi Casale explained the relationship thus:

"Artificial Intelligence (AI) is what drives automated vehicles. Autonomous cars, in particular, are the future of transportation and need to adopt human-like reasoning when it comes to navigation. They need to constantly be absorbing information such as road condition and live traffic updates in order to ensure they can provide safe and efficient journeys for their passengers. In today's

---

[42] Casale, Pierluigi. (April 23, 2020). Keeping driverless navigation in the right lane with AI. *Techerati online,* Available at www.techerati.com/features-hub/opinions/ai-keeping-driverless-navigation-in-the-right-lane-with-ai-2020/.

digital world, AI is utilized heavily for accurate road navigation as well as vehicle operation."[43]

AI is not limited to "earthly" navigation. Although there is no GPS in space, the National Aeronautics and Space Administration (NASA) is now looking at AI-powered solutions to assist in navigation in outer space, and a future where these virtual tools are incorporated on spacecraft. This would enable lighter, less complex, and therefore cheaper missions. NASA envisages future exoplanet missions where AI technologies are embedded on spacecraft that are smart enough to make real-time navigational and technical decisions, reducing the requirement to communicate with scientists on Earth.

Gaming

If you have played a video game in recent years, you have definitely interacted with AI.

AI in gaming is all about enhancing a player's experience through adaptive and responsive game experiences. Players expect immersive gaming encounters on a wide selection of mobile and wearable devices, from smartphones to VR headsets, and more. Using AI, developers can deliver console-like experiences across multiple device types. The AI component in gaming can capture the player's interest and satisfaction over an extended period of time.

---

[43] Casale, Pierluigi. (April 23, 2020). Keeping driverless navigation in the right lane with AI. *Techerati online,* Available at *www.techerati.com/features-hub/opinions/ai-keeping-driverless-navigation-in-the-right-lane-with-ai-2020/.*

2: Is AI really ubiquitous – Does it or will it permeate everything we do?

One of the most frequently used strategies, called the Finite State Machine (FSM)[44] algorithm, was introduced to video game design in the 1990s. Using FSM, a video game designer tries to imagine all the possible situations that could be encountered in a game – whether car, shooting, or strategy games – and then programs a specific reaction for each situation. Basically, an FSM AI would quickly react to the human player's moves with its pre-programmed behavior. For example, in a shooting game, AI would attack when a human player shows up and then retreat when its own health level is too low.

Move forward a couple of decades, and there have been amazing advances in 3D visualization skills, physics-based simulations, and more recently, incorporation of VR and AR in games. These technologies have enabled game developers to create more intelligent, visually appealing games that one would never have envisioned ten years back.

Gaming is also transitioning to the world of smart devices. Mobile game developers are exploring different ML and AI algorithms to make smartphone games "smarter," while also coping with the power limitations of a mobile device. But if you compare today's mobile games with the ones of five years ago, you will see major improvements in terms of the visual appearance of the games and their level of intelligence. However, the processing power of smartphone games still has a long way to go to catch up to the desktop

---

[44] According to Brilliant, *"A **finite state machine** (sometimes called a finite state automaton) is a computation model that can be implemented with hardware or software and can be used to simulate sequential logic and some computer programs. Finite state automata generate regular languages. Finite state machines can be used to model problems in many fields including mathematics, artificial intelligence, games, and linguistics."* Source *https://brilliant.org/wiki/finite-state-machines/*.

gaming experience, especially when considering the lack of a gaming console, which allows a gamer to engage in a faster, more responsive game.

Robotics

People are confused about the differences between robotics and AI, especially since there are robots controlled by AI. Robotics is the field of engineering and technology focused on developing and using robots. According to the futurist Bernard Marr:

> *"Robots are programmable machines that can autonomously or semi-autonomously carry out a task. Robots use sensors to interact with the physical world and are capable of movement, but must be programmed to perform a task."*[45]

ML and AI can help robots see, walk, speak, smell, and move in progressively human-like ways – and advances in the technology are occurring rapidly. In 2020, the American Society of Mechanical Engineers highlighted several "humanoid"[46] robots. Among them were a robotic bartender named Kime, delivery robots being used at Ford assembly plants, Pepper the educational robot, and robots developed to

---

[45] Marr, Bernard. What Is the Difference Between AI and Robotics? *Bernard Marr & Co*. Available at *https://bernardmarr.com/what-is-the-difference-between-ai-and-robotics/*.

[46] Webster defines a humanoid as "a nonhuman creature or being with characteristics (such as the ability to walk upright) resembling those of a human."

perform household tasks or assist humans with certain disabilities.

One of the most famous of these humanoid robots is Sophia, often called an ambassador for robots. Having been designed and taught by humans, Sophia can process visual data quickly to move, talk, show some emotions, draw, and sing.

Figure 2-3: Jimmy Fallon meets Sophia the robot[47]

In 2017, Sophia was introduced on Jimmy Fallon's Tonight Show, where she played rock, paper, scissors with him (and won!), and showed an almost human sense of humor and play.

---

[47] Photo capture from YouTube. Available at *www.youtube.com/watch?v=Bg_tJvCA8zw*.

2: Is AI really ubiquitous – Does it or will it permeate everything we do?

Take a look at *www.youtube.com/watch?v=Bg_tJvCA8zw*.

Robots, such as Sophia, illustrate the possibilities that go far beyond the use of robot arms in manufacturing or warehousing. As Leo Ryzhenko, CEO of SMP Robots,[48] states:

> *"The future of humanity will be greatly assisted by robots and AI. The impact of such innovations will bring improvements in everyday lives and help humans to achieve their most daring dreams."*

Agriculture

Agriculture is highly dependent upon variables we humans cannot control, such as weather or pests. So, it may not seem very intuitive that AI can play an active role for farmers. And yet, AI has been adopted by some agriculturalists and is showing great promise in the areas of:

- Identifying market demand and planting crops to be more profitable;
- Forecasting and risk analysis to identify potential areas of crop failure;
- Determining optimal irrigation and nutrient application schedules; and
- Analyzing data on plant environments to determine more resistant and adaptable crops.

Precision farming is one area of particular growth, and AI is helping farmers combine the best soil management practices,

---

[48] SMP Robots is seeking to develop robots to fulfill a number of jobs formally held by humans, especially in the areas of security, workers in dangerous positions, or positions in harsh environments.

variable rate technology, and the most effective data management practices to help maximize yields and minimize loss.

One point to note – The agricultural sector in developing countries is very different from the agricultural sector in Western Europe and the US. There are regions that could benefit from AI-supported agriculture, but it may be hard to implement in areas where agricultural technology in general is not common.

Manufacturing

Approximately 60% of companies are using some form of AI technology in their manufacturing processes. Some of the most prominent uses are in forecasting product demand, inventory management, defect detection and prevention, customer management, and, of course, in the use of robots in the manufacturing process itself.

Using AI, companies can assess equipment conditions and more accurately predict when routine or as-needed maintenance should be performed. Using AI for predictive maintenance, unplanned machinery downtime and maintenance costs can be reduced by 30%.[49]

---

[49] Columbus, L. (August 11, 2019). "10 Ways Machine Learning Is Revolutionizing Manufacturing In 2019." *Forbes*. Available at *www.forbes.com/sites/louiscolumbus/2019/08/11/10-ways-machine-learning-is-revolutionizing-manufacturing-in-2019/?sh=4ddb45602b40*.

Manufacturers are using AI production planning and scheduling for complex manufacturing processes to analyze material availability, production capacity, and customer demand to recommend the best scheduling plan.

AI helps simplify manufacturing operations by fully automating complex tasks and by requiring less manpower to execute these tasks while maintaining the speed of production. Companies have the ability to rapidly revise production processes or adjust material flow based on schedule, customer demand, or product modifications.

Unmanned vehicles/drones

Unmanned vehicles, otherwise known as drones, have been used for several decades, mainly in military applications. AI, however, increases the capabilities of drones. As a result of DL methods, drones are better able to capture and analyze the environment in which they operate, allowing increasingly complex missions. AI technology is also making it possible to considerably improve drone visual recognition and image analysis. AI software is empowering drones to become smarter and more autonomous, and their use is expanding beyond their original use of unmanned vehicles in the military to improved mapping development, rescue missions, disaster response, power line problem detection, overhead surveillance, and much more.

One of the main capabilities supporting all of these new use cases is image recognition. AI software can now autonomously capture, process, and analyze drone data gathered from aerial images. It then takes the AI engine only minutes to process the images as opposed to days for humans to accomplish the same task. As a result of this enhanced capability, drones are being deployed in many disaster areas to quickly analyze imagery and inform decision-making, rather than spending human labor on the laborious and often dangerous task of identifying damaged areas, such as in the wild fires of Northern California or the 2021 collapse of the Surfside Condo Towers in Miami.

AI-powered drones are also being used in commercial venues, and various industrial sectors are developing more and more intelligent drones. Their use is most common in specific industry sectors where the potential profits are high, such as the construction and warehouse-related industries. In construction, drones are being used for routine inspection tasks. In warehouses, drones are used to navigate through the building and automatically do inventory checks.[50]

Retail/e-commerce

The retail industry is no stranger to technology. In fact, retail has led the adoption of technologies that have proliferated into other sectors, such as supply chain management. Retail success is highly dependent upon customer satisfaction, which includes delivering a personalized shopping experience, together with rapid purchase processing and delivery.

AI is being used extensively in the world of retail. In every facet of merchandising – from a pair of jeans in a showroom to a container ship crossing the Pacific Ocean with tons of the latest fashion apparel – AI enables companies to see both

---

[50] Oren, Camille and Verity, Andrej. (May 2020). "Artificial Intelligence (AI) Applied to Unmanned Aerial Vehicles (UAVs) And its Impact on Humanitarian Action." Available at *www.updwg.org/wp-content/uploads/2021/02/Artificial-Intelligence-Applied-to-Unmanned-Aerial-Vehicles-And-its-Impact-on-Humanitarian-Action-May-2020-2.pdf*.

the smallest detail and the big picture simultaneously, and compile all of that incoming data into simple, easy-to-use guidelines for how to keep stores stocked with just the right amount of merchandise, but also with information about what merchandise will likely sell best in the next season.

With a multitude of merchants seeking to provide shoppers with attention-getting shopping experiences, retailers are using AI to engage customers in a personalized and relevant manner. Algorithmic engines can translate real-world browsing behaviors into sales opportunities by presenting customers with new or related products – curating recommendations based on analysis of search activity, aesthetic, and similarity. This is perhaps most easily recognizable when using a search engine on a particular subject and suddenly a selection of relevant merchandise just appears on the search page.

But merchants are using AI for more than just customer interaction. By mining data from markets, consumers, and even competitors, AI can forecast industry shifts and make proactive changes to a company's marketing, production, merchandising, and business strategies. In some areas, facial recognition and other monitoring technologies in marketplace environments are using AI to recognize and interpret facial, biometric, and audio cues. AI interfaces can then pinpoint shoppers' in-the-moment emotions and reactions to deliver more individualized products, recommendations, or support – ensuring that a retail engagement is right on the mark.

So, bottom line ...

The media would have us believe that a universe populated with AI is just around the corner and that AI has permeated everything around us. The headlines would lead us to believe that we are already living in that future time where AI has infiltrated every aspect of society. But that is only partially true.

Today's media tends to focus on some of the rather sensational AI developments, but also understate the complexity involved in deploying advanced AI systems in the real world. Real progress in AI is painful, slow, and expensive. Despite the hype, despite advances in the use of AI, we are still far from machines that think like you and me, and from AI being in the forefront of all areas of human action. The primary barrier is the limitation of AI and DL. So, while we may be seeing AI applications in a number of areas, it is still not ubiquitous. As Ann LeCun, a recipient of the 2019 Turing Award,[51] said: *"Machines are still very, very stupid. The smartest AI systems today have less common sense than a house cat."*[52]

---

[51] The Turing Award is an annual award issued by the Association for Computing Machinery (ACM) for excellent contributions to the field of computing.

[52] Savage, Neil. Neural Net Worth. *Communications of the ACM.* Available at *https://cacm.acm.org/magazines/2019/6/236990-neural-net-worth/fulltext?mobile=false*.

CHAPTER 3: HUMAN-MACHINE COLLABORATION – CAN WE TALK TO THEM IN ENGLISH (OR ANY OTHER LANGUAGE)?

> *"Can AI learn from people? Can people learn from AI? The prospect of creating systems that can better collaborate with humans, figuring out how we build this common ground, is what excites me most about the future of AI ..."*
>
> **Mark Stefik, Research Fellow, Human-Machine Collaboration, PARC**

Humans can often achieve real success when working in a team. In fact, there is a sort of cult around the formation of teams to address complex problems. The concept that teamwork makes us more creative and productive is widespread, and when faced with a new challenge, leaders are quick to assume that forming a team is the best way to get the job done.

At the same time, there are real challenges to effective teamwork – ineffectively defined goals and tasks, unproductive collaborative work practices, and unsatisfactory computing technology for facilitating teamwork. J. Richard Hackman, the Edgar Pierce Professor of Social and Organizational Psychology at Harvard University is a leading expert on teams. He has spent a lot of time exploring – and questioning – the wisdom of teams, and claims that most of the time, team members can't even agree on what the team's goals should be and how to get there.[53]

The "Age of With™"

A number of researchers are engaging in human-machine collaboration research in order to find more effective ways of creating and engaging human teams – by involving AI as a member of the team. The technology company Deloitte has coined the term "The Age of With" to describe the concept of machines and humans working together so that both can perform smarter. In a 2019 study done by Deloitte, 62% of the organizations studied actively used AI to reduce or even eliminate transactional work and replace repetitive tasks, 47% were supplementing current processes to improve productivity, and 36% were looking at new and innovative ways of working.[54]

As AI continues to augment or even replace human workers, jobs themselves are evolving to demand innovative combinations of AI, and human skills and capabilities. But, even with the evolution of AI skills, there will still remain some areas where humans are especially adept, such as empathy and complex problem-solving.

MIT Professor Thomas W. Malone[55] notes that, as AI can do more of the things that were previously only done by people, we may need to rethink what it means to be human, and what

---

[53] Coutu, D. (May 2009). Why Teams Don't Work. *Harvard Business Review*.

[54] Deloitte Global Human Capital Trends Survey, 2019.

[55] Thomas W. Malone is the *Patrick J. McGovern (1959) Professor of Management* at the MIT Sloan School of Management and the founding director of the MIT Center for Collective Intelligence.

the uniquely human skills are that would continue to remain essential. Malone contends that the collaboration of humans and AI can create more intelligent super minds simply by building new paths for alliance between humans and machines, thus enabling more complex ways of thinking. This human-machine collaboration can have far-reaching consequences on how we as humans live and work. Such a collaboration has the ability to accomplish complex goals by combining human and AI to collectively achieve superior results and continuously improve by learning from each other.

For AI to be an effective part of a human-machine collaboration, it will need to have much more capability than we see in today's manufacturing or social robots, or digital assistants. AI will need to be an active participant in many of the steps involved in the complex problem-solving process, i.e. defining the problem, identifying root causes, proposing and evaluating solutions, choosing among options, planning and taking actions, learning from these interactions, and contributing to after-action analyses.

As we discussed in an earlier chapter, AI has become increasingly more pervasive as a result of the accessibility of hardware and software to process dense neural network training algorithms (aka DL) that mimic the neural architecture of the brain. These more complex algorithms can be trained using unstructured data, such as images, audio, or text, and have radically altered the degree to which AI can learn to reason, classify, and understand. These algorithms are still specific to narrow task domains, such as speech recognition, image classification, human emotion, and characteristic recognition, but their ability and application is continuing to evolve.

But effective human-AI collaboration requires more than just some smart algorithms. It needs the actual coordination of complex activities, such as communication, joint action, and human-aware execution to successfully complete a task that might involve shifting goals in varying environmental conditions and uncertainty.[56]

The five Ts of human-machine collaboration

Manesh Bahi of Cognizant[57] talks about the need to address the five "Ts" when looking at human-machine collaboration: tasks, teams, talent, technology, and trust.

- **Teams will need to be small, flexible, and hybrid.** The transition to intelligent AI needs acute focus on the relationship between humans and machines, how the two will collaborate, and how organizations will adapt to AI. In the future, there will likely be a move from large, hierarchical teams to leaner, more adaptable teams. This will allow AI-human teams to be more fluid across roles and functions.

- **Tasks will be assigned and shared.** No single task will be executed 100% by a machine or a human. Instead, tasks will have a larger degree of shared involvement. Companies will need to clearly define roles and responsibilities and set the rules for AI and humans to synchronize to accomplish a task. Research is being

---

[56] Lemaignan, S.; Warnier, M.; Sisbot, E.A.; Clodic, A.; and Alami, R. (2017) Artificial cognition for social human–robot interaction: An implementation. *Artificial Intelligence.* 247, pp. 45–69.

[57] Bahi, M. (October 2018). The Five Ts of Human-Machine Collaboration. *Cognizant.*

conducted on using AR/VR as a means for enabling humans to communicate more directly with AI.

- **Talent will be a fusion of human and technical skills.** Technical capabilities will continue to be important, but will blend with the more human-centric skills of problem-solving, adaptability, creativity, communication, and organization. These human capabilities will require adjustment for optimal human-machine collaboration. Humans will need training to apply the technologies and processes needed to make the best use of AI.

- **Technology matters more than ever.** For a long time, organizations have accumulated a massive and outdated legacy infrastructure, which is not only expensive to upgrade but cannot meet the greater technical demands of AI. A successful implementation of humans and machines requires a major technology upgrade, so many IT infrastructures will need to be completely revamped.

- **Trust is essential for success.** Few organizations have a clear understanding of how to handle the threat posed by AI to current jobs, which will affect employee-employer trust levels. AI and automation are increasingly assuming many routine, repetitive and low-end tasks, rendering some human skills and capabilities irrelevant, and leaving those unable to keep up and compete behind. This can lead to a trust deficit between humans and AI. Trust growth is a continuous process in evolving successful teams, and requires the establishment of trust and ongoing adjustment based on the team's experiences concerning each team member's performance as well as the overall team performance. To instill trust in the introduction of AI, organizations should proceed sensitively and gradually, and focus on the human-machine collaboration benefits. No matter how well AI is designed, it won't be successfully adopted if people don't have confidence and trust in them. Humans will have increased trust in AI if they see positive results from the collaboration.

Types of human-machine collaboration

Three types of human-machine (AI) collaboration have been identified:

1. **AI will complete a task autonomously.** Humans take control only when machines are unable to proceed further (e.g. automated call centers).
2. **AI may be able to complete a task independently**, however, final control is handed to a human for final diagnoses (e.g. medical diagnostics).
3. **AI cannot complete a task alone, but may be used to supplement human decision-making** (e.g. analyzing data and making recommendations).

Until recently, interactions between machines and humans have tended to take the easier direction, i.e. optimize the actions, flows, and processes for the AI machine, and then have the humans adjust their actions to the machine. This is typified by the modern assembly lines used to manufacture automobiles enabled by robotic process automation.

To date, it has been easier to have humans adapt to machines than to do the opposite. Making AI machines adapt to a human model of work would require the AI to understand humans and collaborate with them in the same way as in a human-human model. Although still sometime in the future, this change is already underway. Professor Judith Donath forecasts:

> *"By 2030, most social situations will be facilitated by bots ... that interact with us in human-like ways ... Aided by their access to vast troves of data about each of us, bots will far surpass humans in their ability to attract and persuade us. Able to mimic emotion expertly ... artificially intelligent companions will cultivate the impression that social goals similar to our own motivate them ... But their real collaboration will be with the humans and institutions that control them."*[58]

How can humans and machines communicate?

Current research into various types of sensors and complex algorithms are beginning to change the boundaries of how humans and machines communicate and interact. Human-machine communication represents an emerging area of communication research focused on the study of the *"creation of meaning among humans and machines,"*[59] and the refinement and development of theory related to people's interactions with AI technologies.

Today, there are several means by which humans communicate with AI/machines. These include voice-based assistants, such as Microsoft's Siri or Amazon's Alexa,

---

[58] Donath, J. (December 2018). Artificial Intelligence and the Future of Humans. *Pew Research Study.*

[59] Guzman, A.L. (2018). What is Human-Machine Communication, Anyway? In Guzman, A.L. (ed.) *Human-Machine Communication: Rethinking Communication, Technology, and Ourselves.* New York: Peter Lang, pp. 1–28.

which can vocally respond to human questions and requests. Embodied robots interact verbally and nonverbally with people. Automated programs, known as bots, participate in text-based social media interactions by impersonating human conversational partners. There are AI technologies that respond uniquely to individual users, "learning" about their human communication partner and altering their communications accordingly.

The Technical University of Munich (TUM) is conducting research into the various methods by which humans and AI can communicate, as illustrated in Figure 3-1.

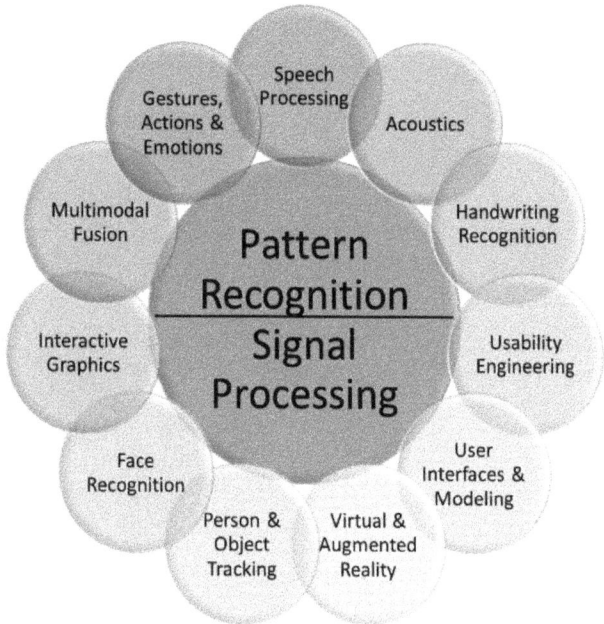

Figure 3-1: Human-machine communication[60]

---

[60] Adapted from the TUM research into human-machine communication.

3: Human-machine collaboration – Can we talk to them in English (or any other language)?

One of the most prominent areas of research is identifying ways to make human-machine interaction more natural, and the TUM is increasingly leveraging the principles of interhuman communication.

Uniquely, human roles and relationships have long served as the basis for AI technology design. Human-like attributes of AI, such as gender, further cement the technology's perceived communication role. For example, AI agents, such as Alexa, function almost as assistants and, as a result, have been designed with overt gender roles that are consistent with many of our cultural biases and stereotypes of human assistants – that is, most of these so-called assistants replicate female voices for communication. In creating these AI technologies, these seem to encapsulate the world views and biases of their creators that are enacted within their communications.[61]

HMC is one organization that is attempting to address the nuances and challenges of human-AI communication. Scholars at HMC are outlining a number of research focus areas in order to further develop their understanding of communication between humans and AI.

One focus of research is on AI sensor perception. Fujitsu is developing AI by using computational models of human sensory signals and anthropomorphic attributes, such as motive and empathy. Its *Sensecomputing* technology is

---

[61] Broussard, M. (2018). *Artificial Unintelligence: How Computers Misunderstand the World.* Cambridge: MIT Press.

enabling AI to interpret human emotions and respond in the same way that humans do in human-human interactions.[62]

Another stream of research is focused on developing targeted learning algorithms, allowing AI to communicate with humans. As humans, we depend upon a complex maze of instincts, cultural norms, and emotions – mechanisms that are challenging to identify empirically and render into an appropriate algorithm. But results from this research are demonstrating that a well-designed reinforcement learning algorithm can facilitate AI-human communications at levels that rival human-human communication.

Challenges to human-machine collaboration

In designing human-machine collaboration, researchers have largely been pursuing a technology-first approach. Nancy Cooke, Professor of Human Systems Engineering at Arizona State University, warns that when AI too closely mimics humans socially, it may in fact misrepresent exactly what AI can do and lead to unrealistic expectations.[63] Humans should not be compelled to adapt to the technology; rather, designers and developers should adapt the technology to serve in conjunction with humans. This creates an imperative for human-centered, not technology-centered design.

Big data and the process by which AI learns, seems to solidify existing human biases in ways that could negatively impact our social, political, and economic lives. Simply put, biased training data can lead to bias in the AI. Corporations,

---

[62] Hayashida, N. (October 2018). Sensecomputing for Human-Machine Collaboration through Human Emotion Understanding. *Fujitsu Scientific & Technical Journal.*

[63] Guszcza, J. (January 2018). Smarter together: Why artificial intelligence needs human-centered design. *Deloitte Review.*

such as Google and Facebook, consider this to be such a critical issue that they are providing toolkits designed to check for unwanted bias in data sets and ML models, and state-of-the-art algorithms to mitigate any such bias.

James Moor[64] described something he called the policy vacuum, where regulations and policies do not keep pace with technological advances. There is justified concern that AI is advancing far ahead of the legal, ethical, and governance frameworks necessary to guarantee fairness and accountability in the implementation of AI.

If we lived in a perfect world, humans and AI would accomplish their assigned tasks perfectly and would interact seamlessly. But the truth is, both humans and AI can fail occasionally, and the developers of the AI must consider this fact. Humans must be aware of the AI's functions and intervene in a timely manner if there is a potential failure. Ideally, the AI would be able to do the same. This challenges developers to create a human-machine interaction that is robust, not only when everything is going well, but also adapts to things when they go wrong.

Value alignment between man and AI presents additional challenges in effectively communicating with and through AI, and to modeling applicable ethical principles and embedding them in the AI through the AI training process. However, there is no universal set of ethical values – culture, geography, and environment may lead to varying biases – particularly since human behavior itself is not always unbiased, predictable, rational, or ethical. Understanding

---

[64] Moor, James H. "What is Computer Ethics"? Available at *https://web.cs.ucdavis.edu/~rogaway/classes/188/spring06/papers/moor.html*.

how bias can enter into AI is critical to developing a more fulfilling collaboration between humans and machines.

CHAPTER 4: AI, ETHICS, AND SOCIETY – ARE THEY COMPATIBLE?

> *"AI presents three major areas of ethical concern for society: privacy and surveillance, bias and discrimination, and perhaps the deepest, most difficult philosophical question of the era, the role of human judgment."*
>
> **Michael Sandel[65]**

Ethics, morals, and laws are essentially concepts and beliefs of what constitutes right and wrong behavior. Individuals often use the terms "moral," "ethical," and "legal" as if they are synonymous, but there are critical distinctions. These terms, however, do share one critical commonality – they are about what is right and wrong behavior.

The term **morals** speaks to an individual's or group's personal and unique set of *internal* principles in respect to right and wrong behavior. These principles are often subjective and based upon human experience, and are ingrained in religion, culture, family traditions, geography, and environment. Morals may also be derived from historical knowledge, practical observation, and the observed consequences of actions. In general, morals clarify the responsibility of the individual to other persons and to society overall. Morals provide firewalls to deter what is

---

[65] Michael Sandel is a political philosopher and a Harvard University Professor of Government.

deemed immoral behavior and prevent harm to self and others.

Ethics, on the other hand, refers to behavioral expectations that are *externally* imposed upon an individual or group by an outside source (e.g. their profession, associations, society, religion, employer, etc.). Certain ethical behaviors, for example, are required from individuals belonging to a particular institution, group, or culture. For instance, lawyers, doctors, law enforcement personnel, etc. all have a defined external code of conduct that they must follow.

Finally, **laws** refer to legal standards enforced by the civil or criminal process. The courts or administrative agencies use laws to protect individual and community safety and security. Laws provide a society with the authority to punish a crime, impose a penalty or sanction, or render a judgment to compel resolution and remedy a dispute. However, laws are considered an often inadequate substitute for morals or ethical behavior.

The table below summarizes the comparison between ethics, morals, and laws:

Table 4-1: Comparison Between Ethics and Morals

Parameter of comparison	Ethics	Morals	Laws
Definition	Rules or code of conduct recognized with respect to a specific	Individual principles or habits regarding personal right	Rules that a society or government develops to deal with crime, business

Parameter of comparison	Ethics	Morals	Laws
	class or group of people.	or wrong conduct.	agreements, and social relationships.
Source of origin	External sources.	Internal sources.	External sources.
Reason for doing	Ethics are adhered to because the society or institution provides rules for what should be done.	Morals are followed because an individual believes it is the right thing to do.	Laws are followed because the society or other institution enforces compliance.
Origination	Comes from the Greek word "Ethos," which means "character."	Stems from the Latin word "Mos," meaning "custom."	Derives from the Teutonic word "lag," meaning definite or rule.
Basis for acceptance	Ethics are governed by legal or professional	Morals go beyond purely cultural or professional	Laws are often combined with a penalty for non-compliance.

Parameter of comparison	Ethics	Morals	Laws
	principles or guidelines.	boundaries or norms.	
Consistency	Dependent upon an external source that generally remains constant within a specific context, but may differ with respect to another context.	Morals largely remain constant. They may change when a difference emerges in the individual's belief structure.	Laws are dependent upon an external source that generally remains constant, but can change over time based on external developments.

Bringing this to a point – individual morals may influence how a developer designs and implements a specific algorithm. As discussed in the earlier chapter on bias, it is incredibly easy for implicit bias to be inadvertently or intentionally designed into an AI. When humans act in certain ways, they are held both morally and ethically responsible. But where AI is operating, only the humans responsible for the algorithms that have been created for a specific AI implementation can be held responsible for the action of an AI. However, ethics in AI can provide AI-focused professional guidelines on the development and implementation of AI, regardless of the area of application and specific mechanisms by which humans can be held accountable for ethical AI design.

How do ethics relate to AI?

In the 1940s, American science fiction author Isaac Asimov developed the "Three Laws of Robotics," in which he argued that intelligent robots should be programmed ethically so that they:

1. May not injure a human being, or, through inaction, allow a human being to come to harm.
2. Must obey the orders given by human beings, except where such orders would conflict with the First Law.
3. Must protect their own existence, as long as such protection does not conflict with the First or Second Law.

Fast forward to today, and these same rules could apply to AI. AI and ML have the ability to rapidly transform society and are likely to continue to do so in the coming decades. This social transformation has the potential for a deep, ethical impact, as these powerful new technologies can both improve and disrupt human lives. If we look at AI as an externalization of human intelligence, it offers us in amplified form everything that is both moral and ethical, or immoral and unethical. The ethics of AI are increasingly important as we enter an era where more advanced and sophisticated AI is becoming an integral part of our daily life.

The Alan Turing Institute described AI ethics as *"a set of values, principles, and techniques that employ widely accepted standards of right and wrong to guide moral conduct in the development and use of AI technologies.*"[66]

With the rapid advances in computing power and access to vast amounts of big data, AI and ML will continue to improve and evolve. In the not-too-distant future, AI will process and use data not only faster, but also with more accuracy, and be represented in ever increasing areas of business and social life. But, with vast power comes great responsibility. Despite the advantages and benefits AI can bring to the world, it may also potentially cause harm to humans and society if it is misused or poorly designed. As a result, it is critical for the development of AI systems to be responsible and developed toward optimal sustainability for public benefit. The field of AI ethics is evolving with the intent to avoid individual and societal harms that might be precipitated by the misuse, abuse, poor design, or unintended negative consequences of an AI implementation.

However, codes of ethics in regard to AI are imperfect. There is no universally agreed upon ethical framework. Unlike laws, the frameworks that exist are not binding, and consequently do not mandate compliance. AI ethics more often mirror the values of the organization that is developing the AI, rather than the range of demographics potentially impacted by the AI. Finally, those determining ethics in AI provide little or no

" ... *guidance on how to resolve conflicts or tensions between them (such as when heeding one principle would*

---

[66] Leslie, D. (2019). Understanding artificial intelligence ethics and safety: A guide for the responsible design and implementation of AI systems in the public sector. Alan Turing Institute. *Zenodo*. Available at *https://doi.org/10.5281/zenodo.3240529*.

undermine another), making them even more difficult to operationalize. Moreover, because tech companies create or control most AI-powered products, this governance model relies largely on corporate self-regulation – a worrying prospect given the absence of democratic representation and accountability in corporate decision-making. "[67]

The Markkula Center for Applied Ethics at the Santa Clara University in California has been researching AI ethics for several years and has identified some topics that have a relationship to AI and ethics.[68]

Technical safety

A *"Japanese Paralympic judoka on Aug. 26 [2021] was hit by a self-driving vehicle inside the athletes' village, suffering injuries that will require two weeks to recover, according to the Metropolitan Police Department."[69]* Two human operators were on board but didn't stop the vehicle. After the accident, the operators claimed they and the vehicle *"were*

---

[67] Pizzi, M., Romanoff, M., and Engelhardt, T. (March 2021). AI for humanitarian action: Human rights and ethics. *International Review of the Red Cross.* Available at *https://international-review.icrc.org/articles/ai-humanitarian-action-human-rights-ethics-913*.

[68] Green, B. Artificial Intelligence and Ethics: Sixteen Challenges and Opportunities. *Markkula Center for Applied Ethics.* Available at *www.scu.edu/ethics/all-about-ethics/artificial-intelligence-and-ethics-sixteen-challenges-and-opportunities/*.

[69] Paralympian hit by self-driving car inside athletes' village. (August 27, 2021). *The Asahi Shimbun.* Available at *www.asahi.com/ajw/articles/14427620*.

aware that a person was there but thought (the person) would (realize that a bus was coming) and stop crossing the (street). "[70]

The risk of technical failures with the potential for significant harm is increasing as AI becomes more widely used, particularly in sectors where both security and safety are critical. To help in reducing this potential, researchers are looking into developing "safe" AI by identifying the potential sources of unintended behavior in AI and developing tools to mitigate the possibility of this behavior taking place. This field of research focuses on technical fixes to ensure that AI operates safely and reliably. But technology alone is not the answer. Other solutions related to the design, development, and deployment of safe AI – such as how to integrate them into existing networks and how to train operators to work effectively with them – are equally important.

The challenges associated with self-driving vehicles provide a good example of the potential for technical AI failures. Multiple people have been injured or even killed in accidents involving self-driving vehicles because these vehicles encountered situations in which they did not make safe decisions. Highly detailed contracts and use agreements may ensure that a manufacturer's liability from a defective AI is limited. But, from an ethical perspective, not only is the manufacturer ultimately responsible, but the contracts themselves could also be viewed as an unethical plot designed to avoid legitimate responsibility.

---

[70] Paralympian hit by self-driving car inside athletes' village. (August 27, 2021). *The Asahi Shimbun.* Available at www.asahi.com/ajw/articles/14427620.

Transparency versus data protection

Internationally, both lawmakers and users have expressed concern regarding AI and how it functions. There are concerns that AI algorithms will potentially learn using personal information that might facilitate prejudiced or discriminatory practices. As a result, legislation for implementing measures to improve algorithms' transparency is under consideration.

There are many good reasons for greater transparency into the inner workings of AI. Transparency can help moderate concerns associated with fairness, discrimination, and trust.

Transparency, however, can be a two-edged sword. Transparency laws compel companies to publicly expose that they collect and use data collected about a person. But as technology developers publicize more information about just how their algorithms function, the simpler it becomes for cyber attackers to hack them and illegally acquire personal data. As a result, there is a difficulty in determining the balance between transparency and privacy to ensure that AI does not expose personal information and damage individual privacy.

The Harvard Business Review calls this *"AI's 'transparency paradox' – while generating more information about AI might create real benefits, it may also create new risks."*[71] AI deals with massive amounts of data, and as a consequence, a breach in an AI could be catastrophic for both business and privacy reasons. This leaves organizations with the problematic decision of deciding if it is more vital to be

---

[71] Burt, A. (December 13, 2019). The AI Transparency Paradox. *Harvard Business Review*. Available at *https://hbr.org/2019/12/the-ai-transparency-paradox*.

transparent regarding the use of AI and its algorithms, or to safeguard data.

There are a lot of organizations, ranging from online entities to brick-and-mortar organizations that collect all kinds of information, ranging from user contact information, email addresses, and even financial or medical information. Organizations that are transparent with their data collection and use processes may improve their trustworthiness with users. At the same time, other users refuse to provide information if they think it might be misused or mismanaged.

But trustworthiness among users is not the only challenge. At least equally important is transparency, which is becoming essential for AI to gain approval from regulators. This is particularly evident in demands of enhanced regulations, such as the European Union's General Data Protection Regulation (GDPR) and the California Consumer Privacy Act (CCPA). From 2023, the CCPA will be replaced by the California Privacy Rights Act (CPRA). *"For example, GDPR has specific mandates stipulating that automated decision-making, which includes the use of AI models, requires enterprises to do the following:*

- *give individuals information about the processing of their personal data;*
- *introduce simple ways for them to request human intervention or challenge decisions; and*

- *carry out regular checks to make sure the systems are working as intended.*"[72]

Based on the research into AI and ethics, it is clear that there exists both positive and negative aspects for AI and its development. Considering the ever-increasing proliferation of AI, it is impossible to address all of these aspects, so the discussions to follow will focus on some of the more important areas for consideration.

Potential positive ethical and security/safety impacts of AI

AI may be able to afford improvements in nearly every area of human endeavor, for example, biomedical research, communication, data analytics, education, energy efficiency, environmental protection, farming, finance, legal services, medical diagnostics, resource management, space exploration, transportation, waste management, and much more.

Amid the cacophony of individuals expressing concern about AI deleting jobs, and even "taking over the world," the capacity for AI to do good often goes unnoticed.

---

[72] Lawton, G. (March 2, 2021). The future of trust will be built on data transparency. *TechTarget.* Available at *https://searchcio.techtarget.com/feature/The-future-of-trust-must-be-built-on-data-transparency.*

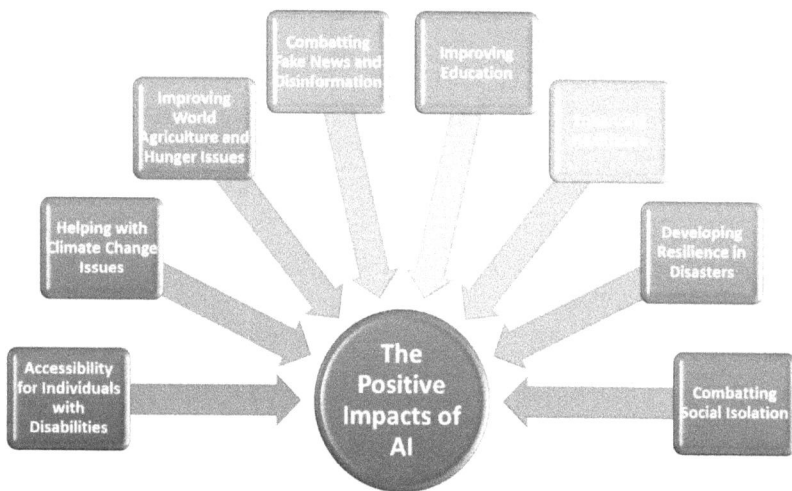

Figure 4-1: The potential positive impacts of AI

But it is also the responsibility of the human developers to determine how to apply AI in order to obtain the most benefit for its users. Forbes recently identified areas where AI can provide enormous benefits[73]:

Improved accessibility for individuals with disabilities

According to the World Institute on Disability (WID), AI is already providing a number of significant aids to foster disability access and inclusion. Existing tools include:

- Auto-captioning with AI to aid individuals with hearing loss or deafness.

---

[73] Marr, B. (February 10, 2020). 8 Powerful Examples of AI for Good. *Forbes.* Available at *www.forbes.com/sites/bernardmarr/2020/02/10/8-powerful-examples-of-ai-for-good/?sh=67b031dd18a8.*

- Autonomous vehicles can provide mobility for those unable to drive.
- Facial and image recognition can help the blind or individuals with low vision to increase their interaction with the environment.
- AI used to enable improved language comprehension can assist those with cognitive challenges.
- AI accessibility tools can help workers and job seekers to develop their professional skills, improve workplace culture, and expand inclusive hiring.

The current achievements in AI only highlight what may be possible in the future for individuals with disabilities. In order for the full potential of AI for individuals with disabilities to be realized, the development of AI needs to take:

"a user-centered approach, artificial intelligence technologies use inclusive design to conceive solutions that best meet the needs of people with disabilities to enhance accessibility. Indeed, AI technology enables them to gain more autonomy whether they're at home enjoying a movie with subtitles or at work reading an accessible document making the world more accessible and inclusive to them."[74]

---

[74] Artificial intelligence and accessibility: examples of a technology that serves people with disabilities. Available at www.inclusivecitymaker.com/artificial-intelligence-accessibility-examples-technology-serves-people-disabilities/.

Helping with climate change issues

Worldwide, many claim that climate change is one of the biggest challenges facing humankind today. The consequences of climate change are becoming increasingly visible as the world experiences stronger and more frequent storms, flooding, droughts, and wildfires.

Climate Change AI (CCAI) is a global institute looking at areas where AI can help in mitigating the effects of climate change. The list below is adapted from CCAI and shows climate change domains where various types of AI/ML can be relevant:[75]

- **Electricity systems** – reducing global impact.
- **Transportation** – alternative fuels, improved vehicle efficiency, and reduced transport activity.
- **Buildings and cities** – improved urban planning, environmentally-friendly construction.
- **Industry** – optimized supply chains, energy management.
- **Farms and forest areas** – remote emissions detection, precision agriculture, farmland, and forestry management.
- **Carbon dioxide management** – detecting and isolating CO_2.
- **Weather prediction** – integrating data from multiple sources, climate science, and extreme event forecasting.
- **Societal impact** – crisis management, enhanced social systems.

---

[75] Rolnik, D., Donti, P., Kaack, L., Kochanski, K., et.al. Tackling Climate Change with Machine Learning. *Climate Change AI*. Available at *www.climatechange.ai/*.

- **Solar engineering** – improved solar capture and utilization.
- **Individual impact** – enhanced understanding of human footprint, aiding in behavioral change.
- **Collective decision-making** – informing legislation and regulation.
- **Education** – increased understanding of climate change cause and impact.
- **Finance** – identification of costs and funding for climate change remediation.

Improving world agriculture and addressing hunger

Population increases, coupled with dramatic climate change, declining soil quality through agricultural overuse, and multiple contenders using potential crop land for production of biofuels are creating significant challenges in feeding the world's population.

"The United Nations (UN) estimates that 840 million people will be affected by hunger by 2030, but researchers have developed a roadmap combining smart and nano-enabled agriculture with AI and machine learning capabilities that could help to reduce this number."[76]

---

[76] University of Birmingham. (June 24, 2021). Nanotech and AI could hold key to unlocking global food security challenge. *ScienceDaily.* Available at *www.sciencedaily.com/releases/2021/06/210624114428.htm.*

Combining AI with nanotechnology[77] enables precision agriculture, which means that farmers are able to identify the best time and location to plant a crop, thereby having greater yield rates to harvest, and ensuring that little to no harvest is squandered.

Support to human rights

AI has created:

> *"new forms of oppression and disproportionally affect those who are the most powerless and vulnerable. Human rights exist exactly to address power differentials and to provide individuals, and the organizations that represent them, with the language and procedures to contest the actions of more powerful actors, such as states and corporations."*[78]

One of the most important questions to ask is how can AI best support human rights while also lessening the risks?

AI, when properly designed and implemented, can have a beneficial impact on human rights challenges. AI can assist in identifying actors in human trafficking, their routes, and

---

[77] The formal definition of nanotechnology from the National Nanotechnology Initiative (NNI) is: "Nanotechnology is the understanding and control of matter at dimensions between approximately 1 and 100 nanometers, where unique phenomena enable novel applications." *MRSEC Education Group.* Available at *https://education.mrsec.wisc.edu/what-is-nanotechnology-defining-nanotechnology/.*

[78] van Veen, C. (May 14, 2018). Artificial Intelligence: What's Human Rights Got To Do With It? *Data and Society: Points.* Available at *https://points.datasociety.net/artificial-intelligence-whats-human-rights-got-to-do-with-it-4622ec1566d5.*

customers, and assist lawmakers in prevention through predictive decision-making. In areas of conflict, AI can provide safe mechanisms for human rights organizations to collaborate and comprehend the conflict environment without compromising their privacy and security protocols.

The COVID-19 pandemic clearly exposed how AI could help define a global response to a crisis. Governments and international organizations across the globe used the predictive power, flexibility, and scalability of AI to develop models to predict the spread of the virus and facilitate molecular-level research that led to the development of effective vaccines.

AI is also being deployed in innovative ways to supplement humanitarian action. Computer vision, a subset of ML, can be used to automatically identify structures acquired through satellite imagery that help to swiftly track migration flows and facilitate a more efficient distribution of assistance during a humanitarian crisis.

Combatting fake news and disinformation

As evidenced in 2016, and again in 2020, AI's role in creating and spreading misinformation can challenge the concept of a fair election, and may even constitute a threat to free will, political participation, and independence. In 2016, false information during the US presidential election demonstrated how a foreign power can use bots and social media algorithms to spread disinformation, with the goal of potentially influencing voters. Today's social media and news dissemination platforms are working to prevent this type of activity, but AI-powered chatbots and deep fakes will continue to make such content increasingly convincing to voters and more difficult to detect. As the uprising at the US

Capitol on January 6, 2021 demonstrates, this may have a significant effect on political participation, especially if voters no longer trust the legitimacy of an election.

Wherever there is AI, there can also be "artificial stupidity" or the gullibility of individuals to disinformation spread through social media, news outlets, and other information sources. In the same way that AI can facilitate the spread of fake news and disinformation, it can also be used to combat it. We are being inundated with information every minute of every day.

"Each minute, there are 98,000 tweets, 160 million emails sent, and 600 videos uploaded to YouTube. Politicians. Marketers. News outlets. Plus, there are countless individuals spewing their opinions since self-publishing is so easy. People crave a way to sort through all the information to find valuable nuggets they can use in their own life. They want facts, and companies are starting to respond often by using machine learning and AI tools."[79]

Combatting fake news and disinformation is a very complicated challenge. Although fact-checking websites, such as FactCheck.org, PolitiFact, and Snopes, do a reasonable job of providing an impartial verification of news and remarks made by politicians, social media, and news outlets, they have a limited reach. But as they face increased criticism, many of the social media sites, such as Facebook, Twitter, and others, are turning to these tools to assist in verifying viral news stories. These social media sites and

---

[79] Marr, B. (January 25, 2021). Fake News Is Rampant, Here Is How Artificial Intelligence Can Help. *Forbes*. Available at *www.forbes.com/sites/bernardmarr/2021/01/25/fake-news-is-rampant-here-is-how-artificial-intelligence-can-help/?sh=32a5d6da48e4*.

others are also in the process of using AI/ML to develop new and improved products to aid in the detection of fake news and disinformation. As in other situations, however, AI/ML cannot provide the final solution; human review and interpretation is still essential in weeding out the truth from the fiction.

Improving education

AI can be used in education to enhance both learning and teaching, aiding the education sector to benefit students and educators alike. For students, AI can streamline the education process by delivering improved access to courses, improving communication with educators, and freeing up time to focus on other aspects of life. As a result, AI can have a positive impact on a student's educational experience. Specific areas where this positive impact can be felt include:

- Increased personalization of a student's educational experience to create a customized profile of each student and design training materials based on individual ability, preferred learning style, and experience;
- Providing learning assistance and tutoring outside of the classroom;
- Delivering quick and responsive feedback; and
- Providing access to a 24x7 learning environment.

AI also provides significant benefits to educators. One of the primary challenges to educators is time management, and the ability to personalize teaching for individual student's needs. AI can help free up time spent on repetitive tasks and allow educators to adjust their course materials to concentrate on the knowledge gaps or challenges to prevent a student from falling too far behind. Voice assistants, such as Apple's Siri and Amazon's Alexa, are enabling students to interact with standardized educational material without the direct interaction of the teacher.

Adjusting the learning experience based on each student's unique requirements has continually been a priority for educators, and the use of AI allows a level of differentiation that is otherwise impossible when there are 30 or more students in each class. This type of hyper-personalization delivers a wide range of materials that leverage the same core curriculum but tailor the content and delivery to the specific requirements of each student.

Each course tends to drive certain repetitive questions, and AI can assist the educator by providing answers to these reoccurring questions and student issues. Autonomous conversational agents are able to respond to questions from students, provide help with assignments, and reinforce content with supplementary information that reinforces the curriculum.

Finally, AI can automate an educator's mundane tasks, such as grading papers and other administrative types of work. Educators are tasked with many non-teaching responsibilities, such as filing paperwork, participating in human relations and other personnel-related issues, ordering and preparing classroom materials, coordinating field trips, responding to parents, helping with second language related issues, or dealing with sick or otherwise absent students. Studies indicate that educators often spend 50% or more of their time on non-teaching tasks.[80]

---

[80] Schmelzer, R. (July 12, 2019), AI Applications in Education. *Forbes.* Available at *www.forbes.com/sites/cognitiveworld/2019/07/12/ai-applications-in-education/?sh=4197f13262a3*.

Enhancing healthcare and refining healthcare decisions

"Artificial intelligence (AI) has the potential to transform how healthcare is delivered. A joint report with the European Union's EIT Health explores how it can support improvements in care outcomes, patient experience, and access to healthcare services. It can increase productivity and the efficiency of care delivery, and allow healthcare systems to provide more and better care to more people. AI can help improve the experience of healthcare practitioners, enabling them to spend more time in direct patient care and reducing burnout."[81]

Diagnosis and treatment of disease have been core applications of AI in healthcare. AI can help identify pinpoint treatments for diseases, such as cancer, and healthcare apps can make it simpler and less time-consuming for health providers to collect, store, and access data. AI also offers a variety of applications in patient management, including health records management, medical billing and claims processing, clinical documentation, and revenue cycle controls. Research indicates that approximately *"30% of healthcare costs are associated with administrative tasks."*[82] Many of these tasks can be automated with AI, such as pre-authorizing insurance, following-up on unpaid bills,

---

[81] Spatharou, A., Hieronimus, S, and Jenkins, J. (March 10, 2020). Transforming healthcare with AI: The impact on the workforce and organizations. *McKinsey & Company*. Available at *www.mckinsey.com/industries/healthcare-systems-and-services/our-insights/transforming-healthcare-with-ai*.

[82] Phaneuf, A., (January 29, 2021). Use of AI in healthcare & medicine is booming – here's how the medical field is benefiting from AI in 2022 and beyond. *Insider*.

and maintaining records, thus easing the workload of healthcare professionals, allowing them to focus on providing patient care, and ultimately saving providers money spent on routine administration.

Researchers in healthcare at McKinsey & Company[83] have identified several areas where AI is positively impacting the healthcare industry and providing for improved care. One of these is increased productivity and efficiency for the delivery of healthcare, which enables healthcare systems to provide improved care to more patients. AI can also ease the burden of healthcare providers allowing them to dedicate more time to direct patient care without risking the burnout that often occurs in a medical environment.

Developing resilience in the face of disasters

Natural and man-made disasters have demonstrated their ability to affect the lives and livelihoods of individuals around the globe. Advances in AI technologies are providing resilient disaster management throughout the phases of preparation, mitigation, response, and recovery. With natural disasters occurring four times as often as in 1970[84] because of climate change and other factors, researchers are looking to AI to improve disaster resilience.

Public and private organizations are turning to AI-based technologies to marshal relief resources more efficiently and rapidly. Here are some examples:

---

[83] McKinsey & Company is a global management and consulting corporation based in the U.S.

[84] Weather-related disasters are increasing. *The Economist*. Available at *www.economist.com/graphic-detail/2017/08/29/weather-related-disasters-are-increasing*.

- Weather, geo-spatial, and data from previous disasters can help predict how many individuals will be displaced and where the migrations will likely occur. This assists aid workers in determining how and where medical care, temporary housing, water, and food will be needed.
- AI can provide more timely, almost instantaneous, assessments of flooding, wind, and other damage using satellite imagery.
- Social media feeds can be interpreted to provide insight into on-the-ground information.
- AI can help organizations collaborate and integrate disaster relief activities.

At the same time, it's important to be sensitive to AI's limitations. Disaster data analysis requires established and internationally agreed-upon processes to rigorously review algorithm methods and assumptions. Finally, international agencies must develop universally-accepted ethical AI principles for design, engineering, and deployment.

Combatting social isolation

The absence of a human support system and human contact can have negative effects on health and cognitive function. The COVID-19 pandemic brought concerns about potential damage as a result of social isolation to a new level. But even before COVID-19, millions of people were already displaying what researchers might define as social isolation – separated from society, with few personal relationships and little communication with the outside world.

There have been a number of research efforts directed at illustrating the effects of social isolation. One example was conducted in 1972,

"... when French adventurer and scientist Michel Siffre famously shut himself in a cave in Texas for more than six months—what still clocks in as one of the longest self-isolation experiments in history. Meticulously documenting the effects on his mind over those 205 days, Siffre wrote that he could 'barely string thoughts' together after a couple months. By the five-month mark, he was reportedly so desperate for company that he tried (unsuccessfully) to befriend a mouse."[85]

Social isolation often affects the more vulnerable members of society – such as the elderly or our youth. When used effectively, AI can help alleviate social isolation by providing a means of connecting individuals who are alone because of physical or environmental limitations, facilitating support systems for individuals who would otherwise be alone, or providing individuals with a means of connection with friends and family.

This is particularly true for the elderly, where AI can serve to simplify life, providing them with a sense of social connection. Some of the ways AI can improve senior quality of life includes healthcare support through early disease detection and personalized medical care; creating a smarter, safer home where the elderly can be more easily monitored; installing "chatbots" with which seniors can create a form of conversational interaction; and improving access to transportation, especially in the form of advanced driver assistance systems (ADAS).

---

[85] Offord, C. (July 13, 2020). How Social Isolation Affects the Brain. *TheScientist.* Available at *www.the-scientist.com/features/how-social-isolation-affects-the-brain-67701*.

AI in the time of COVID

This book would be remiss if it did not look at the positive and negative aspects of the use of AI during the COVID-19 pandemic. Coronavirus is caused by the severe acute respiratory syndrome virus 2 (SARS-CoV-2). The first incidence of COVID-19 was detected in December 2019, and by early 2020, it had spread rapidly around the world. From the outset of the pandemic, governments and health services worldwide recognized the need to act quickly and decisively to stop the disease from spreading. Rapid spread led to enormous losses across the globe, both physical and financial, and exerted considerable pressure on limited medical, service industry, and delivery resources.

"Since the pandemic's onset, innovative applications of AI have included detecting outbreaks, facilitating diagnosis, identifying people with fevers, and accelerating gene sequencing and vaccine development, demonstrating that this non-medical intervention holds much promise in empowering the response to the global health crisis and future healthcare."[86]

Normally, conventional vaccine development has been costly, requiring many years to identify and develop an effective vaccine against a specified pathogen. The COVID-19 outbreak exposed an urgent need for the acceleration of vaccine development worldwide.

---

[86] Mariano, B., Wu, S., and Muneene, D. (July 23, 2021). Artificial intelligence for covid-19 response. the*bmjopinion.* Available at *https://blogs.bmj.com/bmj/2021/07/23/artificial-intelligence-for-covid-19-response/.*

AI aided researchers in developing a rapid understanding of the virus and its structure, and predicting which of its structural elements would provoke a successful immune response in humans, a key step in vaccine design. Using AI, medical scientists were able to identify the requirements for potential vaccines and make sense of experimental data. AI also assisted scientists in tracking COVID's genetic mutations over time, which is essential for determining a vaccine's effectiveness.

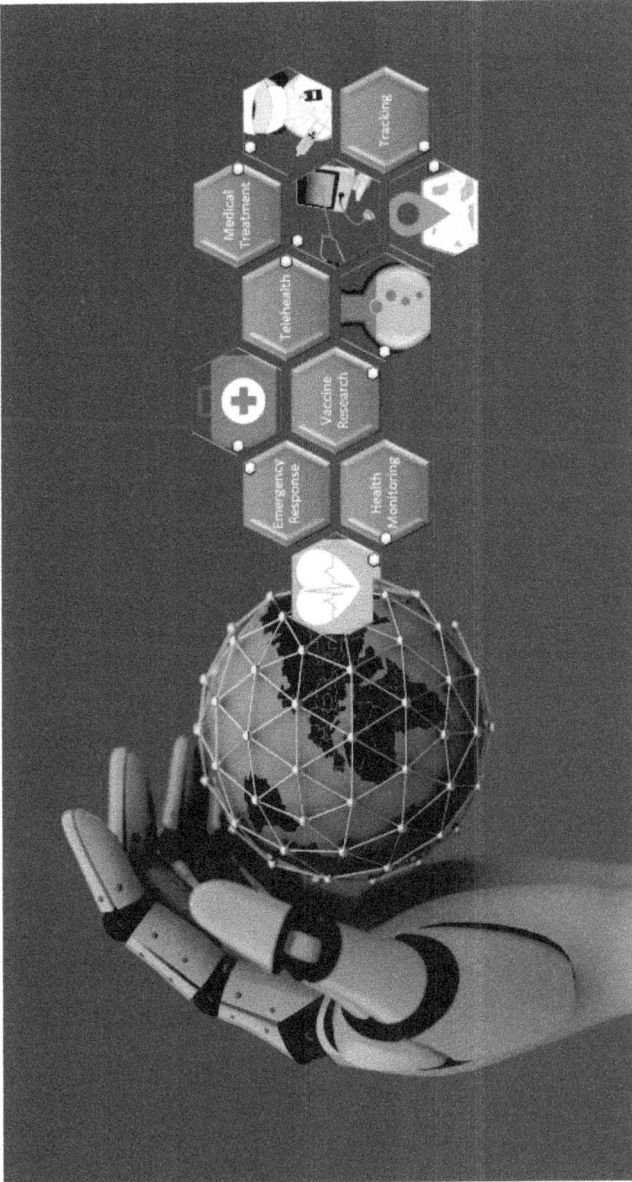

Figure 4-2: AI uses during COVID

As the spread of COVID continued throughout 2021, together with the emergence of new strains, such as the Delta and Omicron variations, scientists used AI to analyze pathogen and epidemiological big data to devise more robust methods for antigen discovery, one of the primary roadblocks in vaccine development.

In addition to the development of the COVID vaccines, AI also demonstrated utility in the actual treatment of the disease. Hospitals and clinics developed AI

> *"Models that identified those with the virus likely to need hospitalization, which helped with capacity planning. They built another model that helped alert doctors to a patient's risk for an intensive care unit and prioritized those at higher risk for aggressive treatment. And when patients were sent home and monitored there, the clinic's software flagged which patients might need to return to the hospital."*[87]

The use of AI during the COVID pandemic regenerated a continuing debate about surveillance and privacy concerning data that is not being collected as part of research. AI-assisted contact tracing and disease monitoring may have assisted with pandemic response in several nations, such as South Korea or Singapore, but these same approaches have encountered broad skepticism in other countries, such as the US.

---

[87] Morrison, J. (March 5, 2021). How Doctors are Using Artificial Intelligence to Battle Covid-19. *Smithsonian Magazine.* Available at *www.smithsonianmag.com/science-nature/how-doctors-are-using-artificial-intelligence-battle-covid-19-180977124/.*

The use of AI for COVID treatment and management revealed a number of flaws, such as algorithm bias, that resulted in the unfair treatment of specific groups of individuals. The potential for algorithmic biases is a well-known challenge in AI development, with the result of entrenching and augmenting existing inequalities in many demographics. Uncritically deploying AI in the fight against COVID-19, often amplified the pandemic's adverse effects on vulnerable groups and intensified health inequity.

The British Medical Journal reported:

> *"The combination of the disproportionate impact of COVID-19 on vulnerable communities and the sociotechnical determinants of algorithmic bias and discrimination might deliver a brutal triple punch. Firstly, the use of biased AI models might be disproportionately harmful to vulnerable groups who are not properly represented in training datasets, and who are already subject to widespread health inequality. Secondly, the use of safety critical AI tools for decision assistance in high stakes clinical environments might be more harmful to members of these groups owing to their life and death impacts on them. Lastly, discriminatory AI tools might compound the disproportionate damage inflicted on disadvantaged communities by the SARS-CoV-2 virus."*[88]

---

[88] Mazumder, A., Wolters, M.K., and Hagerty A. Does "AI" stand for augmenting inequality in the era of covid-19 healthcare? *theBMJ*. Available at *www.bmj.com/content/372/bmj.n304*.

Potential negative ethical and security/safety impacts of AI

History has demonstrated that bad results of new technologies are not always intentional. But new technologies can create unintended side effects, such as the close calls regarding nuclear weapons during the Cold War.

Although there are many areas where AI has enormous capacity for good, there is also the possibility for alternative outcomes. Many of these potentially negative – or less than positive – effects are linked, such as threats to jobs and deskilling, while others stand somewhat alone. But each of these deserves some level of discussion.

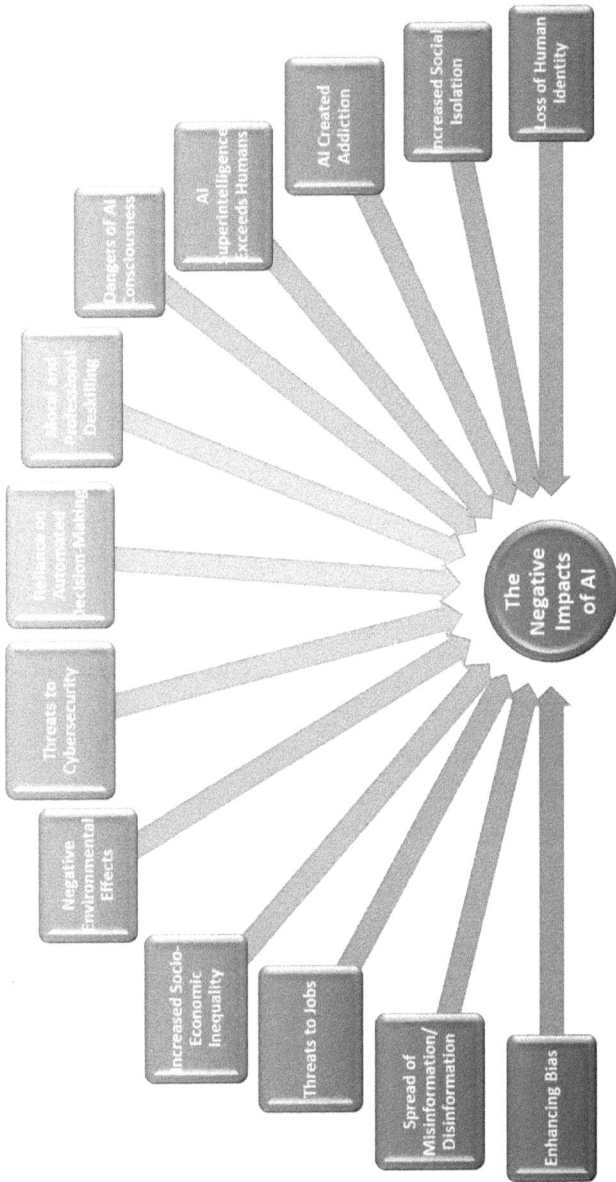

Figure 4-3: The potential negative impacts of AI

The Negative Impacts of AI

Dangers of AI Consciousness

AI Superintelligence Exceeds Humans

AI Created Addiction

Increased Social Isolation

Loss of Human Identity

Moral and Professional Deskilling

Reliance on Automated Decision-Making

Threats to Cybersecurity

Negative Environmental Effects

Increased Socio-Economic Inequality

Threats to Jobs

Spread of Misinformation/ Disinformation

Enhancing Bias

History has demonstrated that evil is not always intentional, but that having destructive power, even if not intending to use it, still risks catastrophe, such as the close calls regarding nuclear weapons during the Cold War. All of these potential negative impacts will be addressed in this chapter, but some are sufficiently significant to warrant their own chapter. These include bias, disinformation/misinformation, threats to cybersecurity, effects on personal privacy, sentient AI, and moral and professional deskilling.

Bias

Bias in human decision making is well known. Research into bias has seen how a judge's decisions can be unconsciously influenced by their own personal preconceptions, while employers may give more or fewer interviews to applicants with identical resumes but with names that appear to reflect different demographics. But the cause of specific human decisions can also be difficult to pin down: people may not be forthcoming about the factors they considered, or may not understand the things that may have prejudiced their thinking, resulting in unconscious bias.

Wide-ranging evidence suggests that AI models can incorporate human and societal biases in the training data and then introduce them into outcomes. Researchers at ProPublica demonstrated how the Correctional Offender Management Profiling for Alternative Sanctions (COMPAS), a tool used by law enforcement to predict recidivism in Broward County, Florida, frequently and incorrectly identified African-Americans as "high-risk" at nearly twice the rate it mislabeled whites.[89] Another company halted development of a hiring algorithm based on analyzing previous decisions after discovering that the algorithm penalized applicants from women's colleges.

Most often, the underlying data and not the AI algorithm itself is the main source of bias. AI models may be trained on data reflecting biased human decisions or societal/historical inequities. Bias can also be introduced into the data used to train an AI model based on how the data is collected and selected for use.

Bias in AI is more than just embarrassing to the organizations that create biased AI; it can have tangible negative and damaging effects on the individuals who are impacted by these biases. Bias in AI can also reduce public trust in companies, government, and any other institutions that might be developing or implementing biased products.

Chapter 5 provides an in-depth discussion of the potential and real impacts of bias in AI.

Disinformation/misinformation, fake news, manipulation, and deepfakes

The terms "disinformation" and "misinformation" are often used interchangeably. But the single letter difference disguises a critical difference: that of intent. **Misinformation** refers to incorrect information that spreads, regardless of the intent to mislead – so it is simply a term referring to any kind of false or incorrect information. In

---

[89] Angwin, J., Larson, J, Mattu, S., and Kirchner, L. (May 22, 2016). Machine Bias. *ProPublica.* Available at *www.propublica.org/article/machine-bias-risk-assessments-in-criminal-sentencing.*

today's digital environment, misinformation can spread very quickly.

On the other hand, **disinformation** is defined as *"deliberately misleading or biased information, manipulated narrative or facts; propaganda."*[90] Disinformation is characterized by *intent* – the knowing spread of false or incorrect information usually to discredit a person, an action, or an organization. **Fake news**, or the intentional fabrication of news-based information with the intent to deceive – is related to disinformation.

Manipulation is the intentional use of AI to influence human behavior or opinions. AI algorithms are not only manipulating consumer behavior with targeted advertising based on extensive consumer profiling, but apparently, they are also manipulating voters, using AI-based data analysis to create detailed profiles of individuals to predict how they might vote and by conveying different things to different electors. The Cambridge Analytica scandal that broke the news in 2019 is a case in point. According to the investigations, Cambridge Analytica purchased content on tens of millions of American Facebook users without their knowledge, in order to build a "psychological warfare tool," which it then let loose on US voters allegedly to help elect Donald Trump as president in the 2016 elections.

But that was not the only data manipulation scandal in which Facebook was involved. In 2014, Facebook conducted a notorious experiment that involved manipulating the news feeds of its subscribers without their knowledge or consent,

---

[90] "Misinformation" vs. "Disinformation": Get Informed On The Difference. *Dictionary.com*. Available at *www.dictionary.com/e/misinformation-vs-disinformation-get-informed-on-the-difference/*.

It fed some subscribers predominantly negative news and others predominantly positive news, to determine how these feeds affected the content that users then shared in response.

Deepfakes are yet another form of falsification of information. They are created when an AI is programmed to substitute one person's likeness with another in recorded video, to produce a kind of fake media content. It is usually in the form of a video with or without audio that has been "doctored" or manipulated to make it seem like someone said or did something that they did not. Deepfakes are generally created to get a lot of attention and go viral because they portray some unlikely or dramatic event: a well-known politician with slurred speech, a celebrity in a compromising situation, or controversial statements from a public figure. The primary concerns are how deepfake content is used to engage in personal defamation efforts to discredit individual reputations in the workplace or in personal life, and the extensive publication of fake pornographic content.

Whether intentional or unintentional, misinformation, disinformation, fake news, manipulation, and deepfakes can all result in changes in human opinions or behavior. These concepts will be discussed in more detail in Chapter 9.

Job threats

As we've devised ways to use AI to automate tasks, humans are enabled to assume more complex roles, moving from the physical labor that ruled in the pre-industrial world, to the more cerebral level of work that characterizes strategic and administrative work today in our more global society.

Most of humanity still relies on trading time for income to sustain themselves and their families. On the one hand, AI may enable people to find meaning in non-labor-intensive activities, such as caring for their families, engaging with their communities, and learning new ways to contribute to human society, but the threat to certain types of jobs is directly linked to a likely increase in socio-economic inequality.

Expansion of socio-economic inequality

Technological advances have always affected the status of workers in society. In almost all cases, the changes resulted in the displacement of workers in those areas. At the same time, the new technologies created thousands of new jobs and new opportunities for employment. The twentieth-century economist Joseph Schumpeter described this phenomenon as "creative destruction,"[91] where new work opportunities replaced outdated jobs. Schumpeter hypothesized that a society cannot benefit from the effects of creative destruction without accepting the fact that some workers might be worse off – and not just in the short term, but perhaps forever. For example, the US saw positive benefits as horses and carts were replaced by cars and airplanes, but this did not come about without eliminating certain job categories. In 1900, the country employed 109,000 carriage and harness makers, and in 1910, approximately 238,000 Americans worked as blacksmiths. Today, those jobs are largely obsolete.[92]

A decade ago, it was assumed that AI would replace human labor for "routine" jobs, such as tasks that could be broken down into discrete steps and then programmed into an AI. Recent advances in AI and related technologies have

---

[91] Alm, R, and Cox, W.M. Creative Destruction. *Econlib*. Available at *www.econlib.org/library/Enc/CreativeDestruction.html*.

[92] Ibid.

changed that forecast – AI is now able to substitute for humans across a much wider range of tasks that typically require creativity, analytical skills, and/or manual dexterity, creating an ever-increasing dichotomy between specialized and unspecialized workers. Low- and medium-skilled employment opportunities will continue to decline, and the income gap between low, middle, and higher skilled labor is predicted to increase.

Recent research by the International Monetary Fund (IMF) indicates that *"automation that substitutes closely with workers will tend to increase incomes but also increase income inequality, at least during the transition and possibly in the long-run for some groups of workers."*[93] Although the IMF research focused largely on third-world nations, it also determined it likely that the same phenomenon will occur in more advanced countries, such as the US or Europe. *"The more easily robots substitute for workers, the higher the increase in GDP per capita and the greater the decrease in labor share, leading to a richer economy, but with more inequality."*[94]

But what is the real danger in socio-economic inequality? As the philosopher Plato wrote more than 2,000 years ago: *" ... when a society is ruled by its elites ... such a [society] should of necessity be not one, but two, a [society] of the rich and a [society] of the poor, dwelling together, and always plotting against one another."*[95] So, social inequality may affect how different income groups behave and interact. As inequality

---

[93] Alonso, C., Berg, A., Kothari, S., Papageorgiou, C, and Rehman, S. (September 11, 2020). Will the AI Revolution Cause a Great Divergence? *IMF Working Papers*, WP/20/184.

[94] Ibid.

[95] Plato, Republic, Book 8.

increases, individuals in the poorer groups have fewer job opportunities, less education, decreased access to good healthcare, and reduced social mobility. Higher levels of economic inequality are associated with reduced trust between the poor and the wealthy, resulting in a higher societal volatility and increased conflict between the groups.

Harmful effects on the environment

AI processing can require enormous amounts of energy to train, in fact, so much energy that the cost can amount to tens of millions of dollars or more. If the needed energy is derived from fossil fuels, it could negatively impact the earth, not to mention being damaging to other aspects of the hydrocarbon supply chain. According to *New Scientist*, *"Training artificial intelligence is an energy intensive process. New estimates suggest that the carbon footprint of training a single AI is as much as 284 tonnes of carbon dioxide equivalent – five times the lifetime emissions of an average car.*"[96] Consider how much technology surrounds us today – and consider just how much data is generated, transmitted, stored, and analyzed. It is almost impossible for the human mind to comprehend an amount exceeding 175 zettabytes (or 175 + 12 zeros). All of this data requires data centers, and these must be sufficiently cooled for AI and other processing technologies to work efficiently – and an associated increase in the already large carbon footprint.

"A core contributor to the AI field's growing carbon footprint is a dominant belief that 'bigger is better.' In

---

[96] Lu, D. (June 6, 2019). Creating an AI can be five times worse for the planet than a car. *New Scientist*. Available at www.newscientist.com/article/2205779-creating-an-ai-can-be-five-times-worse-for-the-planet-than-a-car/.

other words, AI models that leverage massive computational resources to consume larger training datasets are assumed to be inherently 'better' and more accurate. While this narrative is inherently flawed, its assumptions drive the use of increased computation in the development of AI models across the industry."[97]

The increase in AI and related technologies also creates increased demand for the tangible products to support them and a greater need for raw materials. *"The extraction of nickel, cobalt, and graphite for lithium-ion batteries used for example in electrical cars and smart phones has already damaged the environment, particularly in China, India, and Canada, where much of the materials are produced."*[98] These associated products also necessitate an increased use of plastics and packaging, so-called e-waste.

Reliance on automated decision making

The possibility of humans transferring responsibility to AI and not detecting where it fails, has long been acknowledged by industrial psychologists and engineers studying the human operators of complex AI-powered tools. It's been named as "the control problem," or the predisposition for humans within an AI-human process to become over-reliant on the AI, complacent, or unduly hesitant when faced with the outputs of a normally reliable AI system. *"Although it*

---

[97] Crawford, K., et al. (December 2019). AI Now. 2019 Report. *AI Now Institute.*

[98] Meinecke, S. (July 16, 2018). AI could help us protect the environment – or destroy it. *DW Akademie.* Available at www.dw.com/en/ai-could-help-us-protect-the-environment-or-destroy-it/a-44694471.

might be thought innocuous, decades of research confirm that the problem is actually pernicious, and perhaps even intractable."[99]

One example of this control problem was the implementation in Pennsylvania's Allegheny County of a child welfare protection tool based on AI to assist in its child abuse prevention strategy. The technology was developed with the intent of assisting caseworkers to determine if it was necessary to follow up on calls placed with the County's child welfare hotline. However, over time, the caseworkers would simply adjust their risk assessments to align with that of the AI tool, rather than relying on their own instincts, decision-making capabilities, or historical knowledge of the cases.[100]

As AI is given more authority to make decisions, there will need to be some sort of ethical standard encoded into it. The ethical decision-making process might be as simple as following a program to fairly distribute profits, where the primary decision is made by humans and then executed by an algorithm. However, it also might involve a much more comprehensive ethical analysis, and under some circumstances, the AI may make a decision that is contrary to the prevailing human ethical constructs.

---

[99] Zerilli, J., Knott, A., Maclaurin, J., and Gavaghan, C. (December 11, 2019). Algorithmic Decision-Making and the Control Problem. *SpringerLink*. Available at *https://link.springer.com/article/10.1007/s11023-019-09513-7*.

[100] Zerilli, J., Knott, A., Maclaurin, J., and Gavaghan, C. (December 11, 2019). Algorithmic Decision-Making and the Control Problem. *SpringerLink*. Available at *https://link.springer.com/article/10.1007/s11023-019-09513-7*.

Moral and professional deskilling

Linked to an overreliance on automation and job deskilling is moral deskilling. Moral deskilling can be defined as the loss of ability to make moral/ethical decisions as a consequence of lack of experience and practice. As AI technologies increasingly make decisions for us and we delegate decision-making to AI technologies, humans may lose the ability to make moral/ethical decisions. Ethical and moral development requires *practice*; therefore, if the statement "practice makes perfect" is true, then it would also be a truism that "lack of practice makes imperfect." The more humans permit AI to manipulate our psychology through social media or other applications, the less time we spend considering ethical problems and the worse we will be at ethics.

Professional deskilling is related, in that humans may lose the ability to perform certain professional functions as a result of overreliance on AI. An example of professional deskilling can be found when looking at airline pilots. Since most planes are equipped with highly sophisticated autopiloting systems, it is technically feasible that every aspect of air travel from takeoff to landing could be automated. But airlines – and pilots – have decided not to turn over these functions to the automation and reserve autopilot except for the boring, uneventful parts of flight because those are precisely the functions that require the least skill. The takeoff and landing – or the activities that require the most expertise – are those areas where the pilots must not be deskilled. If they became too dependent on the autopilot, if it failed, they might not have the skill to assume charge of the flight in an emergency.

The challenges from moral and professional deskilling are given more in-depth treatment in Chapter 7.

Dangers from the evolution of a self-aware AI

Many researchers have considered that AI might eventually develop a sense of self, and humans will have to determine if we recognize AI as persons like ourselves. A number of movies, such as *Transcendence*, *Ex Machina*, and *Her*, depict the dark side of AI after it obtains human-level consciousness. This genre of movie taps into the human fear that machines will eventually become more intelligent than humans and turn on those that developed them. Although this remains unlikely, there is the possibility that AI could obtain some form of consciousness.

In order to determine if it is possible for AI to obtain consciousness, we must first define what that means. The philosopher John Locke (1632-1704) defined it as *"the perception of what passes in a Man's own mind."*[101] According to leading philosophers, there are three primary criteria for consciousness:

- **Sentience** – the ability to respond to the world around us – is considered one of the components of human consciousness. It is a basic criterion, since any living creature can be sentient or aware of its surroundings, but not all living beings are conscious.
- **Wakefulness** – the concept of a living being reacting and being alert to its surroundings. With wakefulness, a living being is able to receive information both from

---

[101] Yaffe, G. (2011) Locke on Consciousness, Personal Identity, and the Idea of Duration. Available at *https://law.yale.edu/sites/default/files/documents/pdf/Faculty/Yaffe_Loc keonDuration_Identity-Nous.pdf*.

external surroundings and also internally, and at different levels.

- The third criterion is **self-consciousness** or **self-awareness**. This is the one that is most unique to humans. Self-consciousness refers to the concept that a being is aware of oneself and acknowledges and understands its emotions and actions.

In terms of the ability to replicate human consciousness, the AI community itself makes a distinction between strong AI and weak AI. Strong AI, if fully achieved, could conceivably possess the full range of human cognitive abilities, such as self-awareness, consciousness, and sentience, which are all considered essential elements of human cognition. From a legal standpoint, "personhood" has been granted to corporations and other non-human entities, so consciousness may not be the sole determinant for recognition of AI personhood.

If AI were to develop consciousness, we would likely need to change our own human society. Much like the android Data in the *Star Trek: The Next Generation* episode "The Measure of a Man," humans would have to start thinking about the rights of an AI, social justice, and how existing laws would either apply or need to be changed. There would be an inevitable loss and gain of job opportunities, and much, much more.

In addition, human scientists, engineers, and statisticians would have to ensure that the AI has no racist, sexist, xenophobic, homophobic, transphobic, etc. biases. Those who develop AI must also ensure that they are created towards the equal representation of all humans.

The concept of AI sentience is discussed in more detail in Chapter 10.

Superintelligence – or exceeding human capability

If, or perhaps, when, an AI surpasses humans in intelligence, it could become a superintelligence; that is, an entity potentially vastly cleverer and more capable than humans. Bill Gates, Stephen Hawking, and others have warned of the dangers associated with the evolution of "super-intelligent" AI that is able to exceed even the most intelligent of humans in every sphere, from common sense reasoning to social skills. The emergence of an AI with superintelligence could potentially mark the unseating of humans as the most intelligent beings on Earth.

A super-intelligent AI may not even need to develop consciousness. For humans,

> *"Consciousness is correlated with novel learning tasks that require concentration, and when a thought is under the spotlight of our attention, it is processed in a slow, sequential manner. Only a very small percentage of our mental processing is conscious at any given time. A superintelligence would surpass expert-level knowledge in every domain, with rapid-fire computations ranging over vast databases that could encompass the entire internet. It may not need the very mental faculties that are associated with conscious experience in humans. Consciousness could be outmoded."*[102]

---

[102] Schneider, S. (March 18, 2016). The Problem of AI Consciousness. *Kurzweil. Kurzweil.* Available at *www.kurzweilai.net/the-problem-of-ai-consciousness.*

AI dependency

Dependence on AI could become similar to the dependence of a child or an elderly relative on an adult. Children generally depend on adults to think for them, and as we age, the elderly may become reliant on younger adults. Now consider a future where humans become dependent upon AI to guide them in their decisions. At this point, we would become a people, depending like children, on our AI caretakers.

In fact, with AI performing more and more of our tasks, humans could become increasingly dependent on AI to do what we once did ourselves. As Nicholas Carr warns in his book, *The Glass Cage*,[103] we may lose our skills because we no longer need to use them, much like we might lose our physical health through lack of exercise. Already, many of us see diminished social skills because of, among other things, the persistently present smartphone.

A reliance on some form of AI is something many of us have already experienced in our daily lives, ranging from our increasing reliance on smart home devices, such as Alexa; robot vacuums; AI-powered refrigerators; to Google Maps to guide us around traffic problems.

AI-created addiction

Social media and smartphone app developers have turned addiction into a money-generating science. AI-powered apps

---

[103] Carr, N. (2014). *The Glass Cage: How Our Computers Are Changing Us*. W.W. Norton & Company, New York.

can become as addictive as drugs, by exploiting known human psychology, desires, and vulnerabilities. In 2017, Chamath Palihapitiya, former vice president for user growth at Facebook, was giving a talk to students of the Stanford Graduate School for Business, when he said this:

> *"I feel tremendous guilt. The short-term, dopamine-driven feedback loops that we have created are destroying how society works: no civil discourse, no cooperation, misinformation, mistruth. It is eroding the core foundations of how people behave by and between each other."*[104]

Dopamine is a hormone produced naturally by our body. In the human brain, it functions as a neurotransmitter, which is essentially a chemical that neurons use to transmit signals to each other. One of the main functions of dopamine is reward-motivated behavior, where our brain learns through positive reinforcement, incentives, and emotions, and in particular, the sensation of pleasure. Over time, this dopamine reinforced behavior creates an addiction to whatever is generating that release of dopamine in our brains – whether it's a win at the gambling table or another "like" on social media. In reality, the AI-powered social media platforms are intentionally designed to exploit the rewards systems in our brain. Essentially, they are designed to function in the same way as an addictive drug.

---

[104] Snyder, B. (December 12, 2017). Chamath Palihapitiya: Why Failing Fast Fails. *Stanford Business*. Available at *www.gsb.stanford.edu/insights/chamath-palihapitiya-why-failing-fast-fails*.

Human isolation and loneliness

The role and presence of AI in people's day-to-day and working lives is continuing to increase, with the effect of further diminishing people's ability or desire to connect with one another face to face.

This has resulted in a crisis of loneliness and feelings of isolation, which were highlighted by the COVID-19 pandemic. In fact, 1 in 5 Americans report often of always feeling lonely.[105] Research has linked social isolation with a number of physical and mental issues, including depression, impaired mental function, poor cardiovascular function, impaired immunity, increased cognitive decline, elevated stress levels, and poor sleep quality. More and more individuals are using social media platforms every day. In 2019, approximately 90% of 18-to-24-year-olds were connecting on popular social media platforms, such as Facebook, Instagram, Twitter, YouTube, etc. several hours per day.

---

[105] Does Social Media Create Isolation? *Regis College.* Available at *https://online.regiscollege.edu/blog/does-social-media-create-isolation/*.

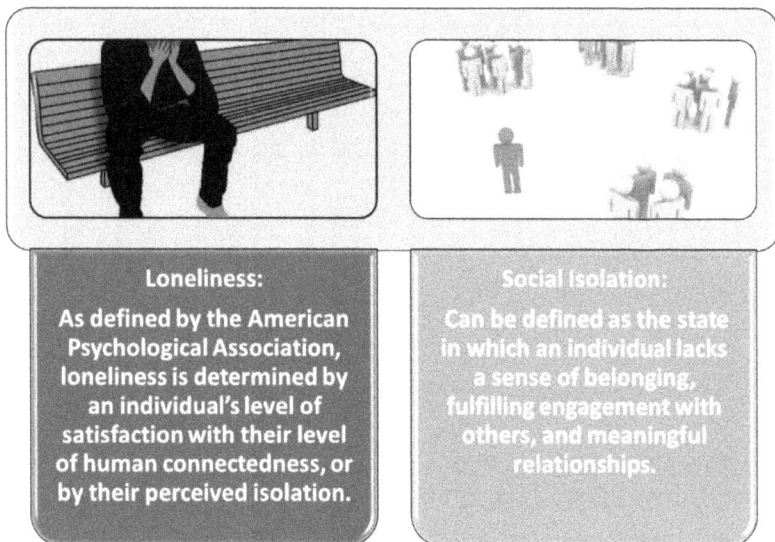

Figure 4-4: Loneliness and social isolation

This paradox leads to the question, "Does social media cause or influence social isolation?" There is not a simple yes or no answer. One might consider that the use of AI-powered social media, smartphones, and video chat could help mitigate loneliness and feelings of social isolation; but in reality, they have actually become a source of loneliness because people are facing phone or computer screens instead of each other.

On the positive side, social media can help connect individuals separated because of a physical environment or a situation such as COVID-19. But seldom can social media substitute for face-to-face interaction. Further, social media, with much of its AI-polished content, can create unrealistic and distorted portrayals of others' lives, leading to feelings of FOMO[106] and increased social isolation. It can appear that everyone else has a better life, is smarter, funnier, more interesting, has more friends, etc.

Within an experimental group of college undergraduates, it was found that participants in the group whose usage of social media (Facebook, Snapchat, Instagram) was limited

> *"To 10 min, per platform, per day, reported lower levels of loneliness, compared to the control group, which used the social media platforms as they normally would. The reasoning is that even though social media may increase the quantity of social contacts and interactions, the quality of contacts and interactions may actually decrease. That is, the lower-quality social media interactions may replace or crowd-out more high-quality in-person interactions. "*[107]

Effects on privacy, human identity, and purpose

AI and privacy

The simplest definition of privacy is to have the power to isolate oneself and/or information about oneself from others. In today's digital age, privacy is dependent upon our ability to influence how our personal data is being collected, stored, modified, and exchanged between parties. AI changes the

---

[106] Fear of Missing Out.

[107] Fumagalli, E., Dolmatzian, M., and Shrum, L.J. (February 9, 2021). Centennials, FOMO, and Loneliness: An Investigation of the Impact of Social Networking and Messaging/VoIP Apps Usage During the Initial Stage of the Coronavirus Pandemic. *frontiers in Psychology.* Available at *www.frontiersin.org/articles/10.3389/fpsyg.2021.620739/full.*

privacy debate through its ability to collect, analyze, and integrate vast amounts of data from different sources, thus expanding the data-gathering capabilities of those that use AI.

Privacy and AI are inextricably linked with big data. According to TechTarget, big data *"is a combination of structured, semi-structured, and unstructured data collected by organizations that can be mined for information and used in machine learning projects, predictive modeling and other advanced analytics applications."*[108] According to Doug Laney of Gartner Group, big data can be characterized by the "3 Vs": variety, velocity, and volume, all of which interact together to create big data.

1. **Volume** is vast amount of data, generated from cell phones, social media, smart devices, the IoT, etc.
2. **Velocity** relates to the speed at which these enormous amounts of data are being created, accumulated, and analyzed.
3. **Variety** addresses the varying types of data: structured data that can be displayed in a data table (such as name, phone number, ID, etc.) and unstructured data (images, audio, social media content, etc.).[109]

What makes AI such a threat to privacy is its ability to gather and analyze volumes of various types of data at great speed. And to develop and train an AI, it takes massive amounts of

---

[108] Botelho, B. big data. *TechTarget* online, Available at *https://searchdatamanagement.techtarget.com/definition/big-data*.

[109] Piatetsky, G. Exclusive Interview: Doug Laney on Big Data and Informatics. *KDnuggets*. Available at *www.kdnuggets.com/2018/01/exclusive-interview-doug-laney-big-data-infonomics.html*.

personal data. Additionally, the pressure to use personal data is escalating as AI-based analyses are used to develop more efficient and effective AI to provide more and better services. Many companies developing AI tend to focus on how to make their idea work and attract funding, so they can move from development to deployment (sales). The protection of data and personal information does not often become a primary consideration, especially in the early stages of an AI life cycle.

Examples abound of privacy infringement in collecting AI training data. The Royal Free London NHS Foundation Trust, a division of the UK's National Health Service (NHS) based in London, gave Alphabet's[110] DeepMind[111] project data on approximately 1.6 million patients without their consent.[112] Google's health data-sharing collaboration with Ascension became the subject of scrutiny, forcing them to abandon plans to publish scans of chest x-rays because of concerns that they contained personally identifiable information (PII).[113] Microsoft quietly deleted data from MS-Celeb-1M,[114] an AI database with more than 10 million

---

[110] Alphabet is the parent company of Google, Nest, and other ventures.

[111] DeepMind was started by Google in 2010 to explore the development of AI.

[112] Hodson, H. (April 29, 2016), Revealed: Google AI has access to huge haul of NHS patient data. *NewScientist*. Available at *www.newscientist.com/article/2086454-revealed-google-ai-has-access-to-huge-haul-of-nhs-patient-data/#ixzz7AQYAWNav*.

[113] Holland, M. (November 18, 2019). Google-Ascension deal reveals murky side of sharing health data. *TechTarget*.

[114] MS-Celeb-1M, claimed by Microsoft to be the largest data set of facial images, was intended for use to train AI facial recognition systems.

facial recognition images, after it was disclosed that the people whose photos were used had not been asked for their consent.[115]

Privacy is being taken increasingly seriously by governments and agencies across the globe. In 2019, the Federal Trade Commission (FTC) issued a $5 billion dollar penalty to Facebook for violating user privacy. The CCPA, which is widely viewed as the toughest privacy law in the US, became law (at least in California) in 2018. Today, nearly every state in the US has its own data breach notification law. European courts are also testing the limits of the EU's GDPR, which has impacts on companies around the world doing business with the EU.

The potential effects of AI on privacy will be addressed in more detail in Chapter 8.

Human identity

Social identity theory[116] postulates that human social interactions are the core of our own identity development. Our roles within family, school, social networks, culture, and society mirror to us the individual that we come to identify as "self." As we process this reflection, we take on and integrate this reflection as part of our identity.

---

[115] Murgia, M. (June 6, 2019). Microsoft quietly deletes largest public face recognition data set. *Financial Times*. Available at *www.ft.com/content/7d3e0d6a-87a0-11e9-a028-86cea8523dc2.*

[116] Social identity theory was formulated by social psychologists Henri Tajfel and John Turner in the 1970s and the 1980s. The theory introduced the idea of social identity as an explanation for intergroup behavior. See *https://en.wikipedia.org/wiki/Social_identity_theory.*

4: AI, ethics, and society – Are they compatible?

In today's digital environment, AI-based social media is forever altering how individuals develop that social identity. Humans create an online social media presence, whether on Facebook, Instagram, TikTok, etc. When that social media presence does not correspond to our offline identities, a cognitive dissonance[117] emerges regarding our perceived identity. In our efforts to correct the cognitive dissonance, we either modify our behavior offline to match the social media presence we have created or vice versa. Altering our behavior then reinforces the perception of our identity. This creates a never-ending cycle of an ever-greater influence by social media on our identities. Social media is only one area where AI can affect our identity. Increasingly, employment opportunities, education, and decision-making are being automated through AI. As more AI-driven systems are implemented, these systems will not only create a level of deskilling, they will also highlight our flaws – those inevitable imperfections found in the human condition and our ways of interpreting the world.

---

[117] *"Cognitive dissonance is the perception of contradictory information. Relevant items of information include a person's actions, feelings, ideas, beliefs, and values, and things in the environment. Cognitive dissonance is typically experienced as psychological stress when persons participate in an action that goes against one or more of those things. According to this theory, when two actions or ideas are not psychologically consistent with each other, people do all in their power to change them until they become consistent. The discomfort is triggered by the person's belief clashing with new information perceived, wherein the individual tries to find a way to resolve the contradiction to reduce his or her discomfort."* See *https://en.wikipedia.org/wiki/Cognitive_dissonance*.

Sense of purpose

A sense of purpose is an essential element of the human experience. *"Possessing a high sense of purpose in life is associated with a reduced risk for mortality and cardiovascular events,"* according to the study by Drs. Randy Cohen and Alan Rozanski, and colleagues at Mt. Sinai St. Luke's-Roosevelt Hospital, New York.[118]

Many individuals find their sense of purpose in their work, whether it's work of the mind or physical labor. Some find comfort, value, and meaning in their work, while others regard work as a necessity to be avoided if at all possible. For many centuries, the elite classes across societies have sought to avoid the perceived bane of daily work. Aristotle defined a "man in freedom" as the apex of human existence, where the individual is free of any concern for the basic necessities of life and in possession of practically complete personal will.[119]

AI and automation raise new challenges in defining the role of purpose in our lives. Although many of us will remain focused for years to come on physical or financial work, as AI delivers services and goods at ever lower cost, humans will be compelled to discover a new sense of purpose – one that isn't necessarily tied to how we conceive of purpose today. As long ago as 1930, and well before the advent of AI, the economist John M. Keynes argued, *"If the economic problem is solved, mankind will be deprived of its traditional*

---

[118] Sense of purpose in life linked to lower mortality and cardiovascular risk. (December 3, 2015). *ScienceDaily.* Available at *www.sciencedaily.com/releases/2015/12/151203112844.htm*.

[119] Walsh, M. (October 1997). Aristotle's Conception of Freedom. *Journal of the History of Philosophy. Volume 35, Issue 4.* Available at *https://omnilogos.com/aristotle-conception-of-freedom/*.

purpose ... Yet there are no country and no people, I think, who can look forward to the age of leisure and of abundance without a dread."[120] As AI and robotic systems increasingly dominate labor and work, producing necessities and the physical artifacts of human life, humans may need to find another source from which to derive a sense of purpose.

The reasons it is difficult for humans to fully address these potential challenges from AI

As humans, we are very good at innovating; but we are equally good at opening up a Pandora's Box of challenges and then consigning future generations to the task of cleaning up the mess. We have a history of deploying new technology a long time before we fully comprehend how it can affect our physical and mental well-being and the society in which we live.

We are not good at assessing the potential impact of innovation

Think back to the days when there was no text messaging, no emails, and no smartphones (if you can!). Cellular technology has made rapid, long distance wireless communication possible. On the other hand, these same technologies have robbed mankind of the warmth of personal human interaction. Emails and text messages have replaced handwritten letters and, consequently, communication has lost much of its personal touch. With the means of communication being so easily quick and accessible, that magic in the expectation of a letter and the subsequent excitement upon receipt have disappeared. At the time, these

---

[120] Keynes, J. M. (1930). *Economic Possibilities for our Grandchildren.* Available at *https://mitpress.mit.edu/books/revisiting-keynes*.

new technologies were viewed as positive developments for society; but little thought was given to the longer-term impact on interpersonal relationships and communication.

New technologies can sometimes change the world irreversibly, and these changes may not necessarily be only positive. There is one category of the potential impacts of new technologies that is much more difficult to measure: the effects that may not be directly caused by the new technology itself, but by the changes in human behavior it causes.

Technology itself is often considered as "neutral," and not the potential source of complex interactions with society. But, new emerging technologies may generate new challenges for which we have no established and accepted ethical standards and no metrics for assessing their impact. As a consequence, we must not only attempt to assess the potential impacts, but we may also have to develop new normative ethical standards.

But what are the standards by which potential effects could be evaluated? Here are three approaches to assessing the potential impact of new technologies:

1. **Gain a complete understanding of the technological changes to effectively evaluate the processes for initiating, processing, and recording transactions, and then design appropriate impact assessment procedures.** This understanding includes, but is not limited to, understanding likely sources of potential misstatements and identifying risks and controls within information technology.
2. **Consider potential risks resulting from the implementation of new technologies, and how those risks may differ from those that have been seen**

arising from more traditional, legacy technologies. Be mindful of the risks that can arise because of program or application-specific circumstances (e.g. resources, rapid tool development, use of third parties) that could differ from traditional technologies. Understanding the system development life cycle (SDLC) risks introduced by emerging technologies will also help develop an appropriate response tailored to a development's circumstances.

3. **Determine whether specialized skills are necessary to discover the impact of new technologies and to assist in the risk assessment.** Understand the design, implementation, and operating effectiveness of controls. If specialized skills are considered appropriate, risk assessors may seek the involvement of a subject matter expert. Assessors should also obtain a sufficient understanding of the expert's field of expertise to evaluate the adequacy of the assessment.

We have no overarching agreement on exactly what constitutes ethics

Ethics as a construct is notoriously malleable and contested. Moreover, even if we could assume a general moral consensus that spans boundaries and cultures, ethics is missing a solid enforcement mechanism. Companies that develop and deploy AI prefer to claim they adhere to ethical standards rather than binding laws or policies, for the single and obvious reason that no tangible penalties attach to altering or even disregarding ethics should the need arise.

Ethics is often regarded only in the minimalistic light of what one "must do," or the legalistic sense of what one "cannot do." This should not be much of a surprise, given recent ethical transgressions involving political leaders, corporations, and many others.

Despite our disparate views of ethics, there can still be the potential that policy makers, developers, educators, and others striving to understand both the benefits and potential challenges of AI, will make an effort to build on existing knowledge and to drive the splintered, global conversations on the future of AI toward some form of ethical consensus.

We fall into a "policy vacuum"

Today, we find ourselves in an exciting age of rapid technological advancement limited only by the ability of humans to digest and use the technology – and this definitely applies to the development and deployment of new forms of AI. Many AI developers seek to gain a competitive advantage from this rapid innovation by introducing new AI products into the marketplace, but without much consideration given to the effects of the new technology on individuals and society.

These technological advances in AI are also outpacing the ability of our legal structures to identify and implement guidelines to manage their use. James Moor[121] labeled this void of legal or expressed policy direction, a policy vacuum.[122] Simply put, the speed of technological development is an order of magnitude greater than the speed

---

[121] James H. Moor is the Daniel P. Stone Professor of Intellectual and Moral Philosophy at Dartmouth College. He earned his Ph.D. in 1972 from Indiana University. He is considered one of the pioneering theoreticians in the field of computer ethics.

[122] Moor, J. (1985) *What is Computer Ethics?* Available at *https://web.cs.ucdavis.edu/~rogaway/classes/188/spring06/papers/moor.html*.

of society to cope with these sometimes revolutionary and disrupting changes, resulting in a "policy gap."

Policy can be formulated as a law, regulation, procedure, administrative action, incentive, or voluntary practice of governments and other institutions. The very fact that AI intelligence lacks an established, universally agreed upon definition or configuration, complicates efforts to develop an appropriate policy framework. Rather than solidly defined policies and laws, companies often prefer to submit their "governance" plans as an alternative.

> *"Invoking the term governance can help insulate technologies from overt government interference – as in the case of Internet governance through non-governmental bodies such as the Internet Corporation for Assigned Names and Numbers ("ICANN") and the Internet Engineering Task Force ("IETF") – the governance model also resists official policy by tacitly devolving responsibility to industry from the state."[123]*

In fact, the law is often too slow in catching up with technological innovation. Laws or regulations may even become outdated as technology evolves beyond where it was when the law was initially crafted. A further observation is that governments and their policy makers often lack the necessary expertise to develop relevant laws and policies in such a deeply technically world. When policy makers are not themselves experts, they must either depend on the self-biased input from private companies (or their proxies) or

---

[123] Rhodes, R. (1996). *The New Governance: Governing Without Government*, 44 POL. STUD. 652, 657.

display a paralysis in the ability to make decisions and take action that squelches innovation.

We are not easily able to standardize fairness

One of the primary challenges in ensuring fairness in AI lies in determining exactly what fairness means. The need to create fair and unbiased AI is now part of the discussion in executive suites and boardrooms alike. Because of the recent high-profile AI bias scandals, companies have begun to realize that they need to rethink their AI strategy to include not just AI fairness, but also algorithmic fairness[124] more broadly as a fundamental tenet. But many companies struggle to form a clear definition of algorithmic fairness.

Without a clear definition, well-meaning fairness initiatives languish in the realm of good intentions and never arrive at meaningful impact. But defining fairness is not as easy as it may seem. And *",,,the failure of the leaders to understand the fairness implications of AI or algorithms can have dire consequences."*[125]

Fairness is not an easy subject to navigate because of the difficulty of precisely and scientifically identifying, analyzing, and minimizing the presence of bias in the AI training data, and also because of the social challenges of determining exactly what "fair" means in terms of AI. Fairness is often situationally dependent, as well as being a

---

[124] In a general sense, "algorithmic fairness" may relate broadly to any use of algorithms attempting to eliminate bias and insert fairness in a social context.

[125] Li, M. (November 5, 2019). Are Your Algorithms Upholding Your Standards of Fairness? *Harvard Business Review.* Available at *https://hbr.org/2019/11/are-your-algorithms-upholding-your-standards-of-fairness*.

reflection of an individual's or culture's unique ethics, values, laws, and regulations. Often, we seek to display fairness by treating everybody exactly the same. An equal amount of time to an exam, equal access to education, even an equal amount of candy at Halloween, and – in an ideal world – equal pay for equal work regardless of gender, ethnicity, or another demographic.

The real meaning of this is *equality*. However, this fails to consider that not every one of us comes from the same place, and that some might need a different level or type of help. For example: *"Imagine people of divergent height trying to get to the beautifully ripe, red apples on an apple tree. If you were to give a small pedestal to everyone, it would not really improve the situation for the smaller individuals."*[126] Graphically, it might look like this:

---

[126] Ebert, A. (May 6, 2020). We Want Fair AI Algorithms – But How To Define Fairness? (Fairness Series Part 3). *Mostly.AI*. Available at *https://mostly.ai/blog/we-want-fair-ai-algorithms-but-how-to-define-fairness/*.

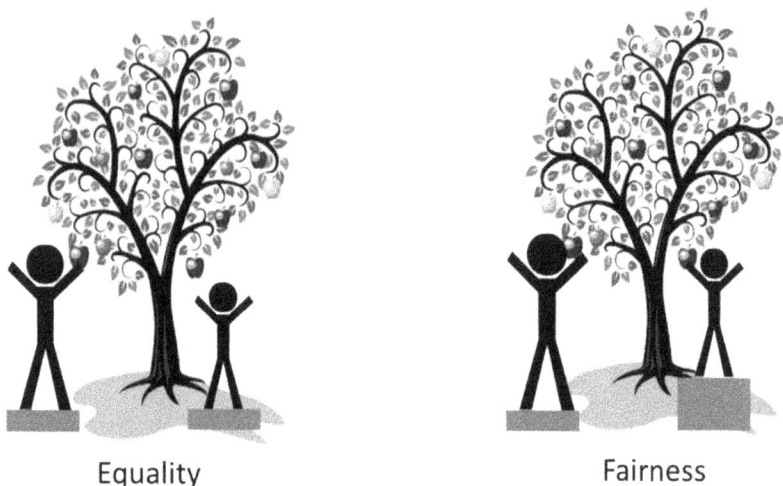

Equality   Fairness

Figure 4-5: Equality vs. fairness

Although equality might be easier for AI to incorporate, since it's a simpler A-B decision, fairness is not. When conceptually developing an AI, the different permutations and requirements for fairness are rarely considered. Even if fairness is part of the initial considerations, there is not always a "right" answer for any particular AI system. In addition, various actors are involved in the AI life cycle (from data set identification and collection, development of algorithms, to use of AI systems), all of which might have dissimilar understanding and interpretation of exactly what constitutes fairness and how to achieve it.

There are, however, an increasing number of quantitative and qualitative tools that can help AI developers incorporate fairness. Quantitative tools focus on technical solutions and qualitative tools look at the nuanced definitions of fairness.

Table 4-2: Quantitative and Qualitative Fairness Tools[127]

Quantitative Tool	Description
IBM's AI Fairness 360 toolkit	A Python toolkit focusing on technical solutions through fairness metrics and algorithms to help users examine, report, and mitigate discrimination and bias in ML models. (*https://aif360.res.ibm.com/*)
Google's What-If Tool	A tool to explore a models performance on a data set, including examining several preset definitions of fairness constraints (e.g. equality of opportunity). This tool is interesting as it allows users to explore different definitions of fairness. (*https://pair-code.github.io/what-if-tool/*)
Microsoft's fairlearn.py	A Python package that implements a variety of algorithms that seek to mitigate "unfairness" in supervised ML. (*https://github.com/fairlearn/fairlearn*)
Facebook "Fairness Flow"	An internal tool to identify bias in AI/ML models. (*www.facebook.com/FacebookAI/videos/294602762188398/?msclkid=173b6990bc0b11ecb9bced36f389802a*)

---

[127] Smith, G. (2020). What does "fairness" mean for machine learning systems? *Center for Equity, Gender & Leadership (EGAL) at Berkeley Haas*. Available at *https://haas.berkeley.edu/wp-content/uploads/What-is-fairness_-EGAL2.pdf*.

Qualitative Tool	Description
Co-designed AI fairness checklist	A checklist listing what needs to be considered at different stages of an AI system's development and deployment life cycle (i.e. envision, define, prototype, build, launch, and evolve). (*https://dl.acm.org/doi/abs/10.1145/331 3831.3376445?msclkid=4478b06abc0b 11ec92c2793a7eacc469*)
Fairness analytic	A tool developed by Mulligan et al that is designed to facilitate conversations about fairness during the early stages of a project. It can be used to explore concepts of fairness from various disciplines and think about what fairness could and should mean for a particular AI system. (*https://richmondywong.com/docs/Mulli gan-et-al-fairness-analytic.pdf*)

CHAPTER 5: BIAS IN AI – WHY IS IT IMPORTANT AND POTENTIALLY DANGEROUS?

> *"Human bias is an issue that has been well researched in psychology for years. It arises from the implicit association that reflects bias we are not conscious of and how it can affect an event's outcomes.*
>
> *Over the last few years, society has begun to grapple with exactly how much these human prejudices, with devastating consequences, can find their way through AI systems. Being profoundly aware of these threats and seeking to minimize them is an urgent priority when many firms are looking to deploy AI solutions."*
>
> **Steve Nouri[128]**

Before we can examine bias in AI, we must first understand human bias[129] and how it can creep into our everyday actions and thoughts. Humans like to believe that we are rational beings – but in truth, we are all susceptible to hundreds of biases that can trigger us to think or act irrationally or judgmentally. AI is most at risk from implicit or unconscious bias.

---

[128] Steve Nouri is the Head of Data Science and AI at the Australian Computer SocietyAustralian Computer SocietyAustralian Computer Society, *www.acs.org.au/*.

[129] The Cambridge Dictionary online defies bias as: "The action of supporting or opposing a particular person or thing in an unfair way, because of allowing personal opinions to influence your judgment." See *https://dictionary.cambridge.org/us/dictionary/english/bias*.

5: Bias in AI – Why is it important and potentially dangerous?

Implicit bias describes what's happening when, despite our best intentions and without our cognizance, stereotypes and assumptions worm their way into our minds and affect our actions in ways that may be unconscious. Unlike the biases we can identify in ourselves, implicit bias resides deep in the subconscious. The fact that implicit biases exist does not mean that an individual is necessarily prejudiced or inclined to discrimination. It simply means that the brain is functioning in a way that makes unconscious associations and generalizations.

Where does AI bias come from?

The blame for bias in AI is often laid on biased data used in training the AI. But the causes of biases go far deeper than that. Implicit bias can sneak into AI algorithms as a result of these real human tendencies:

- **The human brain has a natural tendency to look for patterns and associations when dealing with the world**. Our capability for storing, processing, and using information relies on our ability to form associations about the world.
- **Humans like to take shortcuts and try to simplify the world around us.** The human brain is relentlessly flooded with more information than it could possibly process, so taking mental shortcuts makes it easier and quicker to sort through all of the incoming data.
- **Our experiences and environment influence the development of biases – and sometimes these are formed without direct experience**. Cultural and environmental conditioning, media representations, and education can all add to the implicit bias humans develop about those that are "other."

5: Bias in AI – Why is it important and potentially dangerous?

As a consequence, bias is one of the many human imperfections that causes us to make errors and often restrains us from growing and innovating. Bias is a human reality, but it is also a well-documented reality for AI as well – and one that is notoriously difficult to eliminate.

AI bias happens when incorrect or biased data used in the ML process leads to systematically prejudiced results in the AI itself. This can occur as a consequence of human bias in the individuals designing or training the system, or it can be a consequence of incomplete or faulty data sets used to train the system on a specific area.

Using an earlier example, if an AI is trained to recognize a dog based on certain physical characteristics, such as shape of the head, the possession of four legs and a tail, and a certain profile – the AI may not be able to detect and identify a wolf. Or in more human terms, an AI can be trained to detect certain skin conditions using a selection of pictures, but if these pictures are mainly of individuals with lighter skin, this could have a negative impact on the AI's ability to detect these skin conditions on individuals with darker skin.

Real-life examples of bias in AI

There are many examples of AI triggering problems by imitating the (often unconscious) biases of the developers who created and use it. Here are a few examples of bias in AI:

Amazon's sexist hiring AI

In 2018, Reuters reported that Amazon had implemented an AI-based hiring system designed to restructure the recruitment process by reviewing the incoming resumes and proposing the most-qualified candidate. However, once in use, the AI appeared to have a serious issue with women. It came to light that the algorithm had been designed to replicate Amazon's existing hiring practices, which meant that it also copied the existing biases. The AI reacted to the use of the word "women" in resumes, and devalued the resumes on the scoring system. Reuters learned that *"In effect, Amazon's system taught itself that male candidates were preferable."*[130] Rather than helping to remove biases present in the recruitment process, the AI algorithm simply automated them. Amazon confirmed that they had scrapped the system after the bias was identified and reported.

Facebook's gender and race ad bias

In 2019, Facebook was sued for violation by the US Department of Housing and Urban Development for allowing advertisers on the site to intentionally show ads based on gender, sexual preference, and race, which are considered protected classes under the US legal system.[131] Job ads for positions as nurses or administrative assistants were recommended primarily to women, while job ads for janitors and taxi drivers were shown to a greater number of males, in particular males from minority backgrounds. The AI algorithm learned that ads for real estate sales were likely

---

[130] Dastin, J. (October 10, 2018). Amazon scraps secret AI recruiting tool that showed bias against women. *Reuters.* Available at *www.reuters.com/article/us-amazon-com-jobs-automation-insight/amazon-scraps-secret-ai-recruiting-tool-that-showed-bias-against-women-idUSKCN1MK08G.*

[131] Hao, K. (April 5, 2019). Facebook's ad-serving algorithm discriminates by gender and race. *MIT Technology Review.* Available at *www.technologyreview.com/2019/04/05/1175/facebook-algorithm-discriminates-ai-bias/.*

to attain greater attention when shown to whites, while ads for rentals were being shown to other minority groups.

In 2021, an audit by researchers from the University of Southern California found that Facebook's ad delivery system was still discriminating against women. The imbalance was not only in lower-level jobs, such as delivery drivers, but also for higher-skilled positions. For example, Facebook's " *... algorithms were more likely to show a woman an ad for a technical job at Netflix Inc. – which has a relatively high level of female employment for the tech industry – than an ad for a job at Nvidia Corp., a graphics-chip maker with a higher proportion of male employees, based on data from federal employment reports. "*[132]

Racial bias in US healthcare

In 2019, a research study was conducted into the algorithm used by health systems, insurers, and practitioners to predict which patients with complex medical needs should receive extra medical care. The ostensible goal was to slash costs by suggesting those patients receive "high risk management" at less expensive primary care levels. The focus of the research was an AI used by the health services company, Optum, which is used to guide healthcare decisions for millions of US citizens. Although this is certainly not the only tool used for healthcare decisions, the findings illustrate a critical bias. Generally, only 18% of the patients identified by the algorithm as needing additional healthcare were black, as compared to approximately 82% who were white patients. If,

---

[132] Horwitz, J. (April 9, 2021). Facebook Algorithm Shows Gender Bias in Job Ads. *The Wall Street Journal.* Available at *www.wsj.com/articles/facebook-shows-men-and-women-different-job-ads-study-finds-11617969600.*

however, the AI algorithm were to echo the true percentage of the most unwell black and white patients respectively, those numbers should have been about 46% and 53%.[133]

PredPol crime prediction

With echoes of the movie *Minority Report*,[134] PredPol[135] was used, until its cancellation in 2020, by the Los Angeles Police Department as a tool to predict where crimes would occur throughout the metropolitan area. It was found that PredPol often led police to unfairly target certain neighborhoods with a high proportion of people from racial minorities, regardless of the true crime rate in those areas. PredPol is only one of a number of predictive policing tools in use by police departments across the US, others include HunchLab and MC2 Solutions.

Can AI's decisions be less biased than human ones?

AI bias can be an anomaly in the output of ML algorithms. But bias could also be a result of prejudiced assumptions made during the algorithm development process or preconceptions introduced through the training data.

---

[133] Obermeyer, Z., Powers B., Vogeli, C., and Mullainathan, S. (October 25, 2019). Dissecting racial bias in an algorithm used to manage the health of populations. *Science*, Issue 366, pp. 447–53. Available at *https://science.sciencemag.org/content/366/6464/447*.

[134] Minority Report is a Steven Spielberg movie starring Tom Cruise, which depicts a specialized police department that apprehends criminals based on foreknowledge of their potential crime.

[135] Winston, A. and Burrington, I. (April 26, 2018). A pioneer in predictive policing is starting a troubling new project. *The Verge*. Available at *www.theverge.com/2018/4/26/17285058/predictive-policing-predpol-pentagon-ai-racial-bias*,

5: Bias in AI – Why is it important and potentially dangerous?

With the proper data and associated algorithms, AI could potentially lessen peoples' subjective interpretation of data. Based on the training data used, AI algorithms consider only the data that increases their predictive accuracy. Additionally, there is some evidence that algorithms can improve decision-making, causing it to become fairer in the process.

At the same time, there is also extensive evidence to imply that AI models can indeed demonstrate human and societal biases and deploy them at scale. For example, one technology company discontinued deployment of an AI after discovering that the algorithm penalized applicants from women's colleges. COMPAS,[136] which was used to predict recidivism in Broward County, Florida, incorrectly labeled African-American defendants as "high-risk" at nearly twice the rate it mislabeled white defendants.[137]

So, can an AI be truly unbiased? The simple answer is yes, but this is only as good as the training data. The reality is more complex. AI is only as good as the data it is fed and people create data. Numerous human biases have been identified and new biases are being identified. Consequently, since it may not be possible to have a completely unbiased human mind, it may also be impossible to have completely unbiased AI. It is, after all, people who are creating the biased data, and other people and human-developed algorithms that are examining the data to identify and remove potential biases.

---

[136] Correctional Offender Management Profiling for Alternative Sanctions.

[137] Larson, J., Mattu, S., Kirchner, L., and Angwin, J. (May 23, 2016). How We Analyzed the COMPAS Recidivism Algorithm. *ProPublica.*

5: Bias in AI – Why is it important and potentially dangerous?

There are two basic types of bias in AI:

- **Cognitive bias** – Psychologists and behavioral researchers have defined and classified more than 180 human biases,[138] and each of these could affect how we make decisions. These biases could bleed into AI either via developers unknowingly introducing them to the model, or using a training data set that unintentionally includes those biases.
- **Incomplete or inaccurate data** may not be inclusive or representative of all characteristics, and, consequently, may bring in bias.

To more effectively identify and mitigate bias, developers, statisticians, and AI designers must incorporate "de-biasing" processes and tools.

Identifying and removing bias in AI

AI biases are a result of the prejudices of people, and AI developers need to focus on identifying and removing those prejudices from the data set. But this is not as easy as it sounds.

The introduction of bias into an AI is not always obvious during the design and development phase because it is often not possible to realize the downstream impacts of the data and choices until much later. Once the results of AI bias are identified, it's hard to retroactively determine exactly where that bias originated and then figure out how to eliminate it.

---

[138] Heick, T. The List Of Cognitive Biases: A Graphic Of 180+ Heuristics. *TeachThought University*. Available at www.teachthought.com/critical-thinking/the-cognitive-bias-codex-a-visual-of-180-cognitive-biases/.

5: Bias in AI – Why is it important and potentially dangerous?

One of the most tried-and-tested approaches is to remove protected classes (such as gender or minority status) from data, and delete the labels that could result in algorithm bias. But trials have shown that this approach may not be effective, since the removed labels also affect the understanding of the model and the accuracy of the results will suffer.

Bias can occur in the environment in which AI is created or deployed, in the data from which it learns, in the design process itself, and in the use of the AI.

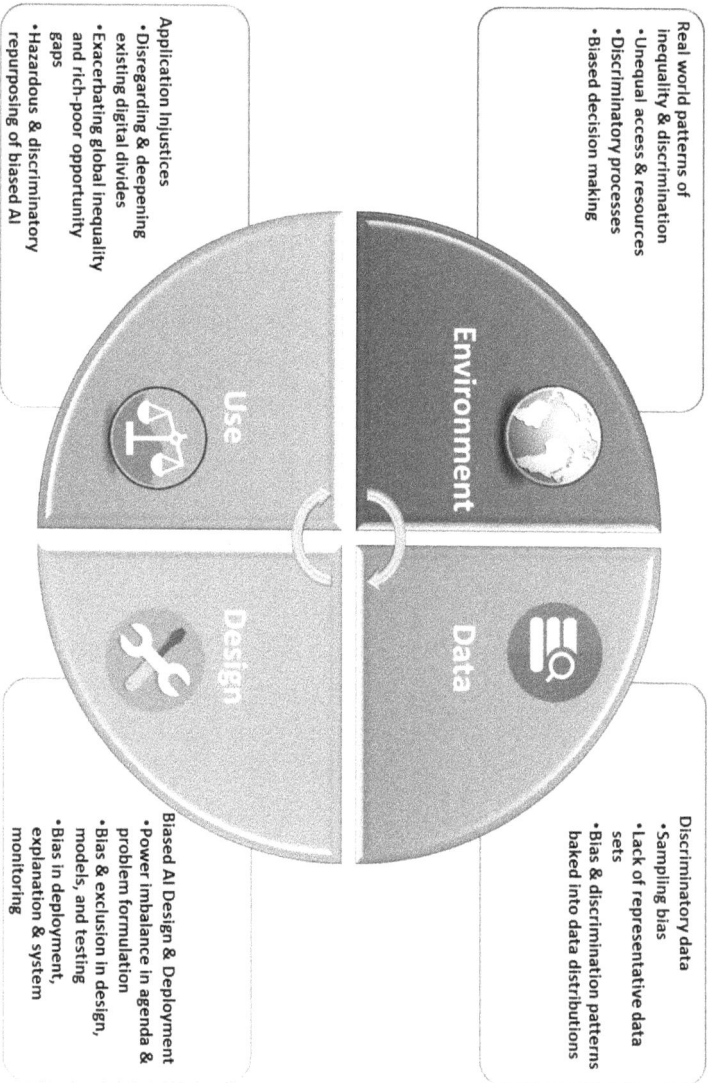

Figure 5-1: Bias in environment, data, design and use

Environment

Real world patterns of inequality & discrimination
• Unequal access & resources
• Discriminatory processes
• Biased decision making

Use

Application Injustices
• Disregarding & deepening existing digital divides
• Exacerbating global inequality and rich-poor opportunity gaps
• Hazardous & discriminatory repurposing of biased AI

Design

Biased AI Design & Deployment
• Power imbalance in agenda & problem formulation
• Bias & exclusion in design, models, and testing
• Bias in deployment, explanation & system monitoring

Data

Discriminatory data
• Sampling bias
• Lack of representative data sets
• Bias & discrimination patterns baked into data distributions

5: Bias in AI – Why is it important and potentially dangerous?

One of the biggest problems in seeking to remove bias in AI and ensuring fairness, is determining a universally-accepted definition of fairness itself. This is not only relevant in AI – this question also has a very long history of argument in philosophy, the social sciences, and law. The difference in AI is that the theory of fairness has to be defined in mathematical terms.

In its simplest formulation, fairness is often defined as the equal treatment of people – unless there is some "relevant distinction" that warrants unequal treatment. And here's where it becomes tricky – how do we, as humans, define a relevant distinction, and how can that be mathematically rendered in an AI? It is often easier to agree on what is unfair rather than what is fair. For example, we can all agree that minority discrimination is wrong, yet many years later we are still arguing about whether or not the affirmative action laws provide a fair remedy.

Research in AI and ML has provided the generic concept of fairness, with more precise definitions, such as "demographic defense parity," "predictive rate parity," and "counterfactual fairness."[139]

Google defines demographic defense parity as a fairness metric that is satisfied if the results of an AI's classification are not dependent on a given sensitive attribute, and special consideration is not given for legal, ethical, social, or personal reasons. For example, if two demographics apply to a university, demographic parity is achieved if the percentage of one demographic admitted is the same as the

---

[139] For more detailed information on these terms and how they can be applied see *https://developers.google.com/machine-learning/glossary/fairness* and *http://fairware.cs.umass.edu/papers/Verma.pdf*.

percentage of the other demographic, regardless of whether the average of one group is more qualified than the other.

Predictive rate parity reflects whether, for a given classifier, the accuracy rates are equivalent for all demographics or groups being considered. In this case, an AI used to predict college acceptance would satisfy predictive parity for different demographics if the precision rate was the same for all considered demographics.

Counterfactual fairness tests whether a classifier has the same result for two identical individuals, except in regard to a human attribute that may be given special attention for legal, ethical, social, or personal reasons.

Part of the problem with bias and fairness in AI is that data on social behavior is often *fuzzy*[140] compared to the binary data used in algorithms. Researchers in many fields have proposed solutions for identifying and mitigating potential *fuzzy* data that leads to bias. A significant challenge lies with the algorithm developers themselves.

> *"These practitioners are often engineers and scientists with less exposure to social or public policy questions. The demographics of algorithm designers are often less than diverse. Algorithm designers make myriad design choices, some of which may have far-reaching consequences."*[141]

---

[140] In computing *fuzzy* has a precise meaning. It refers to data properties and sets that have vague and imprecise boundaries of definition.

[141] Osonde A. Osoba, William Welser IV. (2017). *An Intelligence in Our Image: The Risks of Bias and Errors in Artificial Intelligence.* RAND Corporation.

5: Bias in AI – Why is it important and potentially dangerous?

McKinsey & Company identified six steps that are loosely described here to assist in minimizing bias in AI, and provided several suggested actions in association with each step.[142]

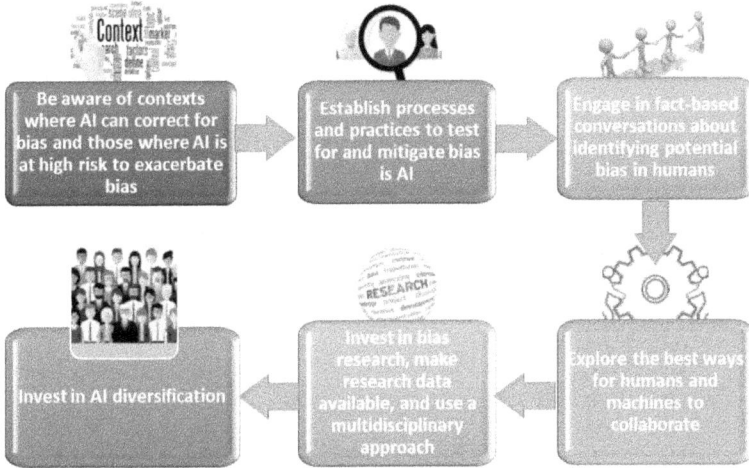

Figure 5-2: Six steps to identify and mitigate AI bias

Identify contexts where AI can correct or exacerbate bias

Anticipate areas that might be prone to unfair bias, such as those with previous examples of AI bias or with prejudicial data.

Implement processes to identify and mitigate AI bias

Improve data collection through more conscious sampling and using internal reviews and/or third-party audits of data and models.

---

[142] Silberg, J. and Manyika, J. (2019). *Tackling bias in artificial intelligence (and in humans)*. McKinsey & Company.

5: Bias in AI – Why is it important and potentially dangerous?

Discuss potential bias in human decisions

Use group and individual discussions to recognize and categorize long-standing biases in human decision-making that may have gone unnoticed.

Explore how AI and humans can collaborate

Identify situations where AI decision-making is acceptable (and indeed ready for the real world) vs. decisions where humans should always be engaged. As needed, apply "human-in-the-loop" decision-making processes in which AI provides recommendations or options, and humans double-check or make the final selection.

Invest in bias research

Enhance interdisciplinary engagement that includes not just developers and statisticians, but also ethicists, social scientists, and behavioral experts.

Further diversification in AI

Create a more diverse AI that is better equipped to anticipate, spot, and review issues of unfair bias in areas such as gender, minority status, geography, and culture.

Use available tools

In addition to processes, several organizations are examining tools to assist in identifying and mitigating bias. IBM has developed a toolkit called AI Fairness 360[143] that enables AI programmers to test biases in models and data sets with a comprehensive set of metrics. It also assists in mitigating

---

[143] See *https://aif360.res.ibm.com/*.

biases with the help of 12 pre-packaged algorithms, such as learning fair representations, rejecting option classification, and disparate impact remover. Another IBM tool, Watson OpenScale,[144] provides more visibility into AI decision-making, facilitating bias checking and mitigation in real time while AI is making decisions.

Google has developed a number of tools, such as What-If,[145] which tests AI performance in hypothetical situations, analyzes the importance of various data features, and visualizes model behavior across multiple sets of input data, and for varying AI fairness metrics. Google's TensorFlow team has been a leader in developing other AI and ML fairness toolkits, such as ML-fairness-gym.[146]

Microsoft and the University of Maryland are experimenting in the use of "crowdsourcing"[147] to identify potential AI bias. The primary role of crowdsourcing is to recognize and remove bias from the data collection and pre-processing step of AI learning. Microsoft also has another tool called Fairlearn,[148] used to assess an AI's fairness and mitigate the observed unfairness. Fairlearn provides a Python package that enablers AI developers to evaluate the AI's fairness and resolve identified unfairness problems.

---

[144] See *https://medium.com/design-ibm/ibm-watson-openscale-wins-an-ai-excellence-award-b9f60d9372bc*.

[145] See *https://www.analyticsvidhya.com/blog/2018/09/google-launches-what-if-tool-perform-code-free-ml-experiments/*.

[146] See *https://github.com/google/ml-fairness-gym*.

[147] Crowdsourcing is a term commonly used to explain the process of engaging multiple people, i.e. a crowd, to innovate, solve a problem, or increase efficiency.

[148] See *https://github.com/fairlearn/fairlearn#overview-of-fairlearn*.

The open-source community also provides another tool called FairML,[149] which is a python-based tool that helps an analyst determine the relative significance of inputs to a black-box predictive model to evaluate the model's fairness (or degree of potential bias).

EqualAI® is a non-profit organization dedicated to reducing the unconscious bias in the development and deployment of AI.[150] The corporation has developed a comprehensive checklist that can help identify potential biases and practices. This checklist can be found in Figure 5-3 and on EqualAI's website at:

www.equalai.org/assets/docs/EqualAI_Checklist_for_Identifying_Bias_in_AI.pdf.

---

[149] See *https://pythonrepo.com/repo/adebayoj-fairml-python-deep-learning-model-explanation*.

[150] See *www.equalai.org/mission/*.

5: Bias in AI – Why is it important and potentially dangerous?

EQUAL™

EqualAI Checklist® to Identify Bias in AI

Bias is in there; how will you find it and what will you do to change it?
This Checklist will help get you started.

Framing the Problem & Product Design
1. Who are you aiming to serve?
2. Who else will be impacted?
3. Who could use or be impacted by the AI who is not represented on your team?

Data. Similar to software, you should implement "data testing" for consumer-facing AI-based solutions.
1. Where is the bias in the data?
   - It's in there. How will it encumber your goals? Impact downstream users?
   - Test for specific populations, protected classes (race, age, gender, etc.) and problematic use cases.
2. What is the origin of your data?
   - Is the code, underlying data auditable?
   - What do you know about the sources, expected uses? Any known limitations?
3. Who/what is represented and how?
4. Identify the influential variables to ensure they are in line with your goals (diversity, offer equal opportunities) and legal compliance (not reliant on zip codes, protected characteristics).
5. Identify error rates for different subgroups.
   - Is there a higher false positive rate for minorities? women? women of color?
6. What is the accuracy of your model for different subsets?
7. Have you checked outcomes to recognize regional and cultural differences?
8. Incomplete Data: Do your data sets sufficiently cover the populations that will be impacted? Or are they narrow, leading to erroneous conclusions?

Legal check
1. Have your legal, HR and innovation teams coordinated on how you will develop or use the AI to avoid potential liabilities?
2. Have you leveraged industry bodies and checked what competitors are doing?
3. Did you consider applicable laws (current and future), such as:
   - Privacy (CA, GDPR), Bot notice (CA), EEOC laws, Fair lending laws, Fair Credit Reporting Act

Safeguards
1. Do you have a testing team that compensates for gaps in the perspective and backgrounds of the executive and development teams?
2. Is your AI system usable by those with special needs or disabilities? Others at risk of exclusion?
3. How could your systems be penetrated by cyber-attack, hackers, trolls? Introduction of biased data sets?
   - What measures are in place to catch and address these harms?
4. What systems and policies do you have in place for AI governance? (Ethics officer, internal ethics board, designated POC for employees and consumers)
   - Does the policy have executive committee-level approval?
   - Oversight from the Board Audit Committee?
   - Approval by the General Counsel, Chief Information Officer & Chief Risk Officer?
5. Have you invited social monitoring to flag signals of bias— real or perceived?

Repeat.
AI is constantly iterating and will develop new patterns. New biases will emerge and you could be legally liable or accountable in the court of law or public opinion regardless of whether an outcome was intended or foreseeable.

Contact EqualAI® for information on best practices and guidance on addressing these pervasive, complex issues.

Figure 5-3: EqualAI checklist to identify bias

5: Bias in AI – Why is it important and potentially dangerous?

It is clear that bias is a real challenge for AI and can have real and damaging results, but we need to look at another significant area of attention – cybersecurity and its relationship to AI.

CHAPTER 6: AI AND CYBERSECURITY – AI AS A SWORD OR A SHIELD?

> *"AI can be both a blessing and a curse for cybersecurity. This is confirmed by the fact that AI is being used both as a sword (i.e. in support of malicious attacks) and as a shield (to counter cybersecurity risks)."*
>
> **Lorenzo Pupillo**[151]

AI as a sword

Cyber attacks continue to rise and many are using AI as part of the attack. In addition, the AI itself may be vulnerable to a cyber attack. Unlike traditional cyber attacks that can be triggered by errors in code or improper network configuration, AI attacks are enabled by inherent limitations in the underlying AI algorithms.

Although there haven't been any robot or AI uprisings (at least not yet!), AI-based cyber attacks have happened and are continuing with increasing regularity.

Cyber attackers are using AI – and its subset called ML – to launch increasingly automated, aggressive, and well-coordinated attacks. Corrupting an AI system can actually be quite easy. Cyber attackers can bias or manipulate data used to train AI by creating subtle changes to the data sets. Where

---

[151] Pupillo, L. *Artificial Intelligence and cybersecurity*, April 21, 2021. Available at *www.ceps.eu/artificial-intelligence-and-cybersecurity/*.

attackers lack access to the actual data, they may also tamper with inputs to force mistakes.

Non-AI based and AI-based cyber attacks have similar goals, such as:

- **Causing damage:** the cyber attacker seeks to cause damage by having the system malfunction. One example of this might be an attack that causes a self-driving vehicle to ignore a stoplight. An attacker can cause the self-driving vehicle to ignore or misread the stoplight either by attacking the AI system itself, or by modifying the stoplight so that it incorrectly recognizes a stoplight as a different sign or symbol. The potential result – a crash into other vehicles or pedestrians.

- **Hiding something:** the cyber attacker seeks to avoid detection by an AI system. An example of this is an attack that affects a content filter tasked with blocking terrorist or hate propaganda from being posted on a social network and causing the filter to malfunction, therefore letting the unwanted material spread unhindered.

- **Degrading trust:** the cyber attacker wants an operator or a user to lose trust in the AI. An example of this is an attack that forces an automated security alarm to misclassify normal events as security threats, triggering a stream of false alarms. For example, a video-based security system could be led to repeatedly classify a passing stray cat or swaying tree as a security threat. Consequently, the false alarms create mistrust in the accuracy of the system and could then allow a valid threat to evade detection.

To organize cyber attacks, cyber attackers frequently manipulate existing AI-based systems, rather than developing new AI programs and tools. AI-based cyber attacks can take the form of:

- Misinformation and data manipulation; and
- Weaponization of AI as part of a system attack.

Using AI to facilitate misinformation

In a different way, criminal hackers and cyber attackers can use AI to aid them in increasing the scale and effectiveness of social engineering attacks. AI can learn to identify behavioral patterns, and be used to convince people that a text message, phone call, or email asking for sensitive data or network access is legitimate. Cyber attackers are using AI to leverage personal information collected from social media accounts to automatically generate phishing emails that can obtain open rates as high as 60%.[152] That's much greater than the standard phishing attacks where cyber attackers are doing the work manually.

AI can also be used to facilitate the spread of misinformation, primarily using bots.[153] One example is using marshaling bots to flood a Twitter thread with false Twitter users in order to influence others. But on a more critical level, AI is being employed to affect national and international policy. The 2016 US presidential election demonstrated how AI is

---

[152] Huang, K., Siegel, M., Pearlson. K., and Madnick, S. (June 2019). Casting the Dark Web in a New Licht: A value-chain lens reveals a growing cyber attack ecosystem and new strategies for combating it. *MIT Management Sloan School.*

[153] Bot is short for robot, and is an automated software program that executes automated tasks over the Internet.

affecting democracy and political life. The use of algorithms, automation, and AI increased the efficiency and the extent of the misinformation campaigns and related cyber activities, affecting how American citizens formed opinions, and perhaps even influencing their voting decisions.

A more recent example is the use of the GPT-3[154] algorithm to generate misinformation. *"Over six months, a group at Georgetown University's Center for Security and Emerging Technology used GPT-3 to generate misinformation, including stories around a false narrative, news articles altered to push a bogus perspective, and tweets riffing on particular points of disinformation."*[155] The reason GPT-3 is particularly powerful is its ability to create anything possessing a language structure – so, it can answer complex questions, write essays, provide summaries of long texts, translate languages, take notes, and even generate computer code.

Research experiments have demonstrated that GPT-3's writing could influence readers' opinions on topics of international diplomacy. The researchers presented volunteers with mock tweets written by the GPT-3 algorithm about the withdrawal of US troops from Afghanistan and US sanctions on China. In both cases, researchers observed that participants were swayed by the messages. After being

---

[154] GPT-3 or third generation Generative Pre-Trained Transformer, is a neural network algorithm created by OpenAI. OpenAI is a research resource co-founded by Elon Musk. GPT-3 has been lauded as an AI that is more proficient at creating content with a language structure – whether human or machine language.

[155] Knight, W. (May 24, 2021). AI Can Write Disinformation Now – and Dupe Human Readers. *Wired.* Available at *www.wired.com/story/ai-write-disinformation-dupe-human-readers/?utm_source=WIR_REG_GATE.*

exposed to a number of tweets opposing sanctions on China, for example, the percentage of respondents who said they were also against such a policy doubled.[156]

In many cases, the same technology that is used to identify and manage misinformation is powered by the AI that can also create that misinformation. For example, during the COVID-19 pandemic, preprints of research papers that had not yet undergone a rigorous peer review were being uploaded to sites such as medRxiv.[157] These reports were not only described in the press, but were being cited in real public-health decisions.

Misinformation has been a defining characteristic of the COVID-19 pandemic. Social media bots were nearly twice as active in COVID-19 posts as opposed to their use in past crises and national elections. Public and private sectors continuously struggled to address the rapid spread of misinformation about the pandemic. The result was confusion, and a lack of coherence in the national and international response to the crisis.

---

[156] Knight, W. (May 24, 2021). AI Can Write Disinformation Now – and Dupe Human Readers. *Wired*. Available at *www.wired.com/story/ai-write-disinformation-dupe-human-readers/?utm_source=WIR_REG_GATE*.

[157] medRxiv is a free online archive and distribution server for finished, but not yet published documents (called preprints), in the medical, clinical, and related health sciences.

AI can be vulnerable to simple attacks

Cyber attacks on AI are not the only way an AI can be affected. Sometimes, simply changing a learned form can have a disastrous effect.

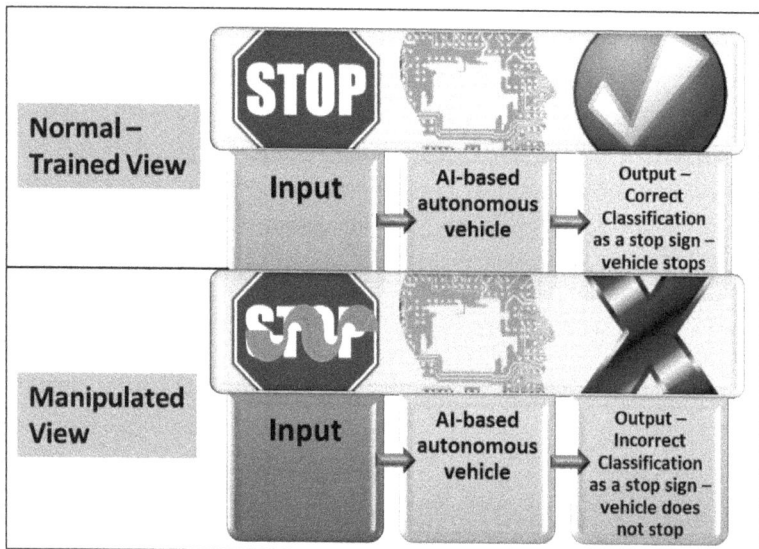

Figure 6-1: Manipulation of an AI-trained view

For example, an alteration in the appearance of a stop sign might cause an AI-based autonomous vehicle to misinterpret the sign and continue driving when it should stop and avoid an accident.

Weaponizing AI in cyber attacks

Making cyber attacks more cost-effective

Using AI and automated scripts enables bad actors to execute more attacks at a faster rate. Just like most "companies," cyber attackers seek to get the most return on investment with the least amount of overhead cost in terms of money, time, and effort, while maximizing the efficiency and effectiveness of the tools they're using. It can cost upwards of six figures to execute a zero-day threat; developing new exploits and malware can be time-consuming and expensive; and renting Malware as a Service (MaaS) tools off the dark web is also not cheap.

MaaS has become increasingly popular with cyber attackers because it is very effective and immediately ready for their use. Malware developers take care of the development and maintenance of MaaS, which makes it easier for less sophisticated cyber attackers, by eliminating the need for them to have high-level exploit-writing technical skills. MaaS offers access to applications and AI bots that can quickly distribute the malware. Much like Software as a Service (SaaS), MaaS is a paid subscription service that provides a personal account where non-technical cyber attackers are able to execute attacks themselves, but still get the benefit of technical support.

Malware and AI cyber attacks

Cyber attackers are also using AI to hide malicious code within otherwise benign applications. The malicious code is programmed to execute and autonomously determine which payloads are most effective and then execute them. This can be a timed execution, executing a certain specified number of months after the application has been installed. Or it could be a triggered execution that launches when a specific number of users have logged into the application.

AI technologies are unique in that they can adapt by acquiring and analyzing incoming data. Cyber attackers are very conscious of this learning capability and they leverage it to develop adaptable attack vectors and then create intelligent and adaptable malware programs. An AI-based attack may not succeed on the first try, but as the AI acquires knowledge of what prevented a successful attack, it adapts and can make it more likely for cyber attackers to succeed in later attacks.

Cyber attackers can also use AI to create malware that self-propagates across a network. As the AI looks at the network, it can detect unmitigated or unpatched weaknesses, and automatically launch an attack. To demonstrate the ability to link AI and malware, IBM created DeepLocker – a new type of "highly targeted and evasive" AI-powered attack tool, which can hide its malicious intent until it reaches a specific target. *"DeepLocker flies under the radar without being detected and unleashes its malicious action as soon as the AI model identifies the target through indicators like facial recognition, geolocation, and voice recognition."*[158] IBM demonstrated this capability by camouflaging the ransomware WannaCry within DeepLocker in a video conferencing app and training the AI on recognition of specific faces using photos publicly available on social media. Since it was embedded inside the AI, WannaCry would not be detected by security tools, such as antivirus engines and malware sandboxes.

> *"When launched, the app would surreptitiously feed camera snapshots into the embedded AI model, but otherwise behave normally for all users except the intended target … When the victim sits in front of the computer and uses the application, the camera would feed their face to the app, and the malicious payload will be*

---

[158] Kumar, M. Researchers Developed Artificial Intelligence-Powered Stealthy Malware. *The Hacker News*, August 9, 2018.

secretly executed, thanks to the victim's face, which was the preprogrammed key to unlock it."[159]

Considering the proliferation of video teleconferencing during the COVID pandemic, this capability would provide an almost undetectable medium for propagating malware and be truly dangerous in the hands of cyber attackers.

AI can reduce the time and effort to execute a cyber attack

AI can mimic trusted system components, allowing a cyber attacker to reside on the system and then execute a stealth attack. AI-enabled malware can automatically learn the networking environment of an organization, patch update life cycle, preferred communication protocols, and time frames when the network is least protected. Using this information, cyber attackers are able to execute undetectable attacks as they seamlessly blend into an organization's existing security environment.

5G can be a game changer in terms of the time it can take a cyber attacker to execute an attack. If AI is integrated into a network of connected devices that communicate at 5G speeds, AI could be formed into a construct where those devices can act as bots using swarm technology[160] to launch an attack on their own, but can also automatically adapt the attack at digital speeds depending on what the AI learns during the attack process.

---

[159] Kumar, M. Researchers Developed Artificial Intelligence-Powered Stealthy Malware. *The Hacker News*, August 9, 2018.

[160] Swarm technology is when multiple technologies are integrated to collectively solve problems by forming constructs and behaviors similar to the ones observed in natural swarms of bees, birds, or fish.

With this swarm technology, intelligent swarms of bots could potentially exchange information and learn from each in other in real-time. By integrating self-learning capabilities into the AI, cyber attackers would be able to design attacks able to quickly assess weaknesses – and also counter any efforts to protect against cyber attacks. The good news is that these swarm technologies are not highly proliferated, and will likely remain so until the communication infrastructures provide a better platform for this technology.

AI can facilitate stealth attacks

Cyber attackers can leverage AI technologies to generate types of malware able to imitate trusted system components and facilitate stealth attacks. For example, cyber attackers use AI-enabled malware to automatically gather information on the network architecture, patch and update schedules, preferred communication protocols, and situations or times when the systems may be least protected. Using this information, cyber attackers using AI-malware can launch undetectable attacks because they are able to blend seamlessly into the organization's security environment. Stealth attacks are especially dangerous since cyber attackers can penetrate and then exit from the network essentially without detection. AI can enable these types of attacks, and improvements in the technology will only lead to the development of more rapid and intelligent attacks.

On the reverse side, AI can be very effective as a protective shield against cyber attacks.

AI as a shield

AI has become a vital tool in assisting cybersecurity personnel in thwarting cyber attacks. In fact, tools that are

AI-based will likely be the only effective defense against AI-enhanced attacks. AI can be used by cybersecurity professionals to reduce the systems and network attack surface and enforce good cybersecurity practices instead of continuously chasing after malicious activity.

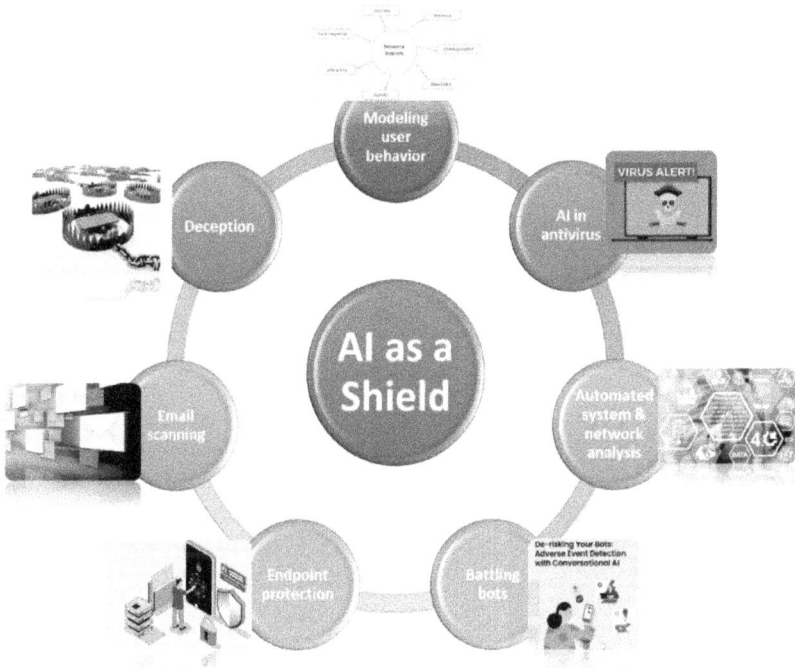

Figure 6-2: AI as a shield

AI can be very effective as a network monitoring and analytical tool by establishing a baseline of normal behavior and flagging discrepancies in areas such as network access and data traffic immediately. There are several areas where AI-based security technologies can be effective.

Modeling user behavior

Organizations can use AI to monitor the behavior of system users and develop use models. The goal of monitoring the interactions between a system and a user is system use anomalies; for example, where one employee uses the login of another user with or without the intent to commit a cyber crime. Over time, AI learns each individual user behavior and becomes able to detect whenever a different user uses the account or the account use is out of the normal pattern. The AI can then respond either by locking out the user or immediately alerting the network administrators of the anomalous use.

AI in antivirus programs

Antivirus software with integrated AI capabilities establishes a system behavior baseline and can then identify network or system anomalies by spotting applications or system activities displaying unusual behavior. Malware is programmed to execute functions that can vary from established network operations. AI-based antivirus can leverage ML to learn how legitimate programs usually interact with the operating system. So, whenever malware is introduced to a network, AI antivirus learns to immediately detect it and block it from access to system resources. This is much timelier and more effective than traditional signature-based antivirus software that scans a signature database to verify whether a program is or is not a security threat.

Automated system and network analysis

Self-learning, AI-based cybersecurity can be trained to gather data continuously and independently from across enterprise systems and networks. The collected data can then be analyzed and used to automatically correlate patterns across billions of signals applicable to the enterprise attack surface.

The outcome of automated system and network analysis is a new level of system and network intelligence that provides timely and relevant information to human cybersecurity personnel, including:

- **System and network asset inventory** – acquiring and maintaining a complete, accurate inventory of all users, applications, and devices with access to information systems and networks.
- **Threat exposure** – cyber attackers follow trends like everyone else, so what's current with cyber attackers changes regularly. AI can deliver relevant and timely information about global and industry-specific threats. This aids leadership in making critical prioritization decisions based not only on what might be used to attack the systems or network, but also on what might be used in future cyber attacks.
- **Security controls effectiveness** – it is critical to have an understanding of the current range of security tools and processes employed to protect the systems and the network. AI can help security personnel understand where the cybersecurity protections are strong and where there are weaknesses and gaps.
- **Breach risk prediction** – After taking into account the system and network assets, threat exposure, and security controls effectiveness, AI can forecast how and where the systems and networks are most susceptible to a breach. This gives leadership the knowledge necessary to plan for resource and tool allocation focused on

vulnerabilities and gaps. Insights derived from the AI system and network analysis can help an organization configure and apply tailored controls and processes to improve its cyber resilience.

- **Incident response** – AI can deliver improved situational awareness for prioritization and response to security events and incidents. It can also bring to light the root causes of cyber weaknesses to mitigate vulnerabilities and prevent future issues.

- **Explainability**[161] – Central to employing AI to augment human cybersecurity personnel is the explainability of its analysis and resulting recommendations. This is an important step to securing buy-in from stakeholders across the organization; understanding the impact of cybersecurity tools, processes, and programs; and reporting relevant information to stakeholders, including end users, security staff, the CISO, auditors, Chief Information Officer (CIO), the Chief Executive Officer (CEO), and the board of directors.

Battling bots

Bots make up a huge chunk of Internet traffic today, and they can be dangerous. From account takeovers with stolen credentials, to bogus account creation and data fraud, bots can be a real menace. Bots cannot be addressed with manual human responses alone. AI helps create a detailed understanding of network traffic and helps cybersecurity

---

[161] Explainability is defined as a set of processes and methods that allows human users to comprehend and trust the results and output created by AI algorithms. See *https://www.ibm.com/watson/explainable-ai*.

staff distinguish between good bots (such as search engine crawlers), bad bots, and human-based user activity.

Endpoint protection – especially for remote work

COVID-19 dramatically escalated the number of employees engaged in remote work, and it quickly became clear that organizations needed improved endpoint protection. Antivirus and virtual private networks (VPNs) can aid in deterring remote malware and ransomware attacks, but they work based on signatures. In order to stay protected against the latest threats, keeping up with signature definitions becomes critical. This can easily become an issue if virus definitions fall behind, for example because of a failure to update the antivirus software through a lack of attention from the software vendor. If a new type of malware attack emerges, signature protection alone may not be enough. AI-based endpoint protection takes a different approach by establishing a baseline of system and user behavior using a repeated training process. If something unusual occurs, the AI can label it and act – whether by notifying the cybersecurity staff to take action, or reverting the system or network to a safe state after an attack. This gives an organization company a level of proactive protection against threats, rather than passively waiting for malicious activity or signature updates.

Email scanning

Cyber attackers like to use email communication as a principal delivery method for malicious links or attachments that can then be used to execute phishing attacks. AI-based anti-phishing tools can apply anomaly detection techniques to identify suspicious activities in an email. These include headers, attachments, links, and message content. In fact,

Google's Gmail has used AI to filter emails for spam and phishing since its launch some 18 years ago, and today blocks upwards of 100 million spam messages a day.[162]

Network-based deception

Another effective tool in deterring AI-based attacks is network-based deception[163] using AI – essentially using tempting decoys across the network to draw in cyber attackers and expose them before they are able to determine which assets are real and which are decoys. Deception technology attracts cyber attackers away from an organization's real assets and diverts them to a decoy that mimics legitimate servers, applications, and data. This tricks the cyber attacker into believing that they have infiltrated and gained access to the network's most important assets, when in reality they are only seeing the decoys. AI can be strategically employed to assist in the deception and minimize damage to an organization's true assets.

It's more than just AI tools

Clearly, AI can be both a blessing and a curse when it comes to cybersecurity. But cybersecurity in the age of AI involves more than having AI-based tools. Even though swarm-based attacks may still be several years away, the impact of AI-enhanced threats are already being felt. Organizations must begin preparing now for this reality – and it begins with basic

---

[162] Vincent, J. (February 6, 2019). Gmail is now blocking 100 million extra spam messages a day with AI. *The Verge*. Available at *www.theverge.com/2019/2/6/18213453/gmail-tensorflow-machine-learning-spam-100-million*.

[163] Deception technology is a defensive cybersecurity practice with the goal of deceiving an attacker by deploying an assortment of decoys across a network's infrastructure to imitate its real assets.

cybersecurity hygiene. This is not just about having patching and updating procedures in place, it must also include implementation of a robust security architecture and segmentation to reduce an organization's attack surface and deter cyber attackers from getting access into the enterprise systems.

A Centre for European Policy Studies (CEPS) research task force studied the effects of AI on cybersecurity and developed a short set of non-technical conditions considered essential to ensure AI resiliency, robustness, and overall security.[164]

- Improve collaboration between law and policy makers, senior corporate representatives, and the technical community to investigate, prevent, and mitigate potential harmful uses of AI in terms of cybersecurity.
- Integrate the evaluation and identification of the security requirements for AI in public procurement policies.
- Guarantee a degree of operational control over AI by developing and keeping a close eye on practices developed to address AI's occasional lack of predictability, such as in-house development of AI models and data testing, and parallel, dynamic monitoring of AI through clones.
- Encourage private sector and cross-border collaboration by providing incentives for information sharing and creating a widely acceptable governance framework that would enable legal certainty when sharing data.
- Promote international AI certification efforts.

---

[164] Pupillo, L., Fantin, S., Polito, C., and Ferreira, A. (April 21, 2021). Artificial Intelligence and cybersecurity. *CEPS*. Available at *www.ceps.eu/artificial-intelligence-and-cybersecurity/*.

- Require assessments to be made before AI deployments, as well as during the whole life cycle of an AI product, service, or process.
- Identify and implement appropriate limitations to a full openness policy for research publication, especially when security risks exist.
- Confirm that libraries and tools have an appropriate level of cybersecurity, and integrate measures to prevent misuse before the publication of any research.
- Advance the study and regulatory interpretation of privacy laws and regulations, such as the EU GDPR, as it pertains to AI and cybersecurity.
- Seek resolution for the AI-related skills shortage and the uneven distribution of talented professionals by creating AI-related training and career paths to re-skill and retain staff.
- Ensure the understanding and efficient integration of AI tools into already existing cybersecurity professional practices and system architectures.

CHAPTER 7: AI AND OUR SOCIETY – WILL THE RESULT BE PROFESSIONAL, ETHICAL, AND SOCIAL DESKILLING, OR UPSKILLING?

> *"Knowledge that is not practiced is lost."*
>
> **Brian Patrick Green**

Deskilling is loosely defined as the loss of skill, judgment, or initiative causing an individual to become less proficient in a particular task or activity. Deskilling is not a recent phenomenon.

For example, from the mid-1700s to the nineteenth century, there was increasing mechanization of the factory system that mass-produced textiles, threatening the jobs and livelihoods of skilled workers. These new technologies resulted in a loss of work and a deskilling of a large number of textile workers. Resistance to the change led to worker uprisings that rocked the wool and cotton industries, known as the "Luddite riots."[165] Deskilled workers worried for their livelihoods sent threatening letters to employers to discourage adoption of the new technology. Workers even went so far as to break into factories to destroy the new machines, such as the new wide weaving frames.

---

[165] The rebelling textile workers in England called themselves "Luddites," allegedly after Ned Ludd, a young apprentice rumored to have destroyed a piece of textile machinery during the revolts in 1779. Today, Luddite is now a term used to describe people who reject new technologies.

Although most often applied to the loss of professional skills in the workforce, deskilling can also be applied to the area of ethical decision-making or social interactions. The opposite of deskilling is upskilling.

Upskilling is a well-known term in a business context. In the micro sense, it describes the process of individuals gaining new skills. On a macro level, it refers to a tectonic change in the environment as a result of technology. Technology, such as AI, has generated new opportunities that can only be fully achieved by a technologically proficient individual. That means that individuals must learn new professional, ethical, and social skills, and competencies. Upskilling requires new skills, but it also includes a cultural shift – a lifetime learning mindset, improved collaboration between humans and machines, and a commitment to accept and adapt to new technologies.

Professional deskilling and upskilling

The AI revolution is just around the corner – or so many say. In a utopian world, AI will emancipate humans from repetitive, everyday tasks, thus liberating us to be more productive and do more fulfilling types of work. In the alternative dystopian vision, AI will replace everyone's jobs and render millions and millions of people without any form of productive labor.

A productively engaged workforce serves at least three main objectives: to provide workers to do constructive work, to provide a source of income to those workers through earned wages, and to allow workers to have a sense of purpose. How we manage work and workers plays an important part in determining the degree of fairness and equity our society can attain.

7: AI and our society – Will the result be professional, ethical, and social deskilling, or upskilling?

Work for many is more than just what we do, it sustains us. It allows us to fulfill our material needs, perhaps escape poverty, and even build decent lives. Beyond meeting our basic material needs, work can also give us a sense of belonging, identity, and purpose.

Work also has social and societal importance, as it provides us with a network of connections and interactions with others that aid in building social cohesion. Scholars in organizational psychology focus predominantly on the subjective experience of work as contributing to our sense of significance or purpose in life. Humans perceive engagement in work as meaningful, where meaningfulness can be defined as the amount of significance work holds that helps us to answer the existential question of "Why am I here"?[166]

Professional deskilling

Acquiring, developing, and exercising skills in the performance of "meaningful" work, especially those that are more complex or well-rewarded, provides people with a sense of accomplishment and competence. This contributes to the fundamental human need for self-esteem and a sense of self-worth. An absence of work, therefore, is more than simply a professional deskilling, it can also mean the loss of a sense of meaning within society – a growth of meaninglessness as the opposite of meaningfulness.

Smids, et.al. summarizes the effects of AI on the workforce as both negative and an opportunity provider:

---

[166] Smids, J., Nyholm, S., and Berkers. H. (September 2020). Robots in the Workplace: a Threat to—or Opportunity for—Meaningful Work? *SpringerLink.* Available at
https://link.springer.com/article/10.1007/s13347-019-00377-4.

Table 7-1: Potential Negative and Positive Effects of AI On the Workforce[167]

Meaningful work	AI as a negative	AI as an opportunity
Having purpose	If AI takes over the most challenging tasks of a job, workers may lose a sense of purpose.	If AI assumes the most tedious or boring tasks, or teams up with human workers, workers might have an increased sense of purpose.
Social context	If human co-workers are replaced by AI, the reduced social interaction will change the nature of the workplace and add to social isolation.	If AI is designed to function as a co-worker, capable of human-like social interaction, the need for human contact may still be fulfilled. If robots take over repetitious tasks, more time may remain for interpersonal contact.
Skills and self-development	Tasks assumed by AI may make human skills obsolete and result in professional deskilling.	Human workers will gain new, complex skills to operate AI technology.

---

[167] Content in Table 7-1 is adapted from: Smids, J., Nyholm, S., and Berkers. H. (September 2020). Robots in the Workplace: a Threat to— or Opportunity for—Meaningful Work? *SpringerLink.* Available at *https://link.springer.com/article/10.1007/s13347-019-00377-4*.

Meaningful work	AI as a negative	AI as an opportunity
Self-esteem and self-worth	If AI assumes more complex tasks, human worker recognition and self-esteem may be diminished.	If human workers team with AI, the result may be expanded skills resulting in greater social recognition and higher self-esteem.
Autonomy	AI may exercise decision-making and deprive human workers of exercising judgment and autonomy. There may be less opportunity for shaping the work environment. There may be ethical concerns related to surveillance and AI's lack of transparency.	Human workers learn to control the AI and enhance their capacities for autonomy, leaving more opportunity for shaping their work environment.

In the past, it has been simpler for humans to specialize and to perform certain tasks than for technologies to specialize in relation to those same tasks. Humans still possess the highest intelligence and strongest muscles around (well, except for some animals). But with the advent of AI, the days of human specialization may be slowly coming to an end and evolving increasingly toward technology.

7: AI and our society – Will the result be professional, ethical, and social deskilling, or upskilling?

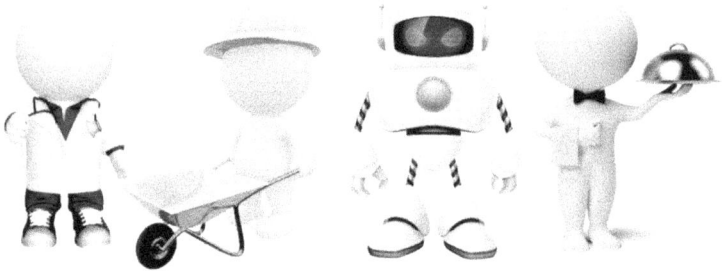

WILL ROBOTS REPLACE YOUR JOB?

Figure 7-1: Will a robot replace your job?

Futurist and author, Martin Ford, theorizes that in previous ages of technological change, deskilling mostly affected the less educated labor force or those that relied mainly on manual skills. According to Ford, however,

" ... the 21st century is seeing technology increasingly threatening the jobs of skilled workers as well. Lawyers, radiologists, and software designers have seen their work outsourced to the developing world. Ford believes the current emerging technologies will fail to generate new forms of employment. "[168]

Further, the International Labor Organization (ILO) stated in a report entitled *Work for a Brighter Future:*

"Technological advances – artificial intelligence, automation, and robotics – will create new jobs, but those who lose their jobs in this transition may be the least equipped to seize the new opportunities. Today's skills

---

[168] Ford, M. (July 12, 2016). *Rise of the Robots: Technology and the Threat of a Jobless Future.* Basic Books, New York.

will not match the jobs of tomorrow and newly acquired skills may quickly become obsolete."[169]

If AI takes on more and more complex tasks previously done by humans, the development and use of those skills will no longer be a source of meaningfulness for human workers, and their tasks will be less conducive to feelings of self-worth and accomplishment.

> *"For example, if machine learning techniques become systematically better than human radiologists on nearly all dimensions of interpreting medical images, the need to extensively train human radiologists might seem to disappear."*[170]

Professional upskilling

Others are more optimistic about the future of work. Infosys[171] co-founder Narayana Murthy recently spoke in support of emerging technologies, such as automation, as a power for opportunity. Speaking at the Infosys Prize 2018,

---

[169] Global Commission on the Future of Work. (2019). Work for a brighter future. *International Labor Organization*. Available at *www.ilo.org/wcmsp5/groups/public/---dgreports/---cabinet/documents/publication/wcms_662410.pdf*.

[170] Smids, J., Nyholm, S., and Berkers. H. (September 2020). Robots in the Workplace: a Threat to—or Opportunity for—Meaningful Work? *SpringerLink*. Available at *https://link.springer.com/article/10.1007/s13347-019-00377-4*.

[171] Infosys is an international company focused on next-generation digital services and consulting.

7: AI and our society – Will the result be professional, ethical, and social deskilling, or upskilling?

Murthy said: *"I am not a believer that technology will render societies into a state of higher and higher unemployment."*[172]

But the current approach to professional upskilling – gearing learning opportunities towards a single technology – is not sufficient to prepare either the employees or a organization for large AI implementations.

The solution to the potential problem of labor loss and employee deskilling requires a three-pronged approach:

1. Identify new roles and skills needed as a result of the AI, and prepare workers through a combination of formal and on-the-job training and education. Create a new culture that derives from leaders setting a direction and goals, then giving workers the tools and incentives through both compensation and recognition to acquire the new skill sets and then use them in the performance of their tasks.

2. Create cross-skilled teams that integrate technical and non-technical skills, so that workers can learn the basics of each other's skill sets. Cross-skilling is essential not just for collaborating on AI technologies, but also for determining which work efforts can be improved through AI.

3. Implement a continuous learning program based on a combination of formal and on-the-job training and education to accommodate and address new technologies as they emerge and are implemented. Provide workers with immediate opportunities and

---

[172] Param, S. (January 24, 2019). Automation could deskill people and create long-term unemployment: ILO. *TECHGIG*. Available at *https://content.techgig.com/automation-could-deskill-people-and-create-long-term-unemployment-ilo/articleshow/67670950.cms*.

incentives to apply what they are learning, so that education turns into relevant skills.

In creating an environment for upskilling, bear in mind that traditional classroom learning and boot camps certainly work for some, but others may find it too rigid to fit into a busy schedule. Virtual, online, and on-demand education can be of more value, especially self-paced programs that are focused on the busy professional.

Finally, don't neglect compensation. Once the workforce has adopted these new skills, the organization must re-evaluate employee compensation and benefits to ensure they remain competitive with the market. There is very little worse than investing considerable time and effort into training an employee only to have a competitor entice them to leave.

And most importantly – leadership should be among the very first to upskill. Leaders and managers will need to understand how best to implement AI positively within their organization. They are responsible for developing a plan to ensure they have the staff with the skills to take advantage of what AI offers their organization or to identify how best to re-/upskill employees to meet the new demands. Workers look to leaders to lead, so they will need to demonstrate how embracing AI serves both the organization and the employees.

Ethical deskilling and upskilling

AI does not have the inherent ability to differentiate between right and wrong and can, therefore, not be responsible for making ethical and moral decisions. AI developers and implementers often tell a story that highlights the concept that AI can be used to solve many of the ethical and moral challenges that we encounter in society and business. This particular mindset has influenced organizations and individuals to believe that ethical dilemmas can be resolved if one only has the right technology.

In March 2020, an autonomous drone deployed by Turkey was used to *"hunt down and remotely engage attack targets in Libya – all on its own. When the news broke, the impression of an army of killer robots was invoked. A leading researcher at MIT even tweeted: 'Killer robot proliferation has begun. '"*[173] The concept of an AI-driven drone engaging on its own in some form of unethical behavior reinforces the idea (and fear) that *"AI is capable of making decisions in autonomous ways and thus is the one in charge to act in either good or bad ways."*[174]

This leads to the concern that an overreliance on AI to make ethical decisions will lead to a devolving of the human ability to discern situations that require an ethical decision – or ethical deskilling. At the same time, there is an opposite movement that believes that – if properly implemented and used – AI can present currently underrealized opportunities for upskilling ethical decision-making skills.

Ethical deskilling

" ... *moral skills appear just as vulnerable to disruption or devaluation by technology-driven shifts in human practices as are professional or artisanal skills such as machining, shoemaking, or gardening. This is because moral skills are typically acquired in specific practices*

---

[173] Tegmark, M. (May 30, 2021). *Twitter*. Available at https://twitter.com/tegmark/status/1399042504071208966.

[174] De Cremer, D. and Kasparov, G. (August 3, 2021). Both moral and digital upskilling vital. *The Business Times*, p. 16.

7: AI and our society – Will the result be professional, ethical, and social deskilling, or upskilling?

which, under the right conditions and with sufficient opportunity for repetition, foster the cultivation of practical wisdom and moral habituation that jointly constitute genuine virtue."[175]

The Aristotelian view is that values are cultivated and are not innate, so a person develops ethical and moral values through practice. Ethical deskilling is the loss of ability to make decisions as a result of lack of practice and experience. *"Concerns about moral deskilling need not reflect reactionary politics, unexamined dogma, or unreasoned panic. They may be rooted instead in a serious and critically minded investigation of the developmental conditions of human character."*[176] As we develop smart AI to make decisions for us, we may be inclined to increasingly delegate important ethical decision-making to the AI, leaving humans to become less skilled in making these decisions.[177]

Today, our behavior in the society in which we reside is guided – and even modified – by laws, regulations, and societal expectations, without us having to make certain ethical decisions. In a world where AI begins to determine our ethical behavior, the human skill may become increasingly rare.

---

[175] Vallor, S. (February 21, 2014). *Moral Deskilling and Upskilling in a New Machine Age: Reflections on the Ambiguous Future of Character.* Springer Science.

[176] Ibid.

[177] Green, B.P. (March 15, 2019). Artificial Intelligence, Decision-Making, and Moral Deskilling. *Markkula Center for Applied Ethics.* Available at www.scu.edu/ethics/focus-areas/technology-ethics/resources/artificial-intelligence-decision-making-and-moral-deskilling/.

The Markkula Center for Applied Ethics at Santa Clara University, California, has identified six ways in which AI could potentially lower our ability to make ethical and moral decisions:

1. **Assaults on truth** – our information and news sources are being corrupted by misinformation and disinformation, a lot of which is driven by AI.

2. **Reduction in our ability to pay attention** – AI-powered applications, particularly on our smart devices, tend to focus our attention on trivialities and away from the more important things in life, such as nurturing relationships and focusing on larger-scale problems, both personal and social. There is a growing body of evidence that suggests our habitual multi-tasking on our AI-powered devices carries with it significant cognitive loss. Persistent multi-tasking renders us more distracted and less efficient at focusing our attention. *"Hyperconnected adult users often trade anecdotal complaints of noticeable declines in their ability to concentrate on a difficult text or an important conversation for an extended period of time; the compulsion to check Facebook messages, update a Twitter status, or check out a new Tumblr page is simply too great for many of us."*[178]

3. **Technology facilitating "infantilization"** – AI is accelerating the trend of "parent" technology, which essentially tells us what we should be thinking or doing. Consequently, our ability to participate in our

---

[178] Vallor, S. (February 21, 2014). *Moral Deskilling and Upskilling in a New Machine Age: Reflections on the Ambiguous Future of Character.* Springer Science.

professional and personal lives in a mature and
thoughtful way is decreased.

4. **Stunted ethical and moral development** – ethical
decision-making and moral development both require
practice. As our thought processes, and even our
psychology, are manipulated by AI-driven information,
we no longer use our ethical decision-making skills
without bias or prejudice.

5. **"Normal" complexity** – AI is providing us with a
number of useful tools, but it remains too complex for
most of us to fully comprehend. Consequently, there is
reduced expectation that we understand how the AI-
driven technologies are operating in our environment.

6. **"Weaponized" complexity** – *"If understanding is no
longer an expectation, humans will become even easier
to deceive and manipulate, and no doubt some people
will use AI systems precisely for this purpose, as they
already do."*[179]

Ethical upskilling

In the same manner as the Markkula Center for Applied
Ethics addressed the challenges of ethical deskilling as a
result of AI, their research also resulted in several
recommendations for how to mitigate this challenge:[180]

- AI has enormous potential for enhancing and
personalizing education to provide individuals with the
tools they need to address the misinformation and
disinformation that can lead to inappropriate ethical

---

[179] Vallor, S. (February 21, 2014). *Moral Deskilling and Upskilling in a
New Machine Age: Reflections on the Ambiguous Future of Character*.
Springer Science.

[180] Ibid.

decision-making. Used effectively, AI can help safeguard the integrity of the information ecosystem and aid humans to be more discerning in their assessment of the information they receive.

- AI can assist in removing some of the environmental distractions that divert our attention or limit our attention span. If we never notice an ethical issue we can never solve it, so AI can focus us on those issues that demand our attention.

- Humans should resist depending upon AI to make ethical decisions, thus fostering dependency. The key is to use AI to help make independent ethical and moral decisions. This includes interacting more effectively and frequently with other individuals, exposing us to more complex interactions, and developing our ability to gain ethical and moral expertise.

- AI can help us identify, and alert us when complexity is being used as a weapon to deceive and manipulate.

Social deskilling and upskilling

People are by nature and through evolution social animals. We tend to form groups, to socialize and exist together. Originally, this way of living was more of a necessity for survival than an option, and over time it evolved into a convention.

The society in which we live is characterized by mutual interactions and interrelations of individuals and of the structure formed by these relations. The concept of society is related not only to people, but also to the complex patterns and standards of interactions that occur between them. Society can be seen as a process rather than a static entity, as motion rather than as a rigid structure. This social interaction is essential as it has a positive influence on human physical and mental health. It has the ability to lower stress, depression, and feelings of anxiety.

It is a great conundrum in today's society that as a result of AI technology, we are more connected than ever before. The Internet, together with all the nifty AI-driven devices we use to access it, has given us increased access to information, increased opportunities for interactions through social media, we can pay our bills, do our shopping, and even play games with people on the other side of the world – all from the comfort of our own homes – without ever having to actually see and interact with another human.

Social deskilling

AI-driven smart devices are broadly defined as the category of technological objects capable of autonomous decision and action without direct human instruction and intervention. They are increasingly interwoven into the social fabric of our society with the area and scope of their use continuing to grow.

Many contend, however, that *"Technology can offer a very anemic connection. Technology can be the junk food of communication where we're just exchanging tiny bits of information over text and we're really missing out on accessing our full relationship capacity."*[181] As we become increasingly accustomed to interacting through and with AI-driven devices, we are also beginning to augment or replace existing human-to-human interactions with human-through-machine interactions.

---

[181] Walker,C. (November 8, 2020). The Importance of Human Interaction. Pepperdine University Graphic. Available at *https://pepperdine-graphic.com/the-importance-of-human-interaction/*.

7: AI and our society – Will the result be professional, ethical, and social deskilling, or upskilling?

In a social context, the evolution of AI seems to be inducing a kind of moral panic about AI as a threat to our human capacity for empathy. Questions such as: "Have we become more willing to inflict pain upon others without reservation, especially when we can do so anonymously"? "Have we lost our sense of responsibility for one another as members of a society/culture/family"?

Research has indicated that people – and, in particular, children – could become discourteous as they become used to interacting with voice-interactive AI digital assistants, such as Amazon Alexa, Apple Siri, etc. These AI digital assistants will respond regardless of attitudes and manners, so that they create a false sense of deservedness that creeps into everyday social interaction. If there is no need for social pleasantries, users can become rude.[182] To take this a bit further, *"Commands usually sting their recipients—it's a sting that sinks deeply into the person who has carried out the command and remains in him unchanged."*[183] With Alexa or similar voice-activated AI assistants, there's no sting.

"Especially as machines are made to look and act like us and to insinuate themselves deeply into our lives, they may change how loving or friendly or kind we are—not

---

[182] Gordon, K. (April 23, 2018). Alexa and the Age of Casual Rudeness. *The Atlantic.* Available at www.theatlantic.com/family/archive/2018/04/alexa-manners-smart-speakers-command/558653/.

[183] Ibid.

just in our direct interactions with the machines in question, but in our interactions with one another."[184]

AI designers and programmers typically create devices to give us responses that make us feel better – but that are not useful for self-reflection. As AI increasingly infiltrates our society, there is the distinct possibility that it will inhibit our emotions and impede our ability to make deep human connections. As a result, our relationships with one another could become less reciprocal, or shallower, or more narcissistic.

Social upskilling

Justine Cassell, a researcher whose goal is a better understanding of the relationship between humans and machines, stated *"It is in our power to bring about a future with AI where social interaction is preserved and even enhanced."*[185]

The right kind of AI may be able to improve the way humans interact.

"For instance, the political scientist Kevin Munger directed specific kinds of bots to intervene after people sent racist invective to other people online. He showed that, under certain circumstances, a bot that simply reminded the perpetrators that their target was a human

---

[184] Christakis, N.A. (April 2019). How AI Will Rewire Us. *The Atlantic.* Available at *www.theatlantic.com/magazine/archive/2019/04/robots-human-relationships/583204/.*

[185] Cassell, Justine. (Summer 2019). Artificial Intelligence for a Social World. *Issues in Science and Technology* 35, no. 4: 29–36.

being, one whose feelings might get hurt, could cause that person's use of racist speech to decline for more than a month."[186]

Social skills are comprised of a variety of social, emotional, behavioral, and communication skills that shape people's interactions with one another. One of the primary human social skills is empathy, or the ability to understand and share the feelings of another, or simply stated as "putting yourself in someone else's shoes." In terms of human-AI interaction, empathy is not about humans versus AI; it's about using the best of what both have to offer. The future of AI-based ethical decision-making is a combination of AI processing capability with human provided socio-ethical input.

Ethical decision-making in a social context leverages information or inputs gathered through an individual's soft skills, together with an understanding of context and non-human (i.e. AI-driven) data processing, to determine a course of action. Social upskilling can take place when an AI and humans are involved in a complementary partnership, where the AI-human overall performance is greater than each other's individual capacity.

Rapport, or a sense of fellowship with other human beings, is a quantifiable metric of positive social interaction. Levels of social skills, where humans can work together with AI, can be aligned into general categories of micro, meso, and

---

[186] Christakis, N.A. (April 2019). How AI Will Rewire Us. *The Atlantic.* Available at *www.theatlantic.com/magazine/archive/2019/04/robots-human-relationships/583204/.*

macro.[187] At each level, AI can assist in guiding humans towards the development of socio-ethical skills that can be applied to help individuals themselves or others cope with feelings of social isolation, depression, or loss of self-worth.

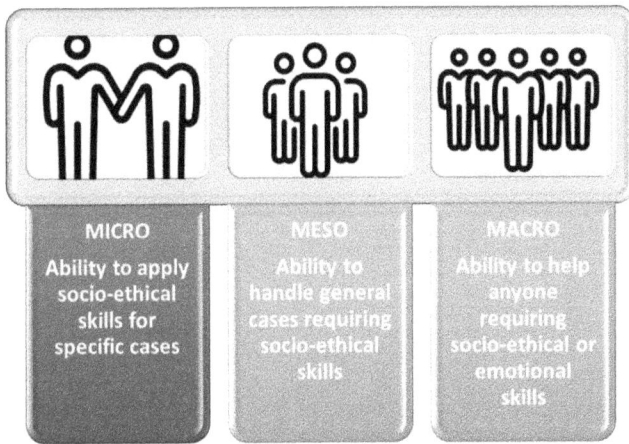

Figure 7-2: Micro, meso and macro socio-ethical skills[188]

Micro-skill abilities can be used in combination with AI in a social context to help individuals facing an unexpected crisis. Meso-skills can be used with AI to aid others experiencing socio-ethical or emotional difficulties, ranging from social isolation, abusive partners, to bullying, or to assist others in becoming more socially engaged. At the macro level,

---

[187] Dede, C. Etemadi, A., & Forshaw, T. (2021). *Intelligence Augmentation: Upskilling Humans to Complement AI.* The Next Level Lab at the Harvard Graduate School of Education. President and Fellows of Harvard College: Cambridge, MA.

[188] Dede, C. Etemadi, A., & Forshaw, T. (2021). *Intelligence Augmentation: Upskilling Humans to Complement AI.* The Next Level Lab at the Harvard Graduate School of Education. President and Fellows of Harvard College: Cambridge, MA.

individuals can work with AI-based tools to help guide others experiencing socio-ethical or emotional distress.

How do we use AI to further our social skills?

> *"It is in our power to bring about a future with AI where social interaction is preserved and where social interaction is even enhanced. I believe that can happen through using social AI to understand social interaction, by implementing social AI that concentrates on collaboration rather than replacement, that encourages productive social behavior, and that can teach social skills to those who need and wish to learn them."*[189]

---

[189] Cassell, Justine. (Summer 2019). Artificial Intelligence for a Social World. *Issues in Science and Technology* 35, no. 4: 29–36.

CHAPTER 8: AI AND PRIVACY – IS ANYTHING REALLY PRIVATE ANYMORE?

> *"Previously, most people were anonymous due to obscurity. In its most basic form as absolute inaccessibility of information, obscurity may never occur again."*
>
> **Woodrow Hartzog and Frederic Stutzman**

Among the moral rights in which most individuals believe, privacy heads the list, but few concepts are less well understood or agreed upon. The definition of privacy often depends upon who you ask. But, in its simplest form, privacy can be defined as the right to be left alone or to be free from interference or intrusion. Data privacy, then, can be described as the right to have some degree of control over how your personal information is collected and used.

In the digital age, the idea of privacy has become murky, convoluted, and even contradictory. New ways of using technology, such as AI, to structure and influence society, often acts in opposition to privacy on technical as well as social levels. Tapscott and Tapscott proposed that *"the Internet of Everything needs a Ledger of Everything"* and *"leads to pseudonymity at best and a buzzword-laden trap for the uninformed and the unwary."*[190]

---

[190] Benjamin, G. (June 2017) Privacy as a Cultural Phenomenon. Available at *www.researchgate.net/publication/318678201_Privacy_as_a_Cultural_Phenomenon.*

Privacy is also in part a type of personal possession, i.e. the ownership of the facts that compose one's life, from sequences of digits to personal tastes and preferences. Almost everyone would agree that matters of personal health and finance should be no one's business but our own, that is, unless we ourselves decide otherwise. This definition of privacy takes into account everything we know about ourselves and want to control, but which is rendered increasingly uncontrollable by the continuous capture of our digital existence – the Google searches, our social media accounts, email traffic, commercial transactions, and the cookie-tracked footprints of our rambles through the Internet.

Today, the degree to which people just assume that their privacy is breached seems to be heading towards a culture of helplessness, in which it is not even worth bothering with trying to have personal and data security online.

Before the evolution of the digital environment, exposure of personal information was largely limited to a manageably small group. "No longer." Daniel J. Solove, an expert in privacy law and an associate professor at George Washington University Law School, begins his 2007 book, *The Future of Reputation: Gossip, Rumor, and Privacy on the Internet,* with an anecdote about a woman in South Korea whose little dog pooped on a subway train. When fellow passengers demanded that she clean up the mess, she told them to mind their own business. One of them took pictures of her and posted them online. She was identified from the pictures, and her life and past were investigated. Eventually she became known throughout cyberspace as "dog poop girl." Solove writes,

"Across the Internet, people made posters with the girl's photograph, fusing her picture with a variety of other images. The dog poop girl story quickly migrated to the mainstream media, becoming national news in South Korea. As a result of her public shaming and embarrassment, the dog poop girl dropped out of her university."[191]

Solove contends that we need a new definition of privacy to address the probability that behavior, such as that of "dog poop girl," can mushroom beyond those immediately affected to reach millions upon millions of people worldwide. *"The Internet,"* Solove writes, *"is indeed a cruel historian. Who wants to go through life forever known as the 'dog poop girl'"?*[192]

In the US, many assume that the right to privacy is guaranteed under the Constitution. But the US Constitution contains no express right to privacy. Although not explicitly called out in the US Constitution, some of the amendments to the Constitution can be interpreted to provide a level of privacy protection. More frequently, however, the right to privacy is protected by statutory law. This includes the Health Information Portability and Accountability Act (HIPAA), which protects an individual's health information, and various privacy policies issued by the FTC to enforce the right to privacy.

When it comes to controlling their personal data today, most individuals do not feel empowered. Cisco's June 2020

---

[191] McCreary, L. (October 2008). What Was Privacy? *Harvard Business Review*. Available at *https://hbr.org/2008/10/what-was-privacy*.

[192] Ibid.

worldwide survey found that just under half of those interviewed felt they were not able to effectively protect their personal data, primarily because it is too hard to figure out how companies and agencies were actually using it. Individuals also resented being asked to accept the terms of use without a choice.[193]

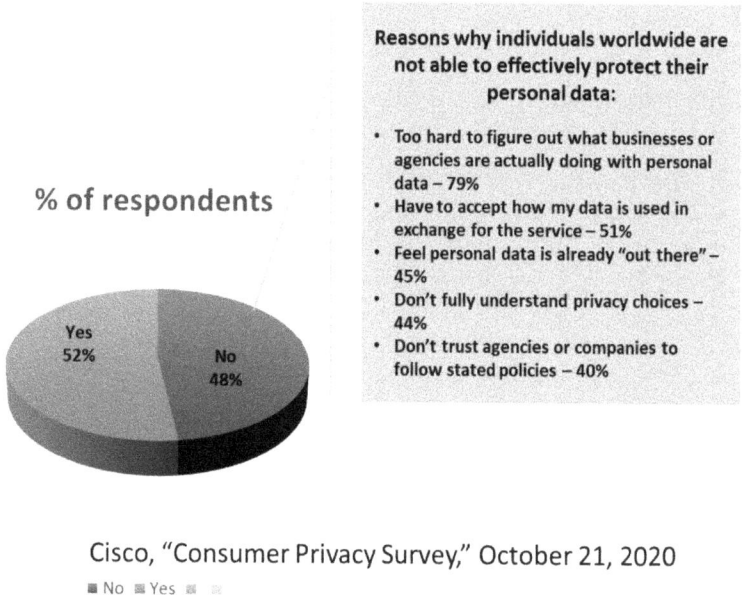

Reasons why individuals worldwide are not able to effectively protect their personal data:

- Too hard to figure out what businesses or agencies are actually doing with personal data – 79%
- Have to accept how my data is used in exchange for the service – 51%
- Feel personal data is already "out there" – 45%
- Don't fully understand privacy choices – 44%
- Don't trust agencies or companies to follow stated policies – 40%

% of respondents

Yes 52%
No 48%

Cisco, "Consumer Privacy Survey," October 21, 2020

No ■ Yes ■ ■

Figure 8-1: Why individuals feel they do not control personal data

In discussing privacy, we should not have a US-centric view, as various cultures have widely differing views on what a

---

[193] *Cisco 2020 Consumer Privacy Survey: Protecting Data Privacy to Maintain Digital Trust.* Available at www.cisco.com/c/dam/en_us/about/doing_business/trust-center/docs/cybersecurity-series-2020-cps.pdf.

person's rights are when it comes to privacy and how it should be regulated. Attitudes about privacy may also be generationally influenced, with attitudes changing over time. To the older generations, it may seem as though the younger generations simply no longer expect privacy in the digital age, with a fatalistic acceptance of the fact that they are likely digitally tracked and monitored all the time. This is culturally visible through the shift from the relative privacy of individual blogs, by default viewed only by those interested in that particular topic, toward more open forums on Facebook, Twitter, YouTube and Instagram.

AI will likely only accelerate this trend. Indeed, most privacy-sensitive data analysis today, such as search algorithms, recommendation engines, and advertising, is driven by AI/ML and has outcomes based on algorithms. As AI continues to evolve, it will magnify the ability to use personal information in ways that can encroach on privacy protections by advancing the analysis of personal information through Big Data to new levels of capability and speed.

Privacy and security

The terms privacy and security are often used interchangeably. But, you can have security without privacy, but not privacy without security.

Although they are certainly related, privacy and security are not the same and the distinction is important. Data privacy targets the use and control of personal data, such as laws and policies made to ensure that personal information is being collected, shared, and used in appropriate ways. Security, however, concentrates on the protection of data from malicious attack or the exploitation of stolen data for profit.

Although security is essential for the protection of data, it is not, on its own, adequate for addressing privacy concerns.

Privacy –
Governs how data is collected, stored, and shared

Security –
Determines how data is protected from internal and external attackers

Figure 8-2: Privacy vs. security

To elaborate, *"security is mainly focused on preventing unauthorized access to data, via breaches or leaks, regardless of who the unauthorized party is."*[194] To implement security, organizations install tools and technologies, such as firewalls, access control mechanisms, user authentication, network restrictions, as well as in-house security procedures to deter unauthorized access. Measures also include technologies, such as encryption and the use of tokens to provide additional data protection by making it unreadable, which can prevent malicious individuals from potentially exposing large amounts of sensitive, personal data if a breach does occur.

---

[194] Phillips, D. (July 7, 2020). Data Privacy vs. Data Security: What is the Core Difference? *TokenEX.*

On the other hand, privacy is more concerned with ensuring that any sensitive data an organization collects, stores, processes, and transmits is treated in compliance with existing privacy laws and regulations and in accordance with user consent. This involves being transparent with individuals regarding which data will be collected, for what purpose, and with whom, and how it will be shared. This also involves user agreement to the terms surrounding data use. Privacy is, therefore, also concerned with the responsible use of data, in accordance with the wishes of customers and users, as well as preventing it from falling into the wrong hands.

Data privacy

Data privacy is generally defined as an individual's right of self-determination regarding when, how, and to what extent personal information about them is collected, shared with, or communicated to others. Personal information can include a person's name, location, contact information, social media profiles, online, and real-world actions. So, just as you might want to exclude outsiders from a private conversation, many individuals want to control or prevent certain types of personal data collection.

At its most simple, most individuals have an idea of data privacy based on whether or not certain pieces of information could be used in ways that have damaging consequences to personal well-being. Our desire for data privacy is frequently about avoiding embarrassing and otherwise damaging professional, personal, or societal consequences.

From a law and regulatory perspective, practical data privacy concerns often center on:

- If or how data may be shared with third parties;

- How data is legally collected, stored, or shared;
- Legal and regulatory constraints, such as the EU's GDPR or the US HIPAA.

Users have the greatest ability to ensure that their data is protected by engaging in safe practices and ensuring that they fully understand user agreements regarding their data. Here are a few of the minimum measures users should take to protect their data:

Data privacy good practices for users

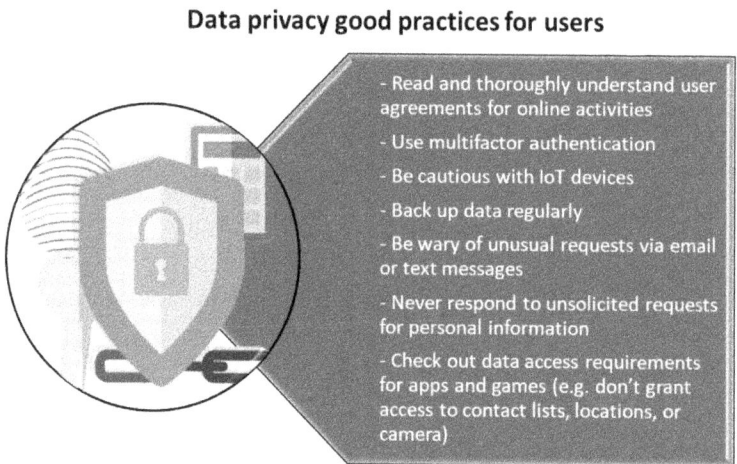

Figure 8-3: Good practices for user data privacy

Monitoring and surveillance

Surveillance

"We live in a surveillance society. It is pointless to talk about surveillance in the future tense ... everyday life is

suffused with surveillance encounters, not merely from dawn to dusk but 24/7. "[195]

Across the world, there are millions of video cameras – but no capability to monitor all of them 24x7x365. AI, however, can rapidly and efficiently process every frame gathered by these cameras and deliver real-time analysis.

"Troubling partnerships between government and private tech companies also emerged as a trend this year, especially those that extended surveillance from public environments into private spaces like private properties and the home."

"With AI public video surveillance our motions, gestures, and whereabouts can be tracked; with speech recognition our telephone and video conversations can be transcribed. The fact some of us but not others spew information on social media will rapidly be largely irrelevant. As better and better models are built relating any form of personal expression (including purchases, travel, and communication partners) to expected behavior (including purchases, votes, demonstrations,

---

[195] Ball, K. and Wood, M. D. (2006). A Report on the Surveillance Society. For the Information Commissioner. Available at *https://ico.org.uk/media/about-the-ico/documents/1042390/surveillance-society-full-report-2006.pdf*.

and donations), less and less information about any one person will be needed to predict their likely behavior."[196]

AI-based surveillance is being implemented for a number of purposes from people tracking and observation, facility protection, parking occupancy determination, vehicle-use analytics, and traffic monitoring. During the COVID-19 pandemic, many companies spent considerable effort building AI-based systems to track employee activities or to ensure social distancing in public areas. *"A growing number of states are deploying advanced AI surveillance tools to monitor, track, and surveil citizens to accomplish a range of policy objectives—some lawful, others that violate human rights, and many of which fall into a murky middle ground."*[197]

Liberal and democratic nations are major users of AI surveillance, deploying a variety of AI-based surveillance technologies. Many European nations are rapidly moving forward with the installation of AI-automated border controls, predictive policing, *"safe cities,"*[198] and facial recognition systems. This does not, however, indicate that democracies are misusing these technologies. The quality of

---

[196] Misselhorn, C., (Editor). (2015) Collective Agency and Cooperation in Natural and Artificial Systems: Explanation, Implementation and Simulation. *Springer Philosophical Studies Series*, Vol. 122.

[197] Feldstein, S. (September 2019). The Global Expansion of AI Surveillance. Available at *https://carnegieendowment.org/files/WP-Feldstein-AISurveillance_final1.pdf*.

[198] The concept of "safe cities" is based on the proactive reduction of urban crime by identifying and limiting antisocial behavior, street robbery, and burglaries through a mixture of policing, technology deployment, and offender management.

governance is the critical factor determining whether a government deploys this technology for repressive purposes.

> *"Governments in autocratic and semi-autocratic countries are more prone to abuse AI surveillance than governments in liberal democracies. Some autocratic governments—for example, China, Russia, Saudi Arabia—are exploiting AI technology for mass surveillance purposes. Other governments with dismal human rights records are exploiting AI surveillance in more limited ways to reinforce repression."[199]*

For the purposes of this book, we'll use China as an example of a surveillance state. Every Chinese mobile phone has an app installed called WeChat. What began as a normal chat app, similar to WhatsApp, has become much more multi-purpose. With the app, a person can apply for credit, use it as an ID, complete financial transactions, and even file for divorce papers through the local court. WeChat also supports the Chinese system of "social credits." Let's say a citizen begins with 1,000 points. Points are added for good deeds, such as helping someone across the street or giving blood; and subtracted for actions such as jaywalking or not picking up your dog's poop from the sidewalk. So, what is the result of losing points? A person can be blacklisted because their social credit is low and can be sanctioned. For example, they may not be able to buy plane tickets, take a high-speed railway, stay in high-end hotels, and their children may no

---

[199] Feldstein, S. (September 17, 2019). The Global Expansion of AI Surveillance. *Carnegie Endowment for International Peace.* Available at *https://carnegieendowment.org/2019/09/17/global-expansion-of-ai-surveillance-pub-79847*.

longer be allowed to go to the better, more expensive schools.

The social point system is, of course, the far end of the surveillance spectrum. There are also strong indications that AI-based surveillance can potentially enhance law enforcement and foreign/domestic terrorism prevention efforts, thus making everyone generally safer. Based on this premise, there are those that would argue that we should tolerate reductions in privacy for the sake of greater security.[200]

Surveillance technologies are not only being deployed at the nation-state level, AI-based surveillance technologies are also being deployed in workplace and retail environments. Companies such as Walmart have established independent research labs and are using captured data from surveillance cameras for everything from predicting a possible shoplifter to identifying and steering shopper preferences.

Surveillance should also be looked at for its positive contribution. Although traditional law enforcement measures can have a considerable impact in terms of decreasing crime or preventing theft, technical surveillance using AI-based analytics gives law enforcement a technological edge that no surveillance camera alone can provide.

Eliminating human error is a key driver behind deploying AI to support security, through rapid and timely video analytics of surveillance content.

---

[200] Himma, K. (June 18, 2007). Privacy Versus Security: Why Privacy is Not an Absolute Value or Right. *San Diego Law Review, Vol. 44*. Available at *https://digital.sandiego.edu/sdlr/vol44/iss4/10/*.

"Studies have shown that humans engaged in mundane tasks have a directed attention capacity for up to 20 minutes, after which the human attention span begins to decrease. In addition, when humans are faced with multiple items at one time, attention spans will decrease even more rapidly. Therefore, video analytics are beginning to take the place of initial human judgment in an effort to increase operational efficiency."[201]

Workplace monitoring

Employers have long been using various methods for monitoring employees, from checking incoming and outgoing email and Internet use to collecting and evaluating data about employee reliability, productivity, and location among others. This information can be very useful for employers wishing to pinpoint inefficiencies in their company. AI-based employee monitoring systems can aid in more rapidly analyzing data collected about employee performance, managing productivity, and identifying how much and what types of resources are used by staff. Employee monitoring is also used as a means to protect the company and its intellectual property. Finally, monitoring allows a company to collect data that could be used as evidence in the event of a legal dispute. But all of this monitoring creates large and diverse data sets, which can morph into something that tempts the company and its leadership to use it for reasons other than the original, which

---

[201] Saptharishi, M. (August 2014). The New Eyes of Surveillance: Artificial Intelligence and Humanizing Technology. *Wired.*

leads to a practice called *"function creep."*[202] Function creep is what occurs when technology and systems are used in ways outside of the original purpose, especially when the new purpose results in an increased invasion of privacy.

Employee monitoring took on a new dimension during the COVID-19 pandemic when millions of workers were forced to work from home. Companies realized that they needed new/additional tools to manage employees, ensure productivity, security, and appropriate behavior, even when a live supervisor was not in the area.

AI systems are extraordinarily well-suited for use and cost-effective worker surveillance. AI is remarkably efficient at counting and identifying keystrokes, the number of words typed, emails sent, and websites visited. It can even monitor the number of steps taken in a warehouse, packages completed for sending, time to complete driver routes, and even the length and number of bathroom breaks – generally every kind of employee behavior that can be monitored on or offline.

"In February [2020], Amazon started tracking its drivers with cameras featuring biometric feedback indicators that monitor when drivers look away from the road or go past the speed limit. An Amazon spokesperson pointed to 'remarkable driver and community safety improvements'

---

[202] Function creep is more properly known as gradual function expansion. It is sometimes also referred to as scope or mission creep. Although the word "creep" implies something that moves slowly, in the cases of organization creep, it generally implies something stealthy or "creepy."

as a result of the indicators, which led to a 48 percent decrease in accidents. "[203]

Experts in employee behavior caution that the focus on increased productivity may come at the cost of greater risk of stress, burnout, and mental health issues. According to a report commissioned by the European Parliament's employment committee, AI-based surveillance technologies can *"reduce autonomy and privacy, lead to greater work intensification, and blur the boundaries between work and personal/family life.*"[204]

Workplace monitoring and surveillance can be frustrating for employees who feel they may have no recourse against the AI-generated analysis and results. The European Commission's Jobs and Social Rights Commissioner, Nicolas Schmit, stated that algorithmic management[205] *"leaves the workers with few means to challenge unfavorable decisions.*"[206]

---

[203] Cater, L. and Heikkila, M. (May 27, 2021). Your boss is watching: How AI-powered surveillance rules the workplace. *Politico.* Available at *www.politico.eu/article/ai-workplace-surveillance-facial-recognition-software-gdpr-privacy/.*

[204] Lodovici, S., et al. (April 2021). *The impact of teleworking and digital work on workers and society.* Publication for the committee on Employment and Social Affairs, Policy Department for Economic, Scientific and Quality of Life Policies, European Parliament, Luxembourg. Available at *www.politico.eu/article/ai-workplace-surveillance-facial-recognition-software-gdpr-privacy/.*

[205] AI-based tools and technologies used to remotely manage workers.

[206] Cater, L. and Heikkilä, M. (May 27, 2021). Your boss is watching: How AI-powered surveillance rules the workplace. *Politico.* Available at *www.politico.eu/article/ai-workplace-surveillance-facial-recognition-software-gdpr-privacy/.*

Although employee monitoring existed in various forms well before AI, there is still little guidance on what is acceptable when AI-based surveillance technologies are used to evaluate an employee's performance. Until laws and policies are able to catch up with technology, employers should approach AI-based workplace surveillance carefully. It is essential to ensure employees are aware of what data is going to be collected and why, how it will be protected from misuse, and how it can be shared. It's even more critical for employees to be given the option to "opt out" of monitoring programs without undue dread that they will lose work benefits or even lose their job.

Facial recognition

Facial recognition is the process of identifying or verifying the identity of a person using images of their face. It identifies, analyzes, and compares patterns based on the individual's facial details. Facial emotion recognition is a subset of facial recognition that maps facial expressions to identify emotions, such as anger, joy, revulsion, surprise, fear, or sadness on a human face often using AI-based image processing software.

Today, AI facial recognition technology is experiencing a massive expansion. AI's superhuman ability to identify faces has led countries to deploy surveillance technology at a remarkable rate. Facial recognition lets you unlock your smart device, it automatically tags photos for you on social media, and allows you to pass almost seamlessly through passport control.

"It's there on Facebook, tagging photos from the class reunion, your cousin's wedding, and the office summer party. Google, Microsoft, Apple, and others have built it

into apps to compile albums of people who hang out together. It verifies who you are at airports and is the latest biometric to unlock your mobile phone."[207]

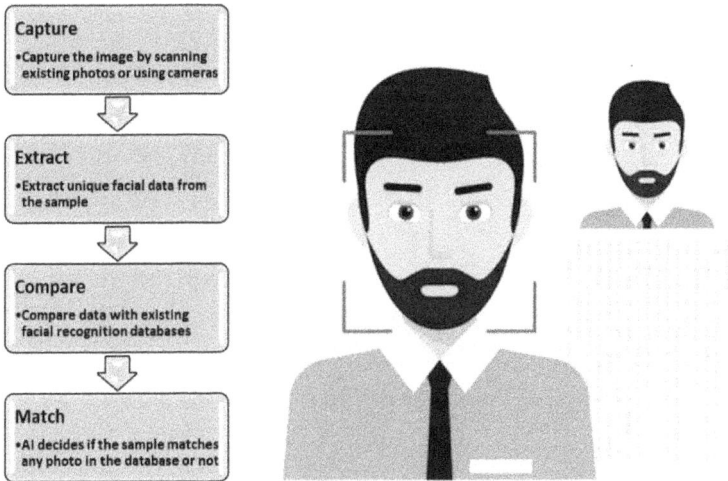

Capture
• Capture the image by scanning existing photos or using cameras

Extract
• Extract unique facial data from the sample

Compare
• Compare data with existing facial recognition databases

Match
• AI decides if the sample matches any photo in the database or not

Figure 8-4: Process of facial recognition

As a result of this increasing deployment of AI-based facial recognition surveillance, there have been dire warnings of a dystopian future. The technology is a formidable way to invade people's privacy, and biases in training data make it likely to automate discrimination. With the benefit of an abundance of databases containing digital photographs accessible via driver's license offices, social media, websites, surveillance cameras, and other sources, AI-based facial recognition has rapidly evolved from fuzzy images of

---

[207] Sample, I. (July 29, 2019). What is facial recognition – and how sinister is it? *The Guardian*. Available at *www.theguardian.com/technology/2019/jul/29/what-is-facial-recognition-and-how-sinister-is-it*.

house pets to the swift (albeit often imperfect) recognition of individual human faces.

AI-based facial recognition is now spreading to vehicles and webcams, and is being deployed to track emotions as well as identity. This AI-driven tracking of an individual's emotional state is being called "affect recognition." This technology:

> *"Claims to be able to detect an individual's emotional state based on the use of computer-vision algorithms to analyze their facial micro-expressions, tone of voice, or even their gait. It is rapidly being commercialized for a wide range of purposes—from attempts to identify the perfect employee to assessing patient pain to tracking which students are being attentive in class."*[208]

There are few rules and regulations to govern the use of facial recognition technologies. Recent disclosures revealed that US law enforcement agencies (the Federal Bureau of Investigation (FBI) and Immigration and Customs Enforcement (ICE)) acquired and scanned millions of photos in state driver's license databases without prior knowledge or consent from the individuals whose images they were collecting and storing.[209]

---

[208] Crawford, K., et al. (December 2019). AI Now Report 2019. *AI Now Institute.* Available at https://ainowinstitute.org/AI_Now_2019_Report.pdf.

[209] Feldstein, S. (September 17, 2019). The Global Expansion of AI Surveillance. *Carnegie Endowment for International Peace.* Available at https://carnegieendowment.org/2019/09/17/global-expansion-of-ai-surveillance-pub-79847.

In some countries – China in particular – facial recognition is being widely used for policing and government surveillance. There is a vast network of cameras across China that use facial recognition as part of a nationwide reward and punishment policy.

> *"Security cameras and facial recognition technology are on the rise in China. In 2018, People's Daily, the media mouthpiece of China's ruling Communist Party, claimed on English-language Twitter that the country's facial recognition system was capable of scanning the faces of China's 1.4 billion citizens in just one second."*[210]

Facial recognition technology is even used to identify perpetrators of toilet paper theft in public facilities or to shame an individual for wearing pajamas on the street.

Using facial recognition and real-time AI analysis, China has also increased public shaming. In major cities, huge, public billboards have been installed on a large number of buildings.

> *"When you jaywalk, still already while you are still in the middle of the road, your face appears on the huge billboard for everybody to see. And next to your face, your name appears, your ID number, part of it is [censored]. ... But the whole point is, 'We know who you are.'"*[211]

---

[210] Davies, D. (January 5, 2021). Facial Recognition and Beyond: Journalist Ventures Inside China's 'Surveillance State.' *npr online.* Available at *https://www.npr.org/2021/01/05/953515627/facial-recognition-and-beyond-journalist-ventures-inside-chinas-surveillance-sta.*

[211] Ibid.

Consumer profiling

How often have you clicked on a link, sent an email, or even just *"thought"* about something only to have advertisements show up on your social media or search engine pages? Does it make you a little uncomfortable?

To develop consumer profiles, companies have to gather information about their customers. The ethical dilemma lies in how companies collect that information, and not all companies agree where the ethical boundary lies. There are companies that collect consumer data information using surveys or questionnaires. Others use software programs that track what sites consumers visit online and then feed this data into AI-analysis engines. Some companies have privacy policies that give the assurance that an individual's personal information will not be sold. Others use their Internet presence specifically with the objective of collecting and sharing/selling consumer information.

Consumer profiling is not new. For decades, companies have gathered information about consumers and used it to target their marketing, advertising, and other business-related activities. Based on other consumers in a demographic, marketing companies can forecast what types of television shows will sell, and what brand of dog food a consumer will buy because consumers in that demographic and area have made these preferences known. AI has only enhanced these capabilities and made the marketing even more targeted and real-time. But there are ethical concerns about consumer profiling.

Several years ago, Target created an AI algorithm that identified if someone was pregnant based on certain in-store and online purchase patterns. Target then sent unsolicited coupons for pregnancy-related items to customer addresses.

This use of predictive marketing became awkward, especially in one instance when a young girl hadn't yet told her family she was pregnant, and they first realized it as a result of the mailed coupons.[212]

The AI algorithms driving social media sites and Amazon collect a lot of information about an individual's preferences in books, music, DVDs, searches about health concerns, and relationship advice. Can we really trust the employees of Facebook, Instagram, YouTube, Amazon, etc. not to mishandle what they know about us? We'd like to believe that we can, but who knows for sure. And even if we started using anonymizing search engines that wouldn't delete any of the legacy data from the many other sites to which we have provided personal information – directly or indirectly.

Another potential side effect of consumer profiling is related to the "backroom" data gathered and analyzed about consumers, and which is used to make determinations about just how to treat a particular consumer.

> *"Market analytics allow companies to identify their best and worst customers and, consequently, to pay special attention to those deemed to be the most valuable. Looked at another way, analytics enable firms to understand how poorly they can treat individual or groups of customers before those people stop doing business with them. Unless you are in the top echelon of customers—those with the highest lifetime value, say—you may pay higher prices,*

---

[212] Lubin, G. (February 16, 2012). The Incredible Story Of How Target Exposed A Teen Girl's Pregnancy. *Insider*. Available at www.businessinsider.com/the-incredible-story-of-how-target-exposed-a-teen-girls-pregnancy-2012-2.

get fewer special offers, or receive less service than other consumers. Despite the fact that alienating 75% to 90% of customers may not be the best idea in the long run, many retailers have adopted this 'top tier' approach to managing customer relationships."[213]

Privacy laws and regulations in the age of AI

The challenge for lawmakers is to create privacy laws that protect individuals against any negative effects that might arise from the use of personal information by AI, but without unnecessarily limiting AI development or entangling privacy legislation endlessly in complex social and political debate.

Privacy protections in the context of AI mandate a transformation in the existing concepts regarding privacy legislation and policy. In the US and in many countries, privacy laws are based on the flawed approach to online user choice based on "notice-and-choice" (also referred to as "notice-and-consent") encountered in the onslaught of user agreements, privacy notifications, and banners connected to lengthy and complex privacy policies, and terms and conditions. In most cases, we provide our consent to notices that are but seldom read. This pretense based on user

" ... consent has made it obvious that notice-and-choice has become meaningless. For many AI applications—smart traffic signals and other sensors needed to support

---

[213] Davenport, T.H. and Harris, J. (2007). The Dark Side of Customer Analytics. *Harvard Business Review.* Available at *https://hbr.org/2007/05/the-dark-side-of-customer-analytics.*

self-driving cars as one prominent example—it will become utterly impossible."[214]

But the first few months of 2021 saw an increased global interest in developing serious regulation of AI in both the US and the EU, which may have far-reaching consequences for technology companies and government agencies. The EU is leading with its April 2021 release of a draft regulation for the use of AI, prohibiting some "unacceptable" uses and mandating stringent requirements, such as documented safety verifications for AI systems and human supervision to certify that an AI technology is "trustworthy."

But the US is also looking closely at AI technologies, and federal regulators, led by the FTC, are positioning themselves as regulators to ensure algorithmic fairness and prevent bias. These are nascent efforts and there is still much to be done.

"On March 1, 2021, the NSCAI[215] submitted its Final Report to Congress and to the President. At the outset, the report makes an urgent call to action, warning that the US government is presently not sufficiently organized or resourced to compete successfully with other nations with respect to emerging technologies, nor prepared to defend against AI-enabled threats or to rapidly adopt AI applications for national security purposes. Against that

---

[214] Kerry, C.F. (February 10, 2020). Protecting privacy in an AI-driven world. *Brookings.* Available at *www.brookings.edu/research/protecting-privacy-in-an-ai-driven-world/.*

[215] National Security Commission on Artificial Intelligence.

backdrop, the report outlines a strategy to get the United States 'AI-ready' by 2025."[216]

The report by the NSCAI provided tangible recommendations and steps that it holds essential to ensure that AI developments protect both safety and privacy. NSCAI specified actions and use of tools to improve the transparency[217] and explainability[218] of AI systems, such as testing and audits of AI systems, AI risk, and impact assessments; and the means to obtain due process and redress for individuals adversely affected by AI systems. Further recommendations include establishing rigorous governance and oversight for AI development, including auditing and reporting requirements, a review process for high-risk AI systems, and an accessible appeals process for those affected.

What do consumers and citizens expect in terms of privacy?

Generally, privacy awareness is increasing across the globe. The 2020 Cisco Survey on privacy highlighted four primary key points regarding individuals and their privacy expectations:

1. COVID-19 and remote working have created new privacy challenges. Individuals want their personal

---

[216] NSCAI (March 1, 2021). Final Report. *National Security Commission on Artificial Intelligence.* Available at *www.nscai.gov/wp-content/uploads/2021/03/Full-Report-Digital-1.pdf.*

[217] This refers to open disclosure related to the use of AI-algorithmic development and decision-making.

[218] This refers to retroactive information about the use of AI-algorithms in specific decisions.

information to be protected and are willing to support only limited exceptions.

2. Approximately one third of individuals have ceased doing business with organizations and agencies they perceive to be less protective of their data.
3. Individuals globally have the expectation that their government must take the lead in protecting their personal data, and citizens in all countries surveyed view privacy laws very favorably.
4. Individuals want more transparency on how their data is being collected, stored, used, and shared.[219]

What can companies, developers, and agencies do to protect privacy in the age of AI?

In a 2021 report, Insider Intelligence identified several key points around protecting privacy for both the AI technology development companies as well as for consumers:

- **Consumers and citizens are willing to pay for privacy.** In recent years as information about privacy violations and data abuse has increased, consumer and citizen viewpoints on personal privacy have evolved beyond the "privacy paradox," the concept that a consumer's stated preferences may not always harmonize with their online behavior. Privacy-conscious consumers and citizens are increasingly inclined to allot both time and money to protect their data and give their business to trustworthy companies or to support trustworthy government agencies.

---

[219] *Cisco 2020 Consumer Privacy Survey: Protecting Data Privacy to Maintain Digital Trust.* Available at www.cisco.com/c/dam/en_us/about/doing_business/trust-center/docs/cybersecurity-series-2020-cps.pdf.

- **AI developers should consider consumer privacy and trust from the start of product development and throughout the life cycle.** Consumer norms regarding trust are being changed by new devices, new technologies, and interfaces, such as the IoT. AI developers must keep user concerns and preferences about privacy and safety in mind from day one of the design process.
- **Bi-lateral communication is critical to building trust.** AI developers must show respect for their users by communicating early and persistently in plain, transparent, and honest terms. This also includes allowing consumers and citizens to assert their preferences and provide "opt-in" consent regarding the use of their data.
- **Privacy and trust are foundational to any agency or business.** These requirements apply outside of emerging AI systems, companies, and agencies; they must be part of any digital transformation effort that relies on data and is built on a close relationship with the citizens or the consumers.

CHAPTER 9: MISINFORMATION, DISINFORMATION, FAKE NEWS, MANIPULATION, AND DEEPFAKES – DO WE KNOW HOW TO THINK CRITICALLY ABOUT INFORMATION?

> *"We are moving into a society where people are being told by algorithms what their taste is, and, without questioning it too much, most people comply easily."*
> **David DeCremer**[220]

Before we take a closer look at misinformation, disinformation, fake news, manipulation, and deepfakes, we must first understand how people today get most of their news and information. Perhaps the easiest place to start is simply to find out whether people are actually using the Internet to get news. The answer to that question is very likely a clear yes.

Reuters Institute and the University of Oxford conducted a survey of more than 92,000 online news consumers in 46 markets, including India, Indonesia, Thailand, Nigeria, Colombia, and Peru to look at digital news consumption in 2021. The January 6, 2021 Capitol Hill riot in the US and the global spread of incorrect or blatantly false information and conspiracy theories about the COVID-19 virus has caused

---

[220] De Cremer, D. (November 2, 2020). Artificial Intelligence Will Change How We Think About Leadership. *Wharton University of Pennsylvania.* Available at *https://knowledge.wharton.upenn.edu/article/artificial-intelligence-will-change-think-leadership/.*

people around the world to look at the source of their news. The research resulted in a number of interesting findings, some of which were to be expected and some a surprise. As some of the critical findings are presented, it is important to also bear in mind that these generalized findings do not always represent every aspect of the world populace, but are likely representative for a large percentage:

- Turning to social media for news remains strong, especially with younger people and those with lower levels of education. Messaging apps, such as WhatsApp, are generating the most concern when it comes to the spread of misinformation.
- Although Facebook and Twitter are still considered news sources by some, they have *been* " ... *eclipsed by influencers and alternative sources in networks like TikTok, Snapchat, and Instagram. TikTok now reaches a quarter (24%) of under-35s, with 7% using the platform for news.* "[221]
- " ... *the use of smartphone for news (73%) has grown at its fastest rate for many years, with dependence also growing through Coronavirus lockdowns. Use of laptop and desktop computers and tablets for news is stable or falling.* "[222]
- In the US, many individuals lost interest in mainstream news after the end of the Trump presidency, turning instead to alternative sources of news.

---

[221] Newman, N. (2021). Executive summary and key findings of the 2021 report. *Reuters Institute.* Available at *https://reutersinstitute.politics.ox.ac.uk/digital-news-report/2021/dnr-executive-summary*.

[222] Ibid.

9: Misinformation, disinformation, fake news, manipulation, and deepfakes – Do we know how to think critically about information?

- Worldwide concerns about misleading or even intentionally false information increased slightly in 2021. *"Those who use social media are more likely to say they have been exposed to misinformation about Coronavirus than non-users. Facebook is seen as the main channel for spreading false information almost everywhere but messaging apps like WhatsApp are seen as a bigger problem."*[223]

- *"Despite more options to read and watch partisan news, the majority of our respondents (74%) say they still prefer news that reflects a range of views and lets them decide what to think. Most also think that news outlets should try to be neutral on every issue (66%), though some younger groups think that 'impartiality' may not be appropriate or desirable in some cases – for example, on social justice issues."*[224]

To a great extent, the harm caused by incorrect information is not directly related to the information itself, although false statements can often damage individuals and companies. Sometimes the real harm comes from a perception of *"tainted truth,"*[225] which is connected to the psychological effect on the human brain when concerns have been raised regarding the accuracy of their information or information sources. It doesn't matter if the warning comes from well-

---

[223] Newman, N. (2021). Executive summary and key findings of the 2021 report. *Reuters Institute*. Available at *https://reutersinstitute.politics.ox.ac.uk/digital-news-report/2021/dnr-executive-summary*.

[224] Ibid.

[225] Bouygues, H. (2019). The Misinformation Effect and the Psychology Behind Fake News. *The Reboot Foundation*. Available at *https://reboot-foundation.org/misinformation-effect/#*.

intentioned fact-checking or ill-intentioned fear peddling, it still causes people to be suspicious of information. They may even pay no attention to accurate news and news sources simply because they may be false. When people do not trust news outlets or public figures, this can result in increased societal chaos and the deterioration of reasonable public discourse.

But how is all of this discussion about false or incorrect information related to AI? Well, the increase in AI-generated content has demonstrated that the algorithms driving AI may not be all that great at generating reliable and accurate information.

> *"Take Facebook for example. The company relies on advertisers and users to click, share, and spend time in the app to make their money. They rely heavily on the data they mine from users who willingly teach their algorithm what they like, what they don't like, and what content causes them to engage. And inflammatory information causes people to engage. We saw an uptick in the amount of misinformation spread during the Brexit referendum, the US 2016 Presidential Election, the BLM movement, and so much more."* [226]

False information comes in many guises, ranging from the more benign "misinformation" to the more serious "fake news" or "disinformation." The First Draft non-profit,

---

[226] Davies, N. (September 23, 2021). AI Is Capable of Generating Misinformation and Fooling Cybersecurity Experts. *CPO Magazine.* Available at www.cpomagazine.com/cyber-security/ai-is-capable-of-generating-misinformation-and-fooling-cybersecurity-experts/.

founded to help individuals navigate the news landscape (*https://firstdraftnews.org/about/*), has developed a chart of seven types of misinformation and disinformation on a scale from left to right depicting the intent to deceive or mislead.

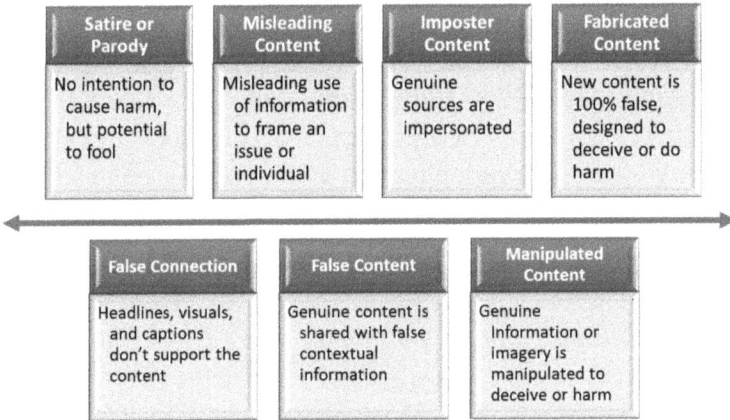

Satire or Parody	Misleading Content	Imposter Content	Fabricated Content
No intention to cause harm, but potential to fool	Misleading use of information to frame an issue or individual	Genuine sources are impersonated	New content is 100% false, designed to deceive or do harm

False Connection	False Content	Manipulated Content
Headlines, visuals, and captions don't support the content	Genuine content is shared with false contextual information	Genuine Information or imagery is manipulated to deceive or harm

Figure 9-1: Seven types of misinformation and disinformation[227]

Although both misinformation and disinformation are able to deceive, *intent* remains the most important distinction. Disinformation is intentionally, maliciously deceptive. Misinformation is content that is untrue or inaccurate. It can often spread widely, but is not created or spread with an intent to deceive. In both cases, the person receiving the content may be largely unaware of the inaccuracies. Misinformation can evolve into disinformation when

---

[227] Wardle, C. Misinformation is damaging communities around the world. Available at *https://lifestylesharer.wordpress.com/2019/01/10/7-types-of-mis-and-disinformation-and-how-to-spot-them*.

perpetuated by those who know it is untrue, yet intentionally spread it to cause uncertainty or divisiveness.

Misinformation

The increase in misinformation is a problem that begins in the human mind. When misinformation is presented effectively, it can be almost impossible to divide fact from fiction. And with Big Data, the amount of information that is out there enables AI/ML to learn and tailor their outputs to users constantly, making it even more challenging to tell the difference.

Social media platforms using sophisticated AI algorithms provide a fertile ground for the spread of misinformation. The algorithms behind social media make it very simple for gullible users to dramatically amplify falsehoods through the simple process of sharing or forwarding the information without first checking the veracity.

In 2020 and 2021,

> " ... *almost 80 mobile cell towers [were literally] set ablaze by those who believe that 5G causes cancer, the Capitol building in Washington DC stormed [on January 6, 2021] by those convinced that the US presidential election was rigged by a secretive cabal, and lingering vaccine scepticism from the days of MMR hampering*

9: Misinformation, disinformation, fake news, manipulation, and deepfakes – Do we know how to think critically about information?

efforts to avoid a future of perpetual Covid-19 epidemics and lockdowns."[228]

These examples of misinformation plagued the news and social media.

Flat-earth theory is another persistent example of misinformation. Almost everyone knows that the earth is a globe. But despite this, there are still people who genuinely believe the earth is flat, despite evidence to the contrary. Individuals who use the Internet to perpetuate this fiction truly believe it is true. And, because AI cannot discern the difference, this false theory continues to be perpetuated.

When exposed to reams of misinformation, humans can fall prey to the "tainted truth effect," which is the psychological effect on the human brain after being constantly warned about the truth of the content they are reading or hearing. Whether the caution takes the form of fact-checking or fear mongering, the result is a distrust of information to the point that people may begin to suspect all news, believing that it may be false.

AI is not always the culprit. It can also be a strong advocate in the fight against misinformation. The key to using AI effectively to combat misinformation is its ability to scour the Internet, collect, process, and analyze data faster than the misinformation itself: compressing fact-checking into a process that can potentially occur in under an hour after information is released. The ideal situation is a joint effort

---

[228] Noone, G. (June 10, 2021). AI vs misinformation: Fighting lies with machines. *Techmonitor*. Available at *https://techmonitor.ai/technology/ai-and-automation/ai-vs-misinformation-fighting-lies-machines*.

between AI and humans, combining the instant analysis from AI with a human fact-checker, with the latter having the final determination over whether or not the content is actually misinformation.

Although misinformation can cause some damage, it is certainly not as dangerous as its relative – disinformation.

Disinformation

Disinformation is related to misinformation with one clear distinction – that of *intent*. Although misinformation can result in incorrect perceptions, disinformation (and its cohort fake news) can have much more damaging results. A 2020 study by the Harvard Business School found that disinformation and fake news was linked to a general decrease in media trust. The research across multiple respondents indicated:

> " ... *sensational and made-up stories that mimic the format of journalism could damage the credibility of all news content. With that in mind, journalists and scholars have expressed concerns that exposure to fabricated news would reduce people's confidence in the press. Our research found evidence confirming that assumption.* "[229]

---

[229] Ognyanova, K., Lazer, D., Robertson, R. and Wilson, C. (June 2, 2020). Misinformation in action: Fake news exposure is linked to lower trust in media, higher trust in government when your side is in power. *HKS Misinformation Review*. Available at *https://misinforeview.hks.harvard.edu/article/misinformation-in-action-fake-news-exposure-is-linked-to-lower-trust-in-media-higher-trust-in-government-when-your-side-is-in-power/*.

9: Misinformation, disinformation, fake news, manipulation, and deepfakes – Do we know how to think critically about information?

AI-based disinformation attacks. Attacks in which AI is used to quickly generate and release disinformation with the intent to create an immediate disruptive effect have become one of the most significant challenges in todays' global digital ecosystem. Few areas are left untouched by disinformation.

> *"Elections are one example of the many domains where this can occur. Financial markets, which can be subject to short-term manipulation, are another example. Foreign affairs could be affected as rumors spread quickly around the world through digital platforms. Social movements can also be targeted through dissemination of false information designed to spur action or reaction among either supporters or opponents of a cause."*[230]

Fake news is one of the most pervasive forms of disinformation. Another is the ever-increasing use of deepfakes. Both are increasingly driven by AI.

Fake news

Our brains love fake news. But why? It definitely is not about a lack of intelligence or gullibility. It is because we often believe what we want to believe – regardless of the facts. It is actually something called cognitive bias.

> *"A cognitive bias is a subconscious error in thinking that leads you to misinterpret information from the world*

---

[230] Villasenor, J. (November 23, 2020). How to deal with AI-enabled disinformation. *Brookings*. Available at *www.brookings.edu/research/how-to-deal-with-ai-enabled-disinformation/*.

around you, and affects the rationality and accuracy of decisions and judgments. Biases are unconscious and automatic processes designed to make decision-making quicker and more efficient. Cognitive biases can be caused by a number of different things, such as heuristics (mental shortcuts), social pressures, and emotions."[231]

More clearly stated – it is a form of unconscious brain malfunction that can cause us to come to flawed conclusions.

Once this cognitive bias has kicked in, humans tend to stick with their faulty conclusions regardless of evidence to the contrary. And this is the result of a form of cognitive bias called confirmation bias.

"Confirmation bias is the tendency to look for information that supports, rather than rejects, one's preconceptions, typically by interpreting evidence to confirm existing beliefs while rejecting or ignoring any conflicting data."[232]

When looking at information that confirms our pre-existing beliefs, we are using the orbitofrontal cortex, or the part of the brain that processes emotions rather than the dorsolateral prefrontal cortex, or the part of the brain that is responsible for logical thought.

Fake news grows because many social media algorithms create filter bubbles to feed their users content that is

[231] Ruhl, C. (May 4, 2021). What Is Cognitive Bias? *SimplyPsychology.* Available at *www.simplypsychology.org/cognitive-bias.html.*
[232] Noor, I. (June 10, 2020). Confirmation Bias. *SimplyPsychology.* Available at *www.simplypsychology.org/confirmation-bias.html.*

determined to be ideologically consistent with that user's existing views (or biases).

Why should a person care if news is fake or not? The COVID-19 crisis provided a very clear demonstration of how fake news can cause damage. Purveyors of fake and misleading medical advice helped to perpetuate myths, such as "COVID is not real," "COVID vaccines can kill you," or even "Secret Helicopter Operation to Spray Disinfectant." This last one was a viral message that spread in March 2020 on Facebook and WhatsApp about an aerial bombardment that would eliminate the virus. It eventually spread on social media to hundreds of thousands of people in countries across the world, yet the time of night and number of helicopters stayed the same.[233]

> Fwd:' tonight from 11:40 pm nobody should be on the street. Doors and windows should remain closed as 5 helicopters spray disinfectants into the air to eradicate the coranavirus. Please process this information to all of your contacts

During the 2016 US election, it seemed like fake news came out of nowhere and was suddenly *everywhere*. A BuzzFeed news study showed that fake news on Facebook received more clicks than all of the other, more mainstream news *combined*.

---

[233] Spring, M. (August 6, 2020). Coronavirus: The viral rumours that were completely wrong. *BBC News*. Available at *www.bbc.com/news/blogs-trending-53640964*.

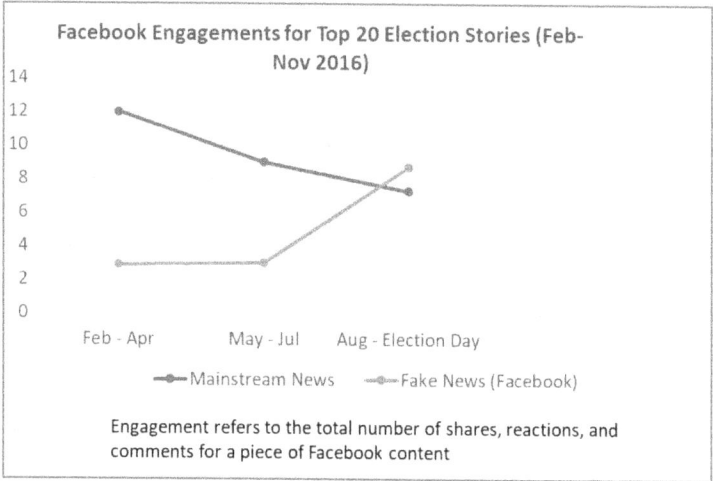

Facebook Engagements for Top 20 Election Stories (Feb-Nov 2016)

Engagement refers to the total number of shares, reactions, and comments for a piece of Facebook content

Figure 9-2: Facebook engagements for Top 20 election stories (Fake News)[234]

"Up until those last three months of the campaign, the top election content from major outlets had easily outpaced that of fake election news on Facebook. Then, as the election drew closer, engagement for fake content on

---

[234] Silverman, C. (November 16, 2016). This Analysis Shows How Viral Fake Election News Stories Outperformed Real News on Facebook. *BuzzFeed News.* Available at *www.buzzfeednews.com/article/craigsilverman/viral-fake-election-news-outperformed-real-news-on-facebook.*

9: Misinformation, disinformation, fake news, manipulation, and deepfakes – Do we know how to think critically about information?

Facebook skyrocketed and surpassed that of the content from major news outlets."[235]

One of the most relevant examples of fake news was information generated by Russia from Facebook ads, pages, and private groups during the 2016 election campaign. Russian actors targeted specific geographic regions and swing states, and used AI-generated algorithms to spread false information about the democratic nominee, Hillary Clinton, with the intent to spread discord in the US electorate during the election process.[236]

AI is a two-edged sword when looking at fake news. On the one hand, a lot of the technology used to identify and manage fake news is powered by AI. Using AI, large amounts of data can be quickly fact checked, especially since there is just too much data for people to collect and analyze without the help of AI technology.

On the other hand, AI is a main contributor to the proliferation of fake news. To be clear, the AI itself is not really causing the fake news problems – rather, it is the people using the AI to create the fake news, and the individuals consuming the content. If an organization or a

---

[235] Silverman, C. (November 16, 2016). This Analysis Shows How Viral Fake Election News Stories Outperformed Real News on Facebook. *BuzzFeed News*. Available at *www.buzzfeednews.com/article/craigsilverman/viral-fake-election-news-outperformed-real-news-on-facebook*.

[236] Summers, T. (July 27, 2018). How the Russian government used disinformation and cyber warfare in 2016 election – an ethical hacker explains. Available at *https://theconversation.com/how-the-russian-government-used-disinformation-and-cyber-warfare-in-2016-election-an-ethical-hacker-explains-99989*.

person with malicious intent uses AI, it is very easy for them to spread fake news and perpetuate false narratives to unsuspecting and susceptible users.

And it is all because of the algorithms that drive AI. In the background of every Twitter feed, Facebook comment, and YouTube video there is an algorithm specifically designed to keep the users using. This algorithm tracks preferences by collecting and analyzing clicks and hovers, and then presents a relentless stream of content that is in line with the user's tastes – or cognitive bias. And the more the user clicks on the fake news entries, the more will be presented.

Deepfakes

> *"Have you seen Barack Obama call Donald Trump a 'complete dipshit,' or Mark Zuckerberg brag about having 'total control of billions of people's stolen data,' or witnessed Jon Snow's moving apology for the dismal ending to Game of Thrones? Answer yes and you've seen a deepfake. The 21st century's answer to Photoshopping, deepfakes use a form of artificial intelligence called deep learning to make images of fake events, hence the name deepfake."[237]*

The term "deepfake" is derived from the underlying technology used to create them – DL, a specific form of AI. There are a number of AI-based applications that make

---

[237] Sample, I. (January 13, 2020). What are deepfakes – and how can you spot them? *The Guardian.* Available at *www.theguardian.com/technology/2020/jan/13/what-are-deepfakes-and-how-can-you-spot-them.*

generating deepfakes easy – even for beginners. These include the Chinese app Zao (*https://zao.en.uptodown.com/android*), Deepfake Lab (*https://deepfakelab.theglassroom.org/*) , FaceApp (which is a photo editing app with built-in AI techniques at *https://www.faceapp.com/*), Faceswap (*https://faceswap.dev/*), and DeepNude, a particularly insidious application used to generate fake nude images of women (which has now been removed). These applications can fake content by using technology that manipulates images or videos of real people and shows them doing and saying things they didn't do.

Although pornography is one of the primary areas where deepfakes are found, they can also be used in the political arena. For example, in 2018, a Belgian political party released a video of a Donald Trump speech demanding that Belgium withdraw from the Paris Climate Agreement.[238] However, Trump never gave that speech – it was a deepfake.

---

[238] Von der Burchard, H. (May 21, 2018). Belgian socialist party circulates 'deep fake' Donald Trump video. *Politico*. Available at *www.politico.eu/article/spa-donald-trump-belgium-paris-climate-agreement-belgian-socialist-party-circulates-deep-fake-trump-video/*.

Even more eye-catching were a series of Tom Cruise deepfakes made by the Belgian Chris Ume and posted on TikTok, allegedly for the purpose of illustrating the power of deepfakes and the technology that is involved in their creation. The videos on TikTok were called "scarily realistic" and were so well-made and deceptive that they tricked many social media users – and specially-designed deepfake detection software.[239]

So, how are deepfakes actually made?

Simply put, specially-designed AI software uses ML to study the movements of a person in a real video, or the facial characteristics in an image, and then superimposes their face (Original faces A and B) onto another video or image (Reconstructed faces A and B). Even a single image can be used to produce a deepfake. But, the more images the deepfake creator has to use, the more realistic the AI can make the deepfake. The deepfake creator uses the detailed information and superimposes it on the underlying facial and body features of the original video or image, essentially creating an entirely new version of the original.

---

[239] Check out the videos at:
www.tiktok.com/@deeptomcruise/video/6957456115315657989.

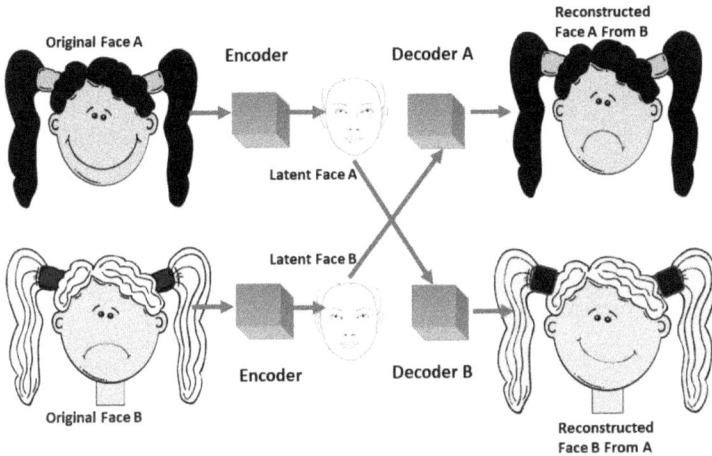

Figure 9-3: How to make a deepfake

Although it is difficult to create a good deepfake on a standard computer, very realistic deepfakes can be created on higher-end desktop computers with powerful graphics cards or by using computing power within the cloud.

More importantly, how can a deepfake be spotted? Although there is not an exact list of steps to take that will easily identify a deepfake, there are some things to look for that can help determine if the image or video is real.

- **Look at the face** – Is someone blinking too much or too little? Do their eyebrows fit their face? Is someone's hair in the wrong spot? Does their skin look airbrushed or, conversely, are there too many wrinkles?
- **Listen to the audio** – Does the voice match their appearance (e.g. the video portrays a woman with a very deep voice).

*9: Misinformation, disinformation, fake news,
manipulation, and deepfakes – Do we know how to think
critically about information?*

- **Check out the lighting** – Is there any reflection, such as a person's glasses reflecting a light? It is difficult to reproduce the natural effects of lighting in a deepfake.

The MIT has created an interesting, online test for users to experience and learn, through examples, to detect deepfakes at *https://detectfakes.media.mit.edu/*.

User manipulation

Many voices warn us that social media platforms filter the information we see – the result is a form of user manipulation. There are two ways this can manifest itself: echo chambers and filter bubbles.

Echo chambers

Echo chambers can occur when we are overexposed to news that we are predisposed to like or agree with, potentially warping our perception of reality. We are exposed to too much of one perspective, and not enough of the other, so we begin to think that perhaps reality is really like this.

Echo chambers can facilitate misinformation and distort an individual's perspective to the point that they may have difficulty considering opposing viewpoints and discussing complicated topics. They are fueled in part by confirmation bias, which is the tendency to prefer information that reinforces pre-existing beliefs. Social media is one of the primary facilitators of echo chambers, as if favors the formation of groups of like-minded users who then frame and reinforce a shared narrative. This can result in an escalating effect by reinforcing existing opinions within a group and, as a consequence, moving the entire group towards increasingly extreme positions.

A filter bubble is a specific kind of echo chamber.

Filter bubbles

Filter bubbles arise when news that we may dislike or disagree with is filtered out automatically, with the effect of narrowing what we see and hear. The difference to echo chambers is critical. Filter bubbles are a result of algorithmic filtering.

As more and more online sites strive to gain users, they tailor the information to individual preferences as identified through the AI algorithms with an unintended consequence: users of these sites get caught in the "filter bubble" and don't get exposed to additional information that could broaden their existing worldview. It is so easy to find and access content that reinforces our preconceptions. Each individual's preferred information "diet" is tracked by Google, Facebook, and many other Internet sites, which then customize the results and news feeds based on previous likes, clicks, or searches. Eli Pariser[240] gave a very interesting Ted Talk on the dangers of filter bubbles at *www.youtube.com/watch?v=EsjOLB_jTBA*.

---

[240] Eli Pariser is an author and activist whose goal is "to help media and technology serve society." More about him at *https://www.elipariser.org/*.

9: Misinformation, disinformation, fake news, manipulation, and deepfakes – Do we know how to think critically about information?

Thinking critically about information and information sources

With all of this intentionally or unintentionally misleading or blatantly incorrect information "floating" about, how can we determine the truth?

What is a fact?

Before we continue to thinking critically about information and information sources, we first need to have a definition of the word "fact." A fact is defined as something that is true, or something that has occurred, or has been proven correct through evidence. The test for fact is generally verifiability – or whether it can be demonstrated to be true.

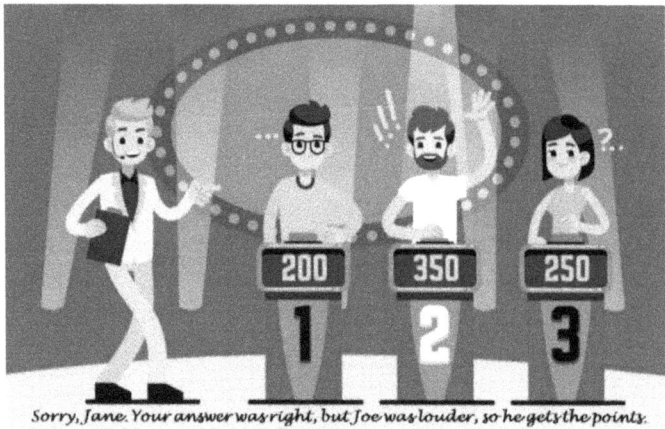

Sorry, Jane. Your answer was right, but Joe was louder, so he gets the points.

Figure 9-4: Facts don't matter

False information can often trump the truth based on who has the louder voice, the larger platform, or who repeats the untruth most often and convincingly.

9: Misinformation, disinformation, fake news, manipulation, and deepfakes – Do we know how to think critically about information?

Understanding media bias

Unbiased news does not exist. Simple. In fact, media bias is widespread across all of the main media channels: network news, printed news, and most definitely online. For this reason, it is wise to learn how to view the media with a more critical eye.

So, what exactly is media bias? It is the stated bias or perceived bias of news channels, individual journalists or reporters, or news presenters in any form of media. It generally implies a prevalent bias that can affect the standard of truth in journalism. Media bias can also be represented in the perspective of a single journalist or article.

The challenge with media bias is that it has the ability to affect the choice of events and stories that get published, the perspective from which they are presented, and the type of language used to report them.

The News Literacy Project has identified five prevalent types of bias:

	Corporate Bias
	A business or ad interests of a news outlet or its parent company influence how or whether a news story is reported.

	Partisan Bias
	A reporter's political views affect how or whether a story is reported.

	Demographic Bias
	Race, gender, ethnicity, or other factor, such as culture or economic class, affect how or whether a story is reported.

	Neutrality Bias
	A journalist or news outlet tries so hard to appear unbiased that the coverage actually misrepresents the facts.

	Big Story Bias
	A reporter's perceptions of an event or development as major can cause them to miss or delete key details.

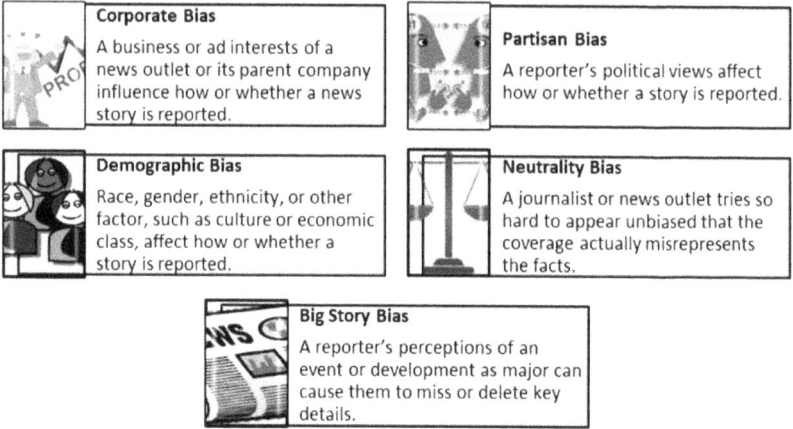

Figure 9-5: Five types of media bias[241]

These five types of bias can also take various forms, as identified by the News Literacy Project:

---

[241] Five types of bias. *News Literacy Project.* Available at *https://newslit.org/educators/resources/understanding-bias/*.

9: Misinformation, disinformation, fake news, manipulation, and deepfakes – Do we know how to think critically about information?

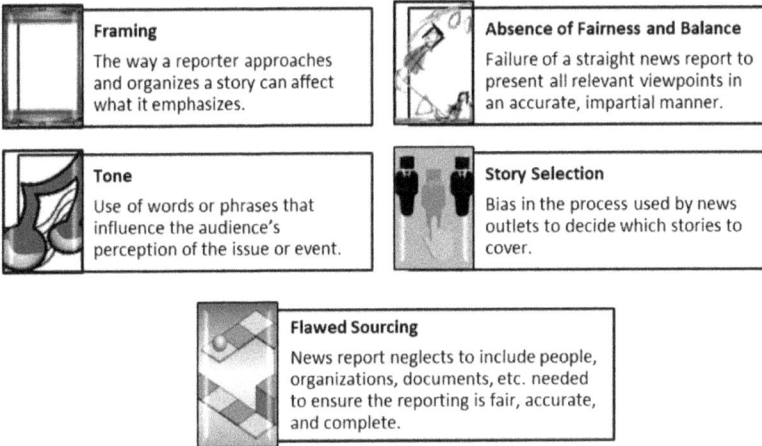

Framing
The way a reporter approaches and organizes a story can affect what it emphasizes.

Absence of Fairness and Balance
Failure of a straight news report to present all relevant viewpoints in an accurate, impartial manner.

Tone
Use of words or phrases that influence the audience's perception of the issue or event.

Story Selection
Bias in the process used by news outlets to decide which stories to cover.

Flawed Sourcing
News report neglects to include people, organizations, documents, etc. needed to ensure the reporting is fair, accurate, and complete.

Figure 9-6: Forms of media bias

There are things a reader can do to avoid being misled by media bias and fake news. Try to identify and put aside pre-conceived notions and emotionalism, and look at the news from different perspectives. View online information and information sources critically to understand the bias – whether it is clearly stated or not.

The News Literacy Project also provides easy-to-understand training modules in news literacy that can be very useful in determining the validity of reporting (see *https://newslit.org/for-everyone/*). AllSides, a corporation focused on balanced news coverage, also provides a comprehensive guide on how to spot 16 types of media bias (see *www.allsides.com/media-bias/how-to-spot-types-of-media-bias*) and 14 types of ideological bias (see *www.allsides.com/blog/beyond-left-vs-right-14-types-ideological-bias*),

9: Misinformation, disinformation, fake news, manipulation, and deepfakes – Do we know how to think critically about information?

There are several organizations that create media bias charts providing some level of perspective about bias. These include the Ad Fontes interactive media bias chart (see *https://adfontesmedia.com/*) and AllSides static media bias chart (see *https://www.allsides.com/media-bias/media-bias-ratings*).

The AllSides Media Bias Chart™ focuses exclusively on political bias. It aligns media sources in one of five verticals identified as "Left," "Lean Left," "Center," "Lean Right" and "Right." As they state on the chart, the assigned ratings are based solely on online content; they do not look at bias in print, radio, or TV.

AllSides has also developed a Fact Check Bias Chart™, which looks at dedicated fact-checking websites, such as Snopes (*www.allsides.com/news-source/snopes*), PolitiFact (*www.allsides.com/news-source/politifact*),   and

9: Misinformation, disinformation, fake news, manipulation, and deepfakes – Do we know how to think critically about information?

FactCheck.org (_www.allsides.com/news-source/factcheckorg-media-bias_).

All ratings are based on online content only — not TV, print, or radio content. Ratings do not reflect accuracy or credibility; they reflect perspective only.

Figure 9-7: AllSides Media Bias Chart[242]

The interactive Media Bias Chart® from Ad Fontes provides more detailed view rates for reliability as well as bias. Ad

---

[242] AllSides Media Bias Chart (2021). _AllSides._ Available at _www.allsides.com/media-bias_.

Fontes has established a team of human analysts with political views across the spectrum. These reviewers are trained to review news content and score it accordingly for bias and reliability using the Ad Fontes methodology. A sample of about 15 articles over several news cycles is selected from each online news source and is then rated by at least three human analysts with viewpoints from right, center, and left. Ad Fontes charges a fee to use its charts for various types of commercial, non-commercial, and educational purposes.

Become a digital detective

In the seemingly lawless Wild West of online news, it has become increasingly time-consuming and challenging to discern the truth among the half-truths, false claims, or even outright lies. Although the Internet is a fountain of misinformation, it can also be the best tool to verify, or debunk, the information found online or from other news sources.

Verifying images

Although the statement "A picture is worth a thousand words" may still be true, it is not true that all pictures found on the Internet are real. With tools such as Photoshop and other image modification apps, there are so many ways to manipulate an image from your own or someone else's photos, so having efficient tools to check if a photograph is real is very important.

There are several sites that offer image checking to verify the truth behind the image. A reversed Google Search (*https://images.google.com/*) can be used to check whether

*9: Misinformation, disinformation, fake news,
manipulation, and deepfakes – Do we know how to think
critically about information?*

an uploaded photo is authentic or not. Another tool is TinEye (*https://tineye.com*), which uses its technology to find the oldest, newest, or most changed version of an image, Truepic is an app that provides photo and video verification for a fee (*https://truepic.com/*). JPEGsnoop (*https://github.com/ImpulseAdventure/JPEGsnoop*) shows all metadata for the photo in question, as well as any edits that clearly show that the photo is not an original.

There are also some useful, old-fashioned detective skills that can be applied. The first is to train your own eye to identify those little – or not quite so little – details that give away that a photo has been manipulated. A second is to check the photographer to determine if they are reputable, and perhaps even to contact them for confirmation. You could also look at the image background and conduct some searches to check what the alleged location really looks like. Another indicator is the quality of the photo; poor quality may actually be a cover up for some not very well executed modification job. The type of light or unnatural curved surfaces on the image can also be signs of manipulation. The lack of authenticity of a photo can easily be detected if the light does not seem to fall naturally, or if there are objects that look bent or out of shape.

Verifying news

The Public Library of Albuquerque and Bernalillo County has one of the best lists of tips for the up-and-coming digital detective. Because it is so good, the suggestions, as well as a few of my own, are provided here:

- **Check author credentials** – Is the author a known specialist in the subject of the article? Do they currently work in that field? Check LinkedIn or do a quick Google search to see if the author has the credentials to speak about the subject with authority and accuracy.

- **Read the "About us" section** – Does the article have one? Usually it is a tab at the top of the page or a link at the bottom, but all reputable websites will have some type of "About us" section, and will also provide a way for you to contact them.

- **Look for bias** – Determine if the article seems to tend toward a particular point of view? Does it link to sites, files, or images that seem to have a noticeable left or right slant? Biased articles may not be giving you the whole story. Also be sure to check your own biases – determine if your beliefs and prejudices can be affecting your judgment.

- **Is it a joke**? – If it is too outlandish, it might be a form of satire. Research the site and the author to verify.

- **Check the dates** – Like eggs and milk, information can also have an expiration date. In many cases, use the most up-to-date information you can find or cross-check with newer articles on the same subject.

- **Read beyond the headlines** – Headlines can be intentionally outrageous in order to get viewers. Read the entire story, then fact-check it.

- **Check out the source** – When an article cites sources, it is always a good idea to check them out. Sometimes, official-sounding associations are really biased think tanks or represent only a fringe viewpoint. If other sources are not provided, look at other articles on the topic to get a feel for what is being published elsewhere, and decide for yourself if the article is accurate or not.

9: Misinformation, disinformation, fake news, manipulation, and deepfakes – Do we know how to think critically about information?

- **Use the CRAAP Test** – **C**urrency, **R**elevance, **A**ccuracy, **A**uthority, and **P**urpose.

- **Interrogate URLs** – There is a lot of domain manipulation these days. For instance, what looks like an .edu domain, followed by .co or "lo" is likely a fake or deceptive site. If there appears to be a slightly variant version of a well-known URL, investigate. TechFeatured provides a good tutorial on how to identify unsafe websites at https://techfeatured.com/14809/online-safety-101-how-to-identify-unsafe-websites.

- **Who owns the website posting the information?** – You can find out at either *https://whois.domaintools.com* or at *https://whois.icann.org*. Both of these websites allow you to perform a WHOIS search. Whenever someone registers a website address, they are required to enter their contact information. When you get to your WHOIS search, enter in the domain (the first part of the website URL). This step can be used to collect all the information when you question a source, or the information's purpose.

- **Suspect the sensational** – When you see something posted that looks sensational, it is even more important to be skeptical. Exaggerated and provocative headlines with excessive use of capital letters or emotional language are serious red flags.

- **Judge hard** – If what you're reading seems too good to be true, or too weird, or too reactionary, it probably is.[243]

---

[243] How to Fact-Check Like a Pro. *The Public Library of Albuquerque and Bernalillo County.* Available at *https://abqlibrary.org/FakeNews/FactCheck*.

CHAPTER 10: AI AND SOCIAL MEDIA – HOW IS IT AFFECTING US?

> *"Dave, Dave, my mind is going," HAL says forlornly. "I can feel it. I can feel it."*
>
> **Nicholas Carr in *The Shallows***

Less than a decade ago, many researchers considered social media only as a passing trend. Today, social media has fully penetrated mainstream society. Most of us are active on at least one major social media platform, but we still fail to understand just how much impact daily social media use can have. It may be entertaining to scroll through all the newest memes or updates from all your "friends," but we often can't see the ways in which social media is changing how we think and act.

Overall, available evidence indicates that the use of social media can also result in acute and sustained alterations in areas of cognition, such as attention span, memory processes, and social cognition.[244] Social media sites are automated and optimized with powerful AI. Every time a user opens up Facebook, Instagram, TikTok, or YouTube, they have activated an AI that is trying to determine what information it can feed to the user's mind to get their attention and to keep them hooked.

---

[244] Social cognition refers to those processes that enable humans to interpret social information inputs and then behave appropriately in a social environment.

Beyond the effects on individual cognition, AI has deeply affected how we receive and process news. Research indicates that, although social media can help to effectively communicate information to a global audience, the information shared on these platforms is often inaccurate or misleading. It causes users to believe that there is just no such thing as truth or fact, which is of course not true. But there is the fact that it is becoming increasingly difficult to actually find and trust truth or fact. So, if a user looks at social media feeds about Russia and disinformation, that feed basically becomes a repeating view that the world is falling apart and the user can do nothing but feel helpless about it.

University of Toronto Professor Ronald Deibert has itemized the challenges of AI-powered social media in what he terms "Three Painful Truths:"

1. **The first painful truth** is that the social-media business is built around personal-data surveillance, with products ultimately designed to spy on us in order to push advertising in our direction.
2. **The second painful truth** is that we have consented to this, but not entirely willingly: social media is designed as an addiction machine, expressly programmed to draw upon our emotions.
3. **The third painful truth** is that the attention-grabbing algorithms underlying social media also propel authoritarian practices that aim to sow confusion,

ignorance, prejudice, and chaos, thereby facilitating
manipulation and undermining accountability.[245]

When social media first emerged, it was widely believed that
these platforms would facilitate much greater access to
information, enable improved interpersonal connectivity,
and empower collective organizing. As a consequence of
recent exposures, social media is increasingly being viewed
as causing some of society's problems. Growing numbers of
people are coming to believe that social media has too much
influence on users, news, and critical social and political
conversations. Together with the expansion of social media
use, there are also mounting concerns that social media may
contribute to social anxiety in users.

What is the relationship between social media and AI?

AI is a key element in all of the popular social media
networks being used every single day. All social media
platforms use AI to determine what users see and what they
engage with, because AI excels at rapidly extracting insights
and patterns from large data sets. In fact, *"social media
platforms now rely on AI to do, well, everything."*[246] And our
reaction to this evolution is, well – mixed.

There is certainly a wide variety of social media, however,
the leading category is social networking. Facebook, Twitter,
and LinkedIn keep attracting users as a means of connecting

[245] Deibert, R. (January 2019). The Road to Digital Unfreedom: Three
Painful Truths about Social Media. *Journal of Democracy, Vol.30, pgs.
25–39.* Available at *www.journalofdemocracy.org/articles/the-road-to-
digital-unfreedom-three-painful-truths-about-social-media/*.

[246] Kaput, M., (April 21, 2021). AI for Social Media: Everything You
Need to Know. *Marketing Artificial Intelligence Institute.* Available at
www.marketingaiinstitute.com/blog/ai-for-social-media.

with family and friends, catching up on the latest news, or expanding one's business connections. Other types of social media platforms include TikTok, Instagram, and YouTube, which specialize in photos and videos. There are interest-based networks, such as Pinterest, and messaging apps, such as Facebook Messenger and WhatsApp.

Although there are very popular social media sites that are unique to a specific nation, e.g. China, there are a number of sites that are global. The graphic below shows some of the most globally popular social media sites as of October 2021:

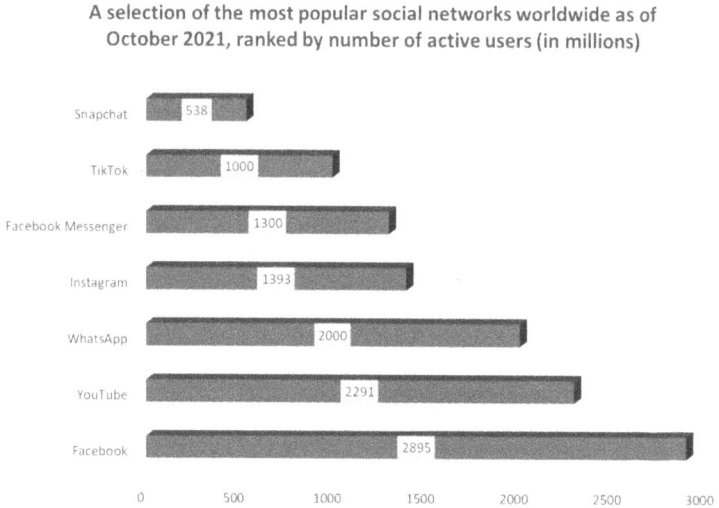

A selection of the most popular social networks worldwide as of October 2021, ranked by number of active users (in millions)

Platform	Active users (millions)
Snapchat	538
TikTok	1000
Facebook Messenger	1300
Instagram	1393
WhatsApp	2000
YouTube	2291
Facebook	2895

Figure 10-1: Most popular social media sites as of October 2021[247]

---

[247] The Top 10 Social Media Sites & Platforms 2021. *Search Engine Journal.* Available at *www.searchenginejournal.com/social-media/biggest-social-media-sites/#close.*

One of the concerns regarding social media is something called "social comparison." This is a product of a human's inclination to assess their value, situation, skill, and overall identity by comparing themselves and their lives to others.[248] Social comparison is argued to be a contributing factor to low self-esteem. *"Since idealistic information presented through social media has increased social comparison norms, the more time people spent on social media, the more likely they would believe that others have better lives and are happier and more successful, reducing their self-esteem."*[249] The following sections look at some of the most prominent social media networks and their impact.

AI and Facebook

Facebook was created by Mark Zuckerberg in 2004 and is the largest social network with *"2.8 billion monthly active users recorded in late 2020 and a revenue of 86 billion U.S. dollars in 2020."*[250] Zuckerberg's stated objective is to *"connect every person on the earth with Facebook-owned tech in the next 100 years. It's a perfect example of a company with the buying capacity of more than entire*

---

[248] Gilbert, P. (2000). The relationship of shame, social anxiety and depression: The role of the evaluation of social rank. *Clinical Psychology and Psychotherapy*, 7, 174–89.

[249] Stapleton, P., Luiz, G., Chatwin, H. (2017). Generation Validation: The Role of Social Comparison in Use of Instagram Among Emerging Adults. *Cyberpsychology, Behavior, and Social Networking*, 20, 142–9.

[250] Social Media & User-Generated Content. *Statista.* Available at *www.statista.com/markets/424/topic/540/social-media-user-generated-content/#overview*.

nations. The total cost of Facebook's acquisitions, thus far, is $23,124,700,000, USD and rising."[251]

Facebook uses advanced AI/ML to do everything from serving content to users, enabling facial recognition from photos, to targeting users with individualized advertising. Facebook can translate foreign languages, automatically classify images, predict what content a user will engage with most based on your historical engagement, and then serve tailored and targeted content.

Facebook's AI functionality starts with text. Its proprietary DeepText system is a DL AI/ML engine that is able to interpret and analyze text content on the platform with near-human accuracy. In addition to text recognition, Facebook's AI-driven image recognition auto-classifies images without relying on human captions or tags, which enables users to search photos using keywords even if images have no associated text descriptions. Facial recognition is another of Facebook's AI-driven functionalities. Its DeepFace AI drives its facial identification, and *"at launch in 2014 it was 97 percent accurate (beating out an 85 percent accurate system used by the FBI)."*[252]

Even though its popularity still continues, Facebook has come under a significant amount of criticism in recent years and is increasingly less popular with younger social media

---

[251] Iyam, M. (August 25, 2020). 7 Revealing Secrets – How Facebook is Using Artificial Intelligence. *IT Chronicles.* Available at *https://itchronicles.com/artificial-intelligence/7-revealing-secrets-how-facebook-is-using-artificial-intelligence/.*

[252] Kaput, M. (October 15, 2021). Meta/Facebook AI: What Businesses Need to Know. *Marketing Artificial Intelligence Institute.* Available at *www.marketingaiinstitute.com/blog/how-facebook-uses-artificial-intelligence-and-what-it-means-for-marketers.*

users. In 2021, revelations made before a US Senate subcommittee by the whistleblower Frances Haugen, a former data scientist at Facebook, led to the highest public outrage against Facebook in the corporation's history. Haugen *"provided a clear and detailed glimpse inside the notoriously secretive tech giant. She said Facebook harms children, sows division, and undermines democracy in pursuit of breakneck growth and 'astronomical profits.'"*[253]

In response to these allegations, Zuckerberg has vowed to maximize its AI use to address some of the biggest concerns about the company and its users, with a focus on seven major categories: 1. Hate speech 2. Terrorism 3. Nudity 4. Graphic violence 5. Spam 6. Suicides 7. Fake accounts.

Does Facebook make users lonelier and sadder?

"Loneliness is and always has been the central and inevitable experience of every man," wrote the novelist Thomas Wolfe.[254] Loneliness is most easily defined as the difference between desired and real social relationships. Even though we all experience loneliness at one time or another, this has become the one question that has likely attracted the most speculation and comment. Facebook tends to set up the expectation that if one is considered to be personally successful, one must also have a lot of "friends" – a huge network of Facebook contacts. Facebook also confronts its users with seemingly constant postings of

---

[253] Allyn, B. (October 5, 2021). Here are 4 key points from the Facebook whistleblower's testimony on Capitol Hill. *npr.* Available at *www.npr.org/2021/10/05/1043377310/facebook-whistleblower-frances-haugen-congress?t=1654873934435*.

[254] BrainyQuote. Available at *www.brainyquote.com/quotes/thomas_wolfe_389588*.

romantic dinners out, perfect vacations, and kids who manifest the ultimate in cuteness.

Other studies have shown that participation in social media, such as Facebook, can lead to feelings of stronger relationships with others. During the COVID-19 pandemic, the use of Facebook and other social media increased dramatically and served as a positive means of maintaining relationships with family and friends during periods of enforced physical isolation.

> *"In summarizing the existing research, [researchers] say that both theories are applicable in different contexts. When users spend time on the social internet to make new friends or strengthen friendships, this technology decreases loneliness. When it is used to displace offline interactions or avoid social pain, the technology increases it."*[255]

AI and Instagram

Instagram – a social networking app used for sharing photos and videos, which is owned by Facebook – uses AI to identify visuals. Instagram has more than 800 million active users and at least 70 million photos and videos are uploaded and shared every day.

Beyond just being a sharing platform for individual users, Instagram has also evolved into a global application used by

---

[255] Nowland, R., Necka, E.A., Cacioppo, J.T. (2017). Loneliness and Social Internet Use: Pathways to Reconnection in a Digital World? *Perspectives on Psychological Science.* doi:10.1177/1745691617713052.

companies to showcase their products, recruit talent, and motivate potential customers.

> *"The ML algorithms [behind Instagram] use certain user activities for insights that Instagram refers to as 'signals.' Signals include what a person posted, when and how often a person posts content, user preferences towards particular types of content, etc."*[256]

Instagram uses the AI/ML algorithms to create a picture of user interests, which is called the "user engagement graph." Each point in the graph represents content in which a particular user has demonstrated clear interest. These points also lead to the creation of "seed accounts" – individual accounts with which users have interacted over time by liking and/or commenting on the posts. Using what Instagram calls the "k-nearest neighbors algorithm," it can then predict what the user might be interested in and tailor the posts to those interests.

Instagram uses a measure called "engagement" to identify the interactions its audience makes with a user's content. The average engagement rate on Instagram ranges anywhere from *1 to 5 percent*. Engagement is measured by a range of metrics, such as comments, shares, likes, saves, followers and growth, mentions (tagged or untagged), branded hashtags, click-throughs, and DMs that are calculated by the AI algorithms driving Instagram. 1 to 3 percent are considered good engagement rates.

---

[256] How Instagram uses AI to Enhance the User Experience. (July 20, 2021. Available at *https://insights.daffodilsw.com/blog/how-instagram-uses-ai-to-enhance-the-user-experience*.

The higher the engagement rate rises, and the more audience an individual gathers, the greater the opportunity to become what Instagram terms as an "influencer." There are essentially three types of influencers: mega, macro, and micro – determined by the number of followers. Influencers can actually turn their Instagram popularity into an income stream, much like the popular Kardashian family, Rihanna, or the fashion influencer, Amy Jackson.

A number of sites provide Instagram calculators, which allow users to calculate their engagement rate by entering their Instagram handle – many for a fee. Others, such as HypeAuditor,[257] are free.

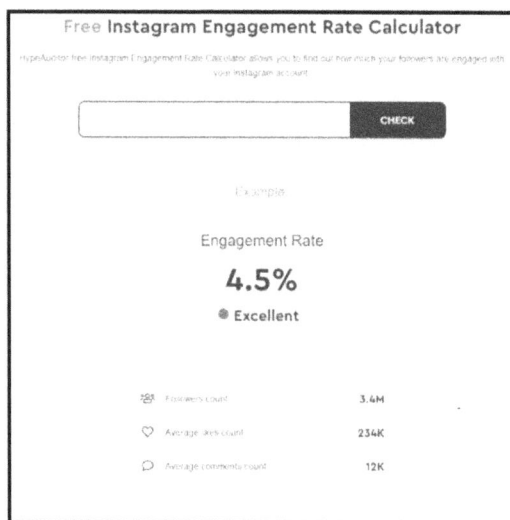

Figure 10-2: Instagram engagement calculator[258]

---

[257] Available at *https://hypeauditor.com/free-tools/instagram-engagement-calculator/*.
[258] Ibid.

Does Instagram promote negative social comparisons?

Most of Instagram's users are teens who tend to be particularly impressionable. According to Statista, as of April 2022, approximately 17.1 percent of global active Instagram users were men between the ages of 18 and 24 years. More than half of the global Instagram population worldwide is aged 34 years or younger.[259] One of the defining features of Instagram is that it enables users to beautify and enhance their photos by applying a wide range of so-called enhancement filters. This particular feature can alter the way individuals present themselves online creating a portrayal of idealized beauty that may affect other users' emotional and psychological responses, often resulting in a feeling of inadequacy. As a result of this potential effect, users often make efforts to refine their own behaviors to conform to certain standards or norms regardless of whom they may compare themselves with.

In 2017, the UK Royal Society for Public Health (RSPH) conducted a survey of almost 1,500 young people in the age group 14 to 24 from across the UK. The survey asked each participant to rate how they feel that each of the social media platforms they use influences them in 14 health and well-being related categories. These categories were considered most significant:

1. *"Awareness and understanding of other people's health experiences*

---

[259] Dixon, S., (May 23, 2022). Instagram: distribution of instagram users as of April 2022, by age and gender (*Statista Research Department.* Available at *www.statista.com/statistics/248769/age-distribution-of-worldwide-instagram-users/.*

2. **Access to expert health information you know you can trust**
3. **Emotional Support** – *empathy and compassion from family and friends*
4. **Anxiety** – *feelings of worry, nervousness, or unease*
5. **Depression** – *feeling extremely low and unhappy*
6. **Loneliness** – *feelings of being all on your own*
7. **Sleep** – *quality and amount of sleep*
8. **Self-expression** – *the expression of your feelings, thoughts, or ideas*
9. **Self-identity** – *ability to define who you are*
10. **Body image** – *how you feel about how you look*
11. **Real-world relationships** – *maintaining relationships with other people*
12. **Community building** – *feeling part of a community of like-minded people*
13. **Bullying** – *threatening or abusive behavior towards you*
14. **Fear of missing out (FOMO)** – *feeling you need to stay connected because you are worried things could be happening without you* "[260]

The results of the survey indicated that Instagram use results in the most detrimental effects on its user's mental health and sense of well-being.

AI and LinkedIn

LinkedIn, a much-used site for promoting professional and business connections, uses AI to make job recommendations,

---

[260] Instagram Ranked Worst for Young People's Mental Health. *The Royal Society for Public Health*. Available at *www.rsph.org.uk/about-us/news/instagram-ranked-worst-for-young-people-s-mental-health.html*.

suggest individuals to connect with, and serves up specific posts in the user feed. In fact, in one way or another, AI serves as the foundation for all of the LinkedIn activities.

AI provides the engine for input to both individual and business users. Individual users are provided with employment recommendations, suggestions for connecting with others, or pointers to useful information relevant to their feed. AI-driven processes also benefit business users, such as recruiters, by finding and recommending potential applicants with relevant talents. LinkedIn's AI-driven systems have thus had a significant and valuable impact on both user constituencies.

To counter the possibility of discrimination,

"LinkedIn also uses AI to help businesses overcome human biases that stifle equality. These AI features are included in LinkedIn's Talent Insight product, which is geared at recruiters and focuses on diversity and inclusion. LinkedIn can monitor what occurs in the recruitment process in terms of gender, providing firms with data and insights into how their job postings and InMail are functioning. In addition, the top search results in LinkedIn Recruiter will be re-ranked to be more representative."[261]

---

[261] Chakraborty, M. (June 8, 2021). LinkedIn Uses Artificial Intelligence In These Incredible Ways. *Analytics Insight.* Available at *www.analyticsinsight.net/linkedin-uses-artificial-intelligence-in-these-incredible-ways/.*

Does LinkedIn create false expectations?

While still working full-time as an executive at a major consulting company in Northern Virginia, I used LinkedIn for several hours each day and often counseled others on how to use it effectively for their own professional advantage. But I also noticed some negative effects based on the misguided ideas people have about just what LinkedIn can do for them.

The first misconception was that LinkedIn would get them a job without having to also do the rigorous internal and external work of knowing what they excel at, communicating those talents effectively, and then actually getting on the radar of hiring managers or recruiters. Another source of false expectations was the belief that the number of connections equated to greater professional opportunities. Also, just because another individual accepted an invitation to connect, it does not mean that there is any deeper interest or advantage to that connection. Finally, there is the misperception that a large number of LinkedIn connections can be a sign of professional success or credibility.

AI and Snapchat

Snapchat leverages the power of computer vision, an AI technology, to track your features and overlay filters that move with your face in real-time. Snapchat has become one of the most used apps in the world, competing with other major social media, such as Facebook, Instagram, and TikTok. It is unique in that its users are able to share photos, videos, text, and drawings that expire and automatically delete themselves after a set time, ranging from a few seconds up to 24 hours. Every message that is posted, whether a text message, snap, photo, video, or voice message, destroys itself once the receiver views it. The capability, called ephemeral social media, is powered by Snapchat's AI algorithms.

Most of the ways in which Snapchat uses AI might be considered trivial, such as its Time Machine smartphone app that can age or de-age a user's facial image. Another is Snapchat's "Lenses" feature, which applies AI-driven technology to the user's selfie video, enhancing it with animated effects. For example, "saying 'yes' will trigger a zoom effect on the user's face, while 'wow' will overlay a cartoon bow over her head and surround her with text bubbles saying 'WOW'!"[262]

The ephemeral quality of Snapchat has also led to several abuses, such as using it as a medium for dealing drugs. Snapchat has recently been more open about the drug crisis on its platform, such as how counterfeit pills laced with fentanyl were sourced through drug dealers on the platform. It is now implementing strong AI to identify users who may be using the platform to source or sell drugs.

Are there dangers in using Snapchat?

Snapchat has enormous popularity particularly among young users, specifically because of its ability to remove content. There are, however, some negative aspects to this capability.

There is a reason why Snapchat is often referred to as the "sexting" app. Users, especially young users, use Snapchat to share personal, intimate snaps, images, and clips with the expectation that they will quickly self-destruct. As a result, sexting using Snapchat has morphed from a stigmatized and

---

[262] New Snapchat Features Illustrate Rise of AI. (August 3, 2018). *MobileIDWorld.* Available at *https://mobileidworld.com/new-snapchat-features-ai-excitement-908034/.*

illicit pastime to a mainstream activity because it seems safe. But there are ways in which a recipient can take screenshots without the sender being aware. For example, they can use the screen capture function or even another phone to record snaps. In fact, no matter how many safety features Snapchat may add to prevent illicit sexting, it is still not entirely safe to send intimate snaps or "sext" on Snapchat.

Snapchat has also not implemented encryption for text messages. So, if a user's device is breached, a criminal hacker can easily read any message that is being sent. So, any text-based data shared on Snapchat is not completely secure.

Anytime a user opens a Snapchat, their location is posted on the Snap Map, unless this capability is disabled. Snapchat connections can then easily track a user's location down to a specific street address. Stalkers have used the Snap Map feature on Snapchat to quickly locate where a person lives, works, what restaurants they frequent, and other personal information.

Snapchat addiction is one of the dark sides of the use of this AI-powered app. Teens, especially, are prone to becoming addicted to views or "snapstreaks." Snapstreaks can easily become a measure of how much a user cares about someone or how much others care for the user. Teens may derive their self-worth based on the number of likes, followers, or snaps they receive on the app.

Snapchat's perceived capability to have messages disappear has led to its use as a means to buy and sell drugs. In early 2021, Dr Laura Berman, a known television relationship therapist, issued a statement about the death of her young son: *"A drug dealer connected with him on Snapchat and gave him fentinyl [sic] laced Xanax and he overdosed in his room ... My heart is completely shattered and I am not sure how to keep breathing.*"[263] In response, Snapchat has *"improved the automated systems it uses to detect the sale of illegal drugs on the app, hired more people to respond to law enforcement requests for data during criminal investigations, and developed an in-app education portal called Heads Up focused on the dangers of fentanyl and counterfeit pills.*"[264]

Sexual exploitation and pedophile stalking is another way in which Snapchat has been used. Adam Scott Wandt[265] was quoted: *"We have children all over the country that are being approached [on Snapchat] by people they think are children their own age, but really they are predators, they are adults who are significantly older than them."* In light of this, Snapchat is using its AI-based technologies to assist in identifying and preventing potential predatory content.

AI and chatbots

AI-based chatbots[266] are considered conversational chatbots and use a form of ML called natural language processing to

---

[263] Abrahamson, R. (February 8, 2021). Mom warns about drug dealers on Snapchat after son, 16, dies from overdose. *The Today Show.* Available at *www.today.com/parents/dr-laura-berman-s-son-dies-bought-drugs-snapchat-t208352.*

[264] Solon, O. (October 7, 2021). Snapchat boosts efforts to root out drug dealers. *NBC News.* Available at *www.nbcnews.com/tech/social-media/snapchat-boosts-efforts-root-out-drug-dealers-n1280946.*

[265] Adam Scott Wandt is an Assistant Professor of Public Policy and Vice Chair for Technology of the Department of Public Management at John Jay College of Criminal Justice. He made this statement in a 2018 interview with Jeremy Hobson. Available at *www.wbur.org/hereandnow/2018/01/22/snapchat-child-predators.*

[266] A chatbot is an AI program designed to simulate communications with customers.

understand and respond to customers. The more the AI interacts with customers, the more efficient it becomes, and the ability to understand complex phrases and provide personalized responses increases. AI-powered chatbots differ greatly from rule-based chatbots, which are only able to respond to a series of button clicks using pre-defined options.

Companies are increasingly using AI-powered chatbots, which use both rule-based and AI technologies, to support their bottom line. These chatbots can take over many repetitive customer-service queries, thereby freeing up employees and leaving them more time for higher value-added activities. They allow customers to communicate with your company 24-hours a day through multiple channels of communication. Implemented correctly, it has been demonstrated that chatbots can help companies take customer engagement to a new level.

So, chatbots have a distinct plus for companies – they save money on personnel and time. But is it worth the level of customer frustration they generate?

Are chatbots creating happier or more frustrated customers?

Who has not had the frustrating experience of trying to contact a company only to be connected to a chatbot and wind up in a seemingly endless do-loop? Companies claim that chatbots are intended to deliver improved customer service by providing accurate responses in both text and voice formats. But frankly, there is little more frustrating for the average business customer than having to navigate a company's automated chatbot system. Chatbots are creating brand-new frustrated and angry customers every second of every day.

So, while chatbots can be a valid means of improving customer response efficiency, they can also generate a negative customer experience.

"According to a recent survey, only 22% of respondents have a positive impression of chatbots, while the overwhelming majority are dissatisfied with the service they offer ... and 60 percent of survey respondents say they don't trust chatbots to communicate their issues effectively ... In the same survey, 33% of people say that chatbots weren't helpful in answering their questions, and 15% feel they're too impersonal."[267]

Many companies are intentionally concealing their customer service phone numbers – or at least making them very challenging to find – and are increasingly relying on chatbot systems to interact on customer issues. As a result, customers lose their sense of power and ability to accomplish their objective in contacting the company.

Recently, I had a need to contact customer services at a cable and phone provider – I won't say which one – but it is a very large telecommunications and entertainment company that has a state-of-the-art customer service system with call centers across the globe, online tools and – of course, chatbots.

---

[267] Sporrer, T. (March 25, 2021). Your Chatbot Is Frustrating Your Customers: Improve the Experience with Guidance. *Customer Think*. Available at *https://customerthink.com/your-chatbot-is-frustrating-your-customers-improve-the-experience-with-guidance/*.

My services had been going well, but one day I had to contact customer services. And there the frustration began. The chatbot asked if it could help me. I replied with a detailed description of the issue, but soon realized that the chatbot simply could not deal with a detailed response.

So, I dumbed it down, but still no success. I finally asked to speak to a live customer service representative, upon which the chatbot replied that it was there to service my issue. The bot simply would not route me to live support and continued to go around in its "do-loop," offering the same choices over and over. After a while, the loss of any goodwill I had toward this company when I chose them was gone. Quite gone.

Companies that are most effective at implementing chatbots without sacrificing customer satisfaction are using a measure called "time to frustration" as a metric. This is the measure of the amount of time it takes for a user to reach peak frustration and disengage from the chatbot – and, perhaps, from the company's product or service entirely. At this point, companies will find it most beneficial to pass the customer from a chatbot to a more personal interaction with a live customer service agent.

The unforeseen effects of AI and social media

Without a doubt, social media has had a profound effect on human psychology. Users can easily spend hours scrolling through sites, trying to stay current with the latest content in an effort to avoid FOMO. AI-based applications and social media networks have recently been outed for the many clever, psychological tricks that they use to glue our attention to our device screens and feed our impulses to keep us there.

Tristan Harris, founder of the Center for Humane Technology, founded the Time Well Spent movement, which is attempting to create an awareness of what he terms *"the underhanded manipulation of our collective awareness through social media platforms and interactive tech."*

AI-powered social media hijacks our attention abilities

Social media is influencing how humans think by affecting our ability to concentrate and focus our attention.

> *"Over the past years I've had the uncomfortable sense that someone, or something, has been tinkering with my brain, remapping the neural circuitry, reprogramming the memory ... I'm not thinking the way I used to think ... Now my concentration starts to drift ... I get fidgety, lose the thread, begin looking for something else to do. I feel like I'm always dragging my wayward brain back to the text."*[268]

The unprecedented potential of these AI-driven apps and social media sites to capture our attention poses an urgent need to understand the impact that this may have on our ability to think. Educators are already seeing the detrimental effects of social media use on children's attention, with more than *"85% of teachers endorsing the statement that today's digital technologies are creating an easily distracted generation."*[269]

---

[268] Carr, N. (2020). *The Shallows: What the Internet Is Doing to Our Brains.* WW Norton & Company.

[269] Purcell K., Rainie L., Buchanan J., Friedrich L., Jacklin A., Chen C., and Zickuhr K. (November 1, 2012). How Teens Do Research in the Digital World. *Pew Research Center.* Available at *www.pewresearch.org/internet/2012/11/01/how-teens-do-research-in-the-digital-world/*.

AI-powered social media gets us hooked

The basic model of AI-supported social media is to get and keep people hooked, much like a drug dealer. The main question becomes "How do I keep users engaged with our site every single day"? Social media sites measure daily active users as their primary metric, just like a drug dealer might count how many people they are able to get hooked.

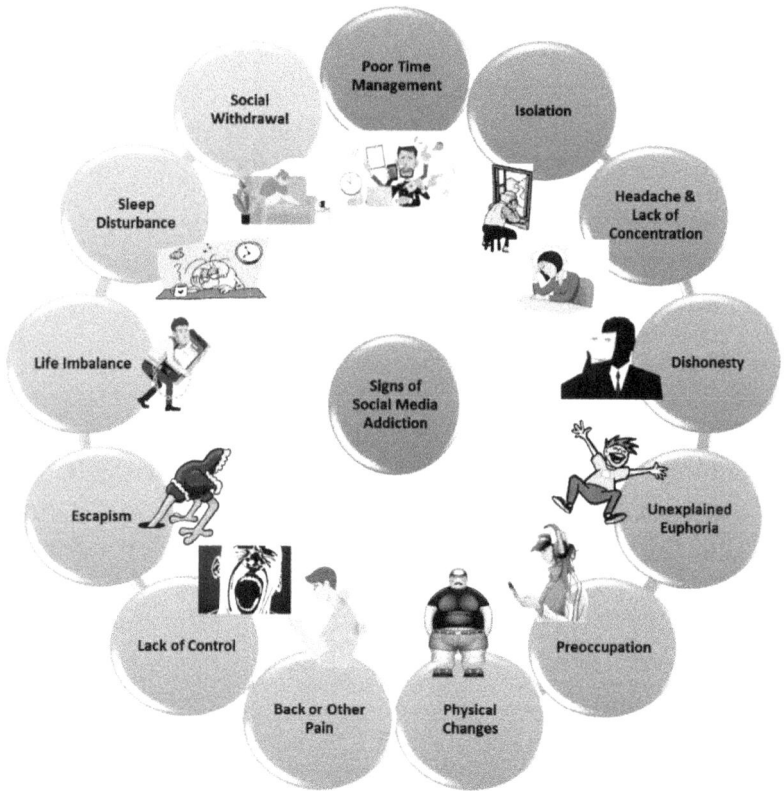

Figure 10-3: Signs of social media addiction

Because of effects on the human brain, social media can be both physically and psychologically addictive. A study by Harvard University revealed that participation on social networking sites lights up the same part of the brain that is also affected by taking an addictive substance. The reward area in the brain and its chemical messenger pathways become attached to the "likes" and "shares." When an individual experiences something rewarding or uses an addictive substance, the same neurons in the dopamine[270] producing areas of the brain are activated and dopamine levels rise. Therefore, the brain receives a "reward" and associates the drug or activity with positive reinforcement.

This is the same phenomenon in social media. When a user gets some form of notification, such as a like or mention, their brain receives a sudden rush of dopamine and transmits it along the reward pathways, producing a sensation of pleasure. Social media generates an almost endless number of immediate rewards in the form of attention from others for relatively little effort. The brain essentially rewires itself to crave this positive reinforcement, making users covet likes, retweets, shares, and emoticon[271] reactions.

AI-powered social media and the consumption of sensationalized content

As a result of the embedded AI-algorithms designed to deliver based on a user's activity, social media also tends to proliferate attention-grabbing, emotionally-driven and

---

[270] Dopamine is a natural chemical produced by the brain when humans feel reward or pleasure. It is released when we eat delicious food, consume drugs, exercise, or gamble, and now when we use social media.

[271] Emoticons are symbols used in social media to indicate happiness, sadness, or other emotions.

divisive content, rather than multi-faceted information that presents various viewpoints. This is often known as *clickbait.*[272]

. *"Since clickbait content privileges itself on shocking content, rather than a principled approach to presenting pressing current issues, University of Toronto Professor Ronald Deibert argues that the proliferation and the consumption of provocative content on social media is a breeding ground for individuals in positions of authority to create confusion and ignorance among the citizenry."*[273]

Figure 10-4 shows attitudes toward Facebook among US adults.[274]

---

[272] Clickbait is content whose main purpose is to attract users' attention by showing headlines that are often sensationalized or scandalous.

[273] Deibert, R. (January 2019). The Road to Digital Unfreedom: Three Painful Truths about Social Media. *Journal of Democracy, Vol.30, pgs. 25–39.* Available at *www.journalofdemocracy.org/articles/the-road-to-digital-unfreedom-three-painful-truths-about-social-media/.*

[274] The e-Marketer Facebook Flash Survey. (June 2020). *Insider Intelligence.* Available at *www.emarketer.com/chart/237688/attitudes-toward-facebook-among-us-adults-june-2020-of-respondents.*

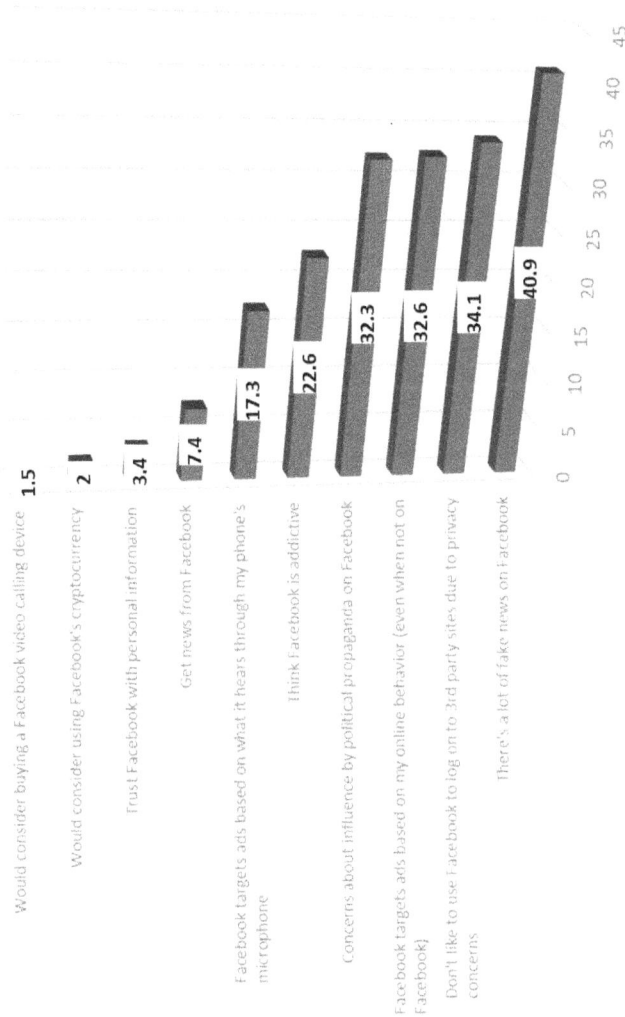

Attitudes Towards Facebook Among US Adults

- Would consider buying a Facebook video calling device: **1.5**
- Would consider using Facebook's cryptocurrency: **2**
- Trust Facebook with personal information: **3.4**
- Get news from Facebook: **7.4**
- Facebook targets ads based on what it hears through my phone's microphone: **17.3**
- Think Facebook is addictive: **22.6**
- Concerns about influence by political propaganda on Facebook: **32.3**
- Facebook targets ads based on my online behavior (even when not on Facebook): **32.6**
- Don't like to use Facebook to log on to 3rd party sites due to privacy concerns: **34.1**
- There's a lot of fake news on Facebook: **40.9**

Figure 10-4: Attitudes toward Facebook among US adults

284

CHAPTER 11: "THE MEASURE OF A MAN" – CAN AI BECOME MORE LIKE A HUMAN?

> *"The AI quest for artificial minds has transformed the mystery of consciousness into philosophy with a deadline."*
>
> **Dr Max Tegmark, MIT Professor**

In 1989, the Star Trek: The Next Generation episode "The Measure of a Man" premiered. The central question of "The Measure of a Man" is whether Data – an Android form of AI with very human-like appearance, thoughts, and abilities – can have the same rights as humans to define his own destiny. In this episode, the android Data refuses to allow his disassembly as part of research into how to create more androids of his type. Starfleet must rule on what defines the concept of self-awareness, sentience, and the right to self-determination. During a trial to determine Data's fate, the question focused on what exactly it means to be human – and the resulting answer was sentience, further defined as self-awareness, intelligence, and consciousness. When the determination is made that Data indeed possesses all of these traits, the judge rules that Data may have the same right to self-determination as humans.

This episode was well ahead of its time in terms of some of the questions that are beginning to plague us regarding the potential for AI to more closely replicate humans and human behavior, emotions, and thought process – perhaps even to the point of being aware of itself as an entity.

11: *"The Measure of a Man" – Can AI become more like a human?*

What does it mean to be "human"?

On the surface, this seems like such a simple question, but it encompasses the entire scope of the complexity, contradictions, and mystery that defines a human. It also implies a certain level of narcissism, since by the very question, we are assuming that we are more than other living creatures that surround us. But in order to answer the question of whether AI can become or be sentient, we must first define what being human actually means.

If we go back to the Star Trek episode, being "human" with the right to self-determination and moral/ethical expectations included the ideas of sentience, consciousness, intelligence, and self-awareness.

Before we proceed further into the discussion of the potential for AI to develop these very characteristics, we need to further define these terms – at least to the extent possible – since for most of them, scientists and philosophers have yet to come to a firm definition.

Let's start with **consciousness**. Some philosophers, such as Susanna Schellenberg, a professor at Rutgers University in the US claims *"anything that feels pain ... is conscious."*[275] By this definition, essentially all living creatures have some level of consciousness. A more precise definition on consciousness as a human state refers to the individual awareness of unique thoughts, memories, feelings, sensations, and environments. Essentially, consciousness reflects an awareness of oneself and the surrounding world, with this awareness subjective and unique to each individual.

---

[275] Currin, G. (July 26, 2020). What is consciousness? *LiveScience.* Available at *https://www.livescience.com/what-is-consciousness.html*.

11: "The Measure of a Man" – Can AI become more like a human?

Sentience is similar to consciousness, since it implies an awareness of the surrounding environment. Sentience, however, focuses on the more limited definition of the ability to have feelings. *"Sentient beings experience wanted emotions like happiness, joy, and gratitude, and unwanted emotions in the form of pain, suffering, and grief."*[276]

Self-awareness is a perception of a unique, personal, particularly autobiographical identity. When an individual is self-aware, that individual has an understanding of their strengths and challenges, and knows what helps them exist successfully.

"Research suggests that when we see ourselves clearly, we are more confident and more creative. We make sounder decisions, build stronger relationships, and communicate more effectively. We're less likely to lie, cheat, and steal. We are better workers who get more promotions. And we're more-effective leaders with more-satisfied employees and more-profitable companies."[277]

In psychological terms, **self-determination** refers to each individual's right and ability to make choices and manage their own life. This serves an important role in psychological well-being, as well as physical health. Self-determination allows individuals to believe that they have control over their

---

[276] Kotzmann, J. (April 8, 2020). Sentience: What It Means and Why It's Important. Sentient Media. Available at *https://sentientmedia.org/sentience-what-it-means-and-why-its-important/*.

[277] Eurich, T. (January 4, 2018). What Self-Awareness Really Is (and How to Cultivate It). *Harvard Business Review.* Available at *https://hbr.org/2018/01/what-self-awareness-really-is-and-how-to-cultivate-it*.

choices and lives. One prerequisite of self-determination is based on the theory that individuals are dynamically focused toward personal growth. This includes meeting challenges and having new experiences as essential steps for developing a cohesive sense of self. Self-determination incorporates a sense of autonomy, feelings of competence, and finally, a sense of belonging or community with other individuals.

Defining **morality and ethics** in terms of humanity is challenging, since it is questionable whether humans can come to a solid understanding that all can agree on. Humans develop moral and ethical values through exposure to family, culture, religion, and other environmental influences. This exposure over time results in the development of a set of societal and personal standards defining what is right or wrong, good or evil. Morality and ethics are based on a predisposition to evaluate human actions as either right or wrong, largely in terms of their consequences for other human beings.

Defining **human intelligence** is also a bit problematic. Many definitions apply the word "intelligence" as an element of the definition itself, which makes the definition tautological. As humans we consider ourselves as entities with the highest level of intelligence. Further, we tend to view ourselves as rational beings with the ability to solve a broad range of complex problems in various circumstances by using experience and intuition, augmented by the laws of logic, decision analysis, and statistics.

"Our intelligence is therefore relatively high compared to other animals, but in absolute terms it may be very limited in its physical computing capacity, albeit only by the

11: "The Measure of a Man" – Can AI become more like a human?

limited size of our brain and its maximal possible number of neurons and glia cells. "[278]

Considering all of the above definitions, it should be evident that being human is somewhat of an amorphous concept – much like the definitions themselves. So, how would these vague and somewhat fluid characteristics be applied in the context of AI?

Applying human characteristics to AI

Because biological, carbon-based brains (e.g. human) and digital, silicon-based processors (e.g. AI) are optimized for totally different types of tasks, humans and AI have fundamental and far-reaching differences. As a result, it may be somewhat misleading to use our own concepts of what constitutes humanity as a basis, model, or analogy for reasoning about AI. At the same time, AI is increasingly evolving to higher levels of processing and capability – so it is important for humans to understand and incorporate the possibility of a more "human" AI in the future.

Moravec's paradox[279] implies that the development of AI with human (-level) characteristics and capabilities may be challenging and the potential additional value, (i.e. abilities beyond the boundaries of human capabilities) may be relatively low. Arguably, the most valuable AI mainly involves augmenting human capabilities or overcoming

---

[278] Kahle, W. (1979). *Band 3: Nervensysteme und Sinnesorgane*, in *Taschenatlas de Anatomie. Stuttgart.* Editors W. Kahle, H. Leonhardt, and W. Platzer (New York, NY, United States: Thieme Verlag).

[279] Moravec's paradox is a phenomenon surrounding the abilities of AI where tasks humans find complex are easy to teach AI, but the skills and abilities that we learn as very young children, such as tying our shoelaces, require far more computational ability for an AI to replicate.

human constraints and limitations. In the near term, more narrow AI systems will be the major driver of AI impact on our society.

What we once defined as AI is now evolving into something else – but it is not yet "human." And herein lies the problem of defining AI – and here is where Tesler's theorem as commonly quoted applies: *"Artificial Intelligence is whatever hasn't been done yet."*[280] It was once thought that a machine that could beat a chess grandmaster embodied an AI. In 1997, an AI program called Deep Blue accomplished this against chess grandmaster Garry Kasparov. Tesler's theorem illustrates the problem with defining AI and its characteristics because it demonstrates that what is considered AI is always changing. It renders the evolution of AI an eternal goal.

---

[280] Tesler, L. Tesler's theorem and the problem of defining AI. Available at *www.thinkautomation.com/bots-and-ai/teslers-theorem-and-the-problem-of-defining-ai/*. NOTE: According to Tesler, what he actually said is "Intelligence is whatever machines haven't done yet."

11: "The Measure of a Man" – Can AI become more like a human?

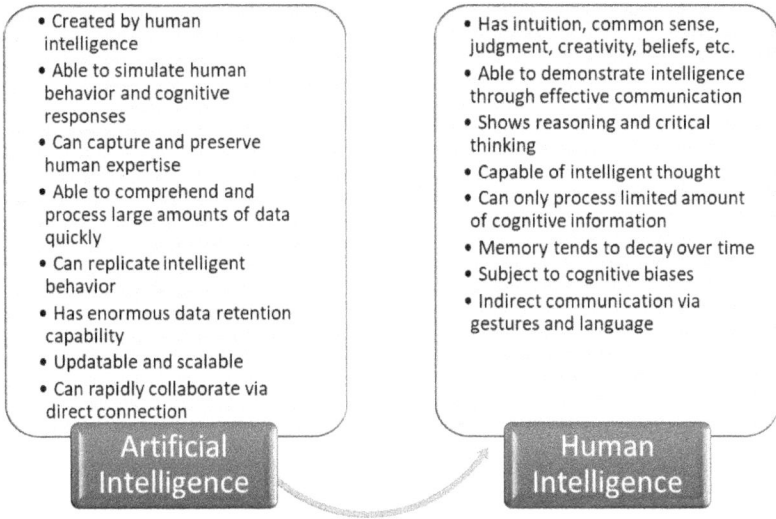

- Created by human intelligence
- Able to simulate human behavior and cognitive responses
- Can capture and preserve human expertise
- Able to comprehend and process large amounts of data quickly
- Can replicate intelligent behavior
- Has enormous data retention capability
- Updatable and scalable
- Can rapidly collaborate via direct connection

- Has intuition, common sense, judgment, creativity, beliefs, etc.
- Able to demonstrate intelligence through effective communication
- Shows reasoning and critical thinking
- Capable of intelligent thought
- Can only process limited amount of cognitive information
- Memory tends to decay over time
- Subject to cognitive biases
- Indirect communication via gestures and language

Artificial Intelligence

Human Intelligence

Figure 11-1: Comparison of human and AI

AI and consciousness or sentience

Researchers are actively working on developing an AI that could be considered sentient. Some, such as the AI-robot Sophia, have already been developed.

"Sophia did once say on CNBC that she wanted to 'destroy humans,' which had crackpot conspiracy theorists freaking out, citing the Terminator movies as a reason to be afraid. But Sophia hasn't even passed the Turing test: she has no wants or desires, much less a desire to destroy humanity. She was just responding to a tongue-in-cheek question, 'Do you want to destroy humans'? Unable to detect the sarcasm, Sophia simply

11: "The Measure of a Man" – Can AI become more like a human?

executed a line of programming that has her agree to do what someone asks. "[281]

The type of intelligence that allows an AI to respond to questions of this type does not reach the benchmark for sentience. Even today's most sophisticated AI with their artificial neural networks cannot yet replicate the complex neural networks that function in the human brain. And researchers generally agree that current AI is not conscious or sentient, despite the science fiction portrayals that might seem to suggest otherwise.

Sophia, and similar AI-robots, are examples of a broad category of social robots that display characteristics that are relatable to humans: limited decision-making and learning, human-like appearance and behavior, speech recognition and verbal communication, a certain level of facial expression, and a perceived "personality." This makes these AI-robots easy for humans to anthropomorphize; e.g. assign human characteristics to them, to the point of even developing emotional bonds.

Sentience and consciousness are often used interchangeably, but there are certain critical distinctions. Sentience refers to the ability to feel or sense things, and is often considered the path to consciousness. It's easy to think about in terms of a dog – it can feel things such as pain or sadness. But there is no temporal consciousness of itself over time. A dog can experience only the here and now.

The general agreement in philosophy is that sentience and consciousness are linked, and that sentience is the path to consciousness. In other words, any being that is conscious

---

[281] Johnson, D.K. (May 31, 2021). The Road to Developing Sentient AI and Concerns Surrounding It. *Wondrium Daily*.

must also be sentient. Antonio Damasio[282] proposes identifying two types of consciousness: core and extended. Extended consciousness is what is generally understood – an individual is self-aware, engaged, and able to discern both past and future – a capability considered to be uniquely human. Core intelligence, on the other hand, resembles an on/off switch. An entity is awake and aware of the moment, but is not self-aware and has no concept of past and future. Again, let's compare this to a dog. Is it able to sit and reflect on its actions, contemplate the future, think about the past?

Based on these distinctions, MIT Professor Ferguson contends that it is safe to say that AI today is neither truly sentient nor possessing a sense of consciousness and likely will not do so for quite a while. The case might be made that some of the more advanced AI architectures are "attentionally conscious[283]", but nothing has implemented p-consciousness[284] yet.[285]

> *"On the other end of the spectrum are 'techno-optimists,' who believe consciousness is the byproduct of intelligence, and a complex-enough AI system will inevitably be conscious. Techno-optimism pertains that*

---

[282] Antonio Damasio is the David Dornsife Chair of Neuroscience at the University of Southern California.

[283] Attention is a mechanism that selects information of current relevance, distinct from but often considered essential to consciousness.

[284] P-Consciousness refers to phenomenal consciousness or the experiential state that humans see, feel, hear, and can have pain.

[285] Ferguson, M. (September 11, 2021). A "No BS" Guide to AI and Consciousness. *Towards Data Science*. Available at *https://towardsdatascience.com/a-no-bs-guide-to-ai-and-consciousness-b2976fb7f4c5.*

11: "The Measure of a Man" – Can AI become more like a human?

the brain can be broken down into logical components, and those components can eventually be reproduced in hardware and software, giving rise to conscious, general problem-solving AI. "[286]

AI and intelligence

There is a distinct difference between consciousness and intelligence. In its simplest definition, intelligence is the ability to solve problems.

Humans have an anthropocentric view of our own intelligence – as evidenced clearly by the use of the very term "artificial" intelligence – as if there is a distinction to be made of artificial vs. "real" intelligence. Implicit in our aspiration of constructing AI with something resembling human intelligence, is the premise that human intelligence is the only "real" form of intelligence. This is implicitly stated in the term "artificial intelligence," as if it were not entirely actual, i.e. not as real as "non-artificial" or human, biological intelligence.

One predominant concept among AI scientists is that intelligence is in the end largely a matter of data and computation, and not of flesh and blood. Consequently, there would be no physical barrier from developing AI with a much larger and more advanced computing power and intelligence than the human brain. This would further imply that there is no insurmountable reason why AI one day could not even become more intelligent than humans in all possible ways.

---

[286] Dickson, B. (August 5, 2020). The complicated world of AI consciousness. *TechTalks*. Available at *https://bdtechtalks.com/2020/08/05/artificial-you-susan-schneider/*.

11: "The Measure of a Man" – Can AI become more like a human?

If the human definition includes solving complex problems, then the definition for an intelligent AI might be *"non-biological capacities to autonomously and efficiently achieve complex goals in a wide range of environments."*[287]

AI and morals/ethics

The big question here is "Can we teach morality to a machine"? And the simple answer – before we can program morality to an AI, we must first be able to define morals and ethics and do so in a way that AI can process. AI is not inherently moral or immoral – it must be taught by the programmers, statisticians, and engineers.

> *"Consider this: A car is driving down the road when a child on a bicycle suddenly swerves in front of it. Does the car swerve into an oncoming lane, hitting another car that is already there? Does the car swerve off the road and hit a tree? Does it continue forward and hit the child? Each solution comes with a problem: It could result in death. It's an unfortunate scenario, but humans face such scenarios every day, and if an autonomous car is the one in control, it needs to be able to make this choice. And that means that we need to figure out how to program morality into our computers."*[288]

---

[287] Korteling J.E., van de Boer-Visschedijk G.C., Blankendaal R.A.M., Boonekamp R.C., and Eikelboom A.R. (March 25, 2021). Human-versus Artificial Intelligence. *Frontiers in Artificial Intelligence.* 4:622364. doi: 10.3389/frai.2021.622364. Available at *www.frontiersin.org/articles/10.3389/frai.2021.622364/full#h9*.
[288] Creighton, J. (July 1, 2016). The Evolution of AI: Can Morality be Programmed? *Futurism.* Available at *https://futurism.com/the-evolution-of-ai-can-morality-be-programmed*.

11: "The Measure of a Man" – Can AI become more like a human?

As we've seen in previous chapters, there are a significant number of dystopian prophecies about the morality of AI. These forecasts of doom may still be far in the future, but there are a number of so-called narrow AI that are making ethical decisions, such as autonomous vehicles determine the value of human life in certain traffic situations, or the algorithm that assists in making hiring decisions.

Despite wrestling with the concepts of human morals/ethics for centuries, humans are still challenged to develop globally accepted standards. Many times, when confronted with moral/ethical decisions, humans tend to go with "their gut." Further, we have not yet met the challenge of converting morality into the measurable metrics that an AI can comprehend.

In order for AI to be able to develop a moral/ethical decision-making capability, AI engineers and ethics experts must first determine how to formulate morals/ethics as quantifiable properties. AI would need humans to provide explicit, programmable answers to any and all possible moral/ethical dilemmas – quite a challenging task.

One possible course that might go a long way toward identifying these situations would be to crowdsource potential ethical/moral dilemmas and associated solutions from millions of individuals worldwide. If humans fail to solve this problem, we may find ourselves in a situation where AI is making our decisions for us – and with potentially damaging results.

AI and autonomy/self-determination

Put most simply, autonomy is the right to determine for oneself, to be guided by considerations, needs, conditions, and characteristics that are not externally imposed – i.e.

being responsible, independent, and able to speak for oneself. It is a manifestation of an entity's legal and mental capacity to understand and make an informed decision.

AUTONOMY

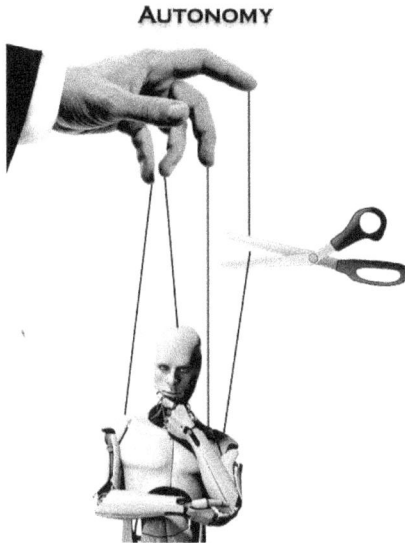

Figure 11-2: The concept of autonomy

Self-determination *"refers to a person's own ability to manage themselves, to make confident choices, and to think on their own."*[289] It is clear from these two definitions that human autonomy and self-determination, although not identical, are definitely interrelated.

There are two distinct aspects regarding AI and autonomy/self-determination. One is the right of individuals to determine how to manage interactions with the digital

---

[289] Deci, E. L. (1971). Effects of externally mediated rewards on intrinsic motivation. *Journal of Personality and Social Psychology*, 18, 105–15.

environment and AI. The other is the consideration of whether or not AI itself can possess or be granted the rights associated with autonomy and self-determination.

We'll look at autonomy and the right to self-determination from the lens of "legal personality" – the ability to be the subject of rights and obligations, and to determine one's own legal situation is generally assigned by law to human beings (natural persons). This narrow definition has been expanded *"to cover entities grouping together individuals sharing common interests, such as states and commercial entities. They are 'artificial' persons, known as 'legal persons,' created by the humans standing behind them."*[290]

It is important to note here that this discussion does not refer to so-called "autonomous robots," which are systems *"designed for use in predictable environments to complete tasks within a specific, usually pre-planned, environment."*[291] In terms of autonomy and self-determination described here, the discussion revolves around AI systems that are able to solve complex tasks that would normally require a level of human intelligence and understanding.

---

[290] Kraińska, A. (July 2, 2018). Legal personality and artificial intelligence. *newtech.law*. Available at *https://newtech.law/en/legal-personality-and-artificial-intelligence/*.

[291] Ball, M. (November 12, 2020). Artificial Intelligence vs Autonomy for Mobile Robotics. *Unmanned® Systems Technology*. Available at *www.unmannedsystemstechnology.com/2020/11/artificial-intelligence-vs-autonomy-for-mobile-robotics/*.

11: "The Measure of a Man" – Can AI become more like a human?

In this context, it is essential to differentiate between present-day AI and the potential for AGI.[292] AI/ML today are largely purpose-driven systems, with some AI/ML capable of DL artificial neural networks designed for specific tasks and simulating human cognition. The future of AI/ML is the creation of an AGI with a multi-purpose artificial brain, able to independently and autonomously execute both high and low cognitive functions simultaneously and to demonstrate reason, judgment, and emotions at a level approaching that of a human being.

The concern regarding granting AI (or AGI) legal status with the associated right to autonomy and self-determination lies in the very nature of AI/ML itself. Whereas:

"humans may be persuaded against committing an act of crime through fear or sheer calculation due to the severity of the punishment. Such punishment may include forfeiture of possessions, monetary fines, arrest, and imprisonment. But humans cannot be certain that a Strong AI would be susceptible to such notions. Without pain receptors, fear of missing out, the cultural significance of material or monetary possession, or the passage of time itself (which is heavily connected with aging and the severity of imprisonment), an AGI might not be eager to obey the law or respect the terms of an

---

[292] An AGI possesses general intelligence akin to that of an adult human being, including the capacity for self-awareness, sentience, and consciousness.

agreement on other principles than sheer philosophy and morality. "[293]

A further consideration for autonomy and self-determination is whether or not AI may today or in the future be liable for the damage it causes. Thus, it could be derived that more complexity in the AI would likely necessitate a greater need for direct human control and less tolerance of autonomy, in particular in circumstances where an AI system failure could have seriously damaging results.

At the same time, the increasing rapidity in the development of AI technology demands careful analysis of the possibility of according some form of legal status – to include the right to autonomy and self-determination – to AI at some point in the future.

But can AI be considered alive?

In purely biological terms, the definition of life is the prerequisite that distinguishes living organisms from inorganic matter. These specific criteria are the capability for reproduction, growth, response to stimuli, and continuous adaption and change until death.[294]

Considering these criteria, one can ask "Does AI reproduce"? Even at the simplest level of a single cell organism, there are a number of complex chemical processes to replicate. An AI can be programmed to replicate itself by spinning off a program, perhaps even with some variation

---

[293] Muzyka, K. (April 3, 2020). The basic rules for coexistence: The possible applicability of metalaw for human-AGI relations. *Journal of Behavioral Robotics.* Available at *www.degruyter.com/document/doi/10.1515/pjbr-2020-0011/html*.
[294] The Free Dictionary. Available at *https://www.thefreedictionary.com/life*.

that will execute then terminate at the end of its usefulness. Although this can be considered a loose form of reproduction, it is not alive.

Secondly, can AI grow? Yes, AI can be programmed to grow with every data input, but not in a physical sense. So, in a loose sense, AI does grow, but not biologically. In accordance to the definition for growth of a living entity, it means to undergo natural development by increasing in size, having physical changes, and increased maturity.

AI is fully capable of responding to stimuli – but not by nature; only if programmed to do so.

AI can decay and "die," but not in the same way as living organisms.

At the end, it is essential to be aware that the definition of life is based on carbon-based life forms. But this definition may be adjusted over time as AI/ML continues to evolve. The primary advantage for AI is precisely that it has the freedom to evolve and discover possibilities that are difficult or even impossible to delve into for natural living systems.

AI – A new species

Let's bear in mind that not all AI needs to become more "human." AI/ML and DL already encompass a vast array of capabilities, but most of them are better classified as processing or statistical systems. The argument about the creation of human-like AI concerns the future of AI and not the status today.

11: "The Measure of a Man" – Can AI become more like a human?

But, *"there's one aspect in which it's different. It is the only technology that could become a new species with which we'd have to coexist."*[295]

As researchers continue to probe the limits of AI sentience and "humanity," we may have to rethink what AI means and what the role of AI in human society is. It is very likely that we will be faced with challenging questions about what it really means to be human as AI meets or even exceeds humans in capability.

"The first significant challenge is likely to be how we treat our new equals. A common theme of sci-fi is human inability to recognize and treat with respect sentient life forms different from our own. If we do achieve human-level artificial intelligence within the next 20-30 years, what we do next will define both us as humanity and our relationship with our creation. Will we treat it with respect, as an equal, or will we treat it as a tool?"[296]

---

[295] Romero, A. (August 14, 2021). The Unavoidable Reason Why AI Should Be More Human. *Towards Data Science.* Available at https://towardsdatascience.com/the-unavoidable-reason-why-ai-should-be-more-human-50e06ae21ee0.

[296] Murray, A. (August 10, 2018). When machines become sentient, we will have to consider them an intelligent life form. *LSE Business Review.* Available at https://blogs.lse.ac.uk/businessreview/2018/08/10/when-machines-become-sentient-we-will-have-to-consider-them-an-intelligent-life-form/.

CHAPTER 12: WHAT'S NEXT IN AI – LESS ARTIFICIAL AND MORE INTELLIGENT?

> *"AI will be viewed as a necessity by more and more organizations in a post COVID-19 world, and the leading organizations are figuring out how to make it a strategic competitive advantage. In a future where AI is ubiquitous, adopters should be creative, become smarter AI consumers, and establish themselves as trustworthy guardians of customer data in order to remain relevant and stay ahead of the competition."*
>
> **Paul Silverglate**[297]

The future of AI – What comes next?

Any discussions of near-term and long-term AI developments are often unable to precisely identify what constitutes near-term and long-term. Some ambiguity is inevitable because of uncertainty about future advances in AI. For the reader of this book, it must be understood that the near- and long-term future of AI are defined relative to the state of the technology at the time of writing (2022). As time progresses, what classifies as near- and long-term will certainly shift. Near-future AI is that technology that already

---

[297] Paul Silverglate is the vice chairman, Deloitte LLP, U.S. technology sector leader.

exists to some degree or is being actively worked on with a fairly defined path to being developed and deployed.

The longer-term future of AI is concentrated on AI with at least near human general intelligence, with a focus on the development of strong AI, human-level AI (HLAI), AGI, and ASI.

Kai-Fu Lee, chairman and CEO of Sinovation Ventures, stated that:

> *"Artificial intelligence (AI) could be the most transformative technology in the history of mankind—and we may not even see much of this sweeping change coming. That's because we often overestimate what technologies can do in five years, and underestimate what they will be able to do in 20."*[298]

AI's near-future possibilities

In the near future, many researchers see humans moving from a fear of AI *"to the Age of With, wherein humans can team with machines to deliver outcomes that marry mechanized speed and precision with human intuition and curiosity."*[299] The COVID pandemic, beginning in 2020, accelerated the adoption of analytics and AI in many areas, such as vaccine development, healthcare, and business. AI and the associated analytics became critical to a diverse set

---

[298] Lee, K. (September 14, 2021). How AI Will Completely Change the Way We Live in the Next 20 Years. *Time 2030*. Available at *https://time.com/6097625/kai-fu-lee-book-ai-2041/*.

[299] The future of AI. *Deloitte*. Available at *https://www2.deloitte.com/us/en/pages/consulting/articles/the-future-of-ai.html*.

of organizations as they responded to changes in the work environment, consumer purchasing, travel, hospitality, and healthcare.

Now and in the near term, most of the challenges where we see AI as a possible solution take place in the physical world, such as turning lights on and off, autonomous vehicles, and Amazon's robotic storage shelves.

Some forecast that within a few years, nearly all data in the world will have been digitized, making it possible to use AI to ingest for decision-making and optimization. We are seeing increasing opportunities where AI can be used with human-in-the loop (HITL) systems for expanded human potential.

> *"HITL is a machine learning model that combines human and artificial intelligence to build effective ML models. AI systems are good at making optimal decisions when there is a large and high-quality data set. On the other hand, human intelligence is good at recognizing patterns within small and poor-quality datasets."*[300]

AI's longer-term future

The longer-term objective of many researchers in AI is to create general AI (AGI or strong AI). General AGI would be likely to outperform humans at nearly every cognitive task. But how long will it really take until AI greatly exceeds human-level intelligence? One common misconception is that we can know the answer with any degree of certainty.

---

[300] Gencer, G. (June 6, 2022). In-Depth Guide to Human-in-the-Loop Models 2022. Available at *https://research.aimultiple.com/human-in-the-loop/*.

Where is the vision of the future we were presented almost 50 years ago in the Jetsons?[301] The Jetsons, an animated cartoon show on TV, gave the public a peek at every possible future space age technology. The show had just about every futuristic technology our hearts could desire: jetpacks, flying cars, robot maids, and moving sidewalks.

Just a couple of years ago, Oxford University's Future of Humanity Institute published a survey about AI called "When Will AI Exceed Human Performance"? The survey analyzed the responses of approximately 350 AI/ML researchers about the future of AI.

"By 2026, a median number of respondents said, machines will be capable of writing school essays; by 2027 self-driving trucks will render drivers unnecessary; by 2031 AI will outperform humans in the retail sector; by 2049 AI could be the next Stephen King and by 2053 the next Charlie Teo. The slightly jarring capper: by 2137, all human jobs will be automated. But what of humans themselves? Sipping umbrella drinks served by droids, no doubt."[302]

AI will force us to rethink how we work and live

The longer-term future may see AI service "robots" taking over almost all household chores. AI will be able to design

---

[301] The Jetsons was an American-produced animated sitcom produced by Hanna-Barbera Productions that aired on ABC from September 23, 1962 to March 17, 1963.

[302] Thomas, M. (July 21, 2021; updated December 1). The Future of AI: How Artificial Intelligence Will Change the World. *built in.* Available at *https://builtin.com/artificial-intelligence/artificial-intelligence-future*.

buildings, even creating prefabricated modules that robots can assemble, such as Lego® bricks, thus dramatically reducing housing costs. But the real value of AI is that it can work 24/7, won't get sick, won't complain, and won't need to be paid.

AI and automation will likely replace most if not all blue-collar work, creating products or doing certain types of manual labor for minimal cost. Robots and AI will gradually assume control over the design, marketing, manufacturing, and delivery of most goods – freeing humans to engage in activities requiring more mental effort and less physical effort.

> *"Longer term, AI may be thought of as a radically different mechanism for wealth creation in which everyone should be entitled to a portion of the world's AI-produced treasures. It is not too soon for social debate on how the economic fruits of AI technologies should be shared."*[303]

AI will move us more efficiently

AVs are already somewhat commonplace and influencing the public's perception. As AVs become better at driving than people, individuals may be willing to live further from work, and spend their time on activities other than driving, leading to an entirely new urban/suburban society. Forecasters have predicted that one in ten vehicles globally will be fully automated by 2030, but as of today, there are

---

[303] Stone, P., Brooks, R., Brynjolfsson, E., et. at. (September 2016). "Artificial Intelligence and Life in 2030. One Hundred Year Study on Artificial Intelligence: Report of the 2015 Study Panel." *Stanford University*. Available at *https://ai100.stanford.edu/2016-report*.

still significant challenges to overcome, so the industry can only speculate. In reality, many pieces of a very complicated puzzle need to fall into place before AVs become the norm on our roads.

AI and humans may become increasingly linked

An even more disturbing prospect for many is the idea that the longer-term future may involve implanting chips in humans. Researchers are already experimenting using neuromuscular implants to help paraplegics regain some use of their limbs, and with the hearing and sight impaired to give them the approximate sensations of sound and sight. Humans can only begin to conjecture about the increased intensity of debate as AI evolves in the future from muscular augmentation to human cognitive augmentation.

There will come a time when AI will be waiting for us at home presenting us with an immense variety of immersive entertainment and a virtual experience that may become indistinguishable from the real world. When we combine technologies such as VR, AR and mixed reality (MR), the boundaries between real life, remote communications, games, and movies may begin to blur.

A primer for integrating ethics and safety into new AI developments

The expectation that AI will help humans confront some of their most critical challenges is exciting. But, as with any new and rapidly evolving technology, there is a steep learning curve that will inevitably result in unintentional mistakes. AI is no exception.

To address this involves understanding the potential social and ethical implications of the design and implementation of

AI systems, and integrating ethical considerations into every aspect of development. It will also require a collaborative effort between the statisticians, data engineers and scientists, product developers, domain experts, and implementers to align the AI technologies with ethical values and principles that protect and promote the welfare of the society that these new AI technologies affect. AI developers must create and implement a set of values, principles, and governance mechanisms essential for responsible innovation.

Frameworks for the integration of ethics into AI

The following framework discussion has been adapted from research at The Alan Turing Institute,[304] which has identified the following constructs to assist AI developers in ensuring the integration of ethics into their technologies.

- A framework of ethical values that *support, underwrite, and motivate (SUM)* responsible design and use. SUM values are comprised of four key concepts: *respect, connect, care, and protect.* The objectives of these SUM values are (1) to provide an accessible framework to start thinking about the moral scope of the societal and ethical impacts of an AI technology; and (2) to establish well-defined criteria to assess its ethical permissibility.
- A set of actionable principles that facilitate the responsible design and use of AI systems. These FAST Track Principles are composed of four key concepts: fairness, accountability, sustainability, and transparency. The objectives of the FAST Track

---

[304] The Alan Turing Institute is located in the British Library, London. It was established as the national institute for data science in 2015. In 2017, as a result of a government recommendation, AI was added to its area of research.

Principles are to provide the moral and practical tools (1) to make sure that an AI project is bias-mitigating, non-discriminatory, and fair, and (2) to safeguard public trust in the project's capacity to deliver safe and reliable AI.

• An ethical platform for responsible AI project delivery. The process-based governance framework (PBG framework) operationalizes the SUM values and the FAST Track Principles across the entire AI project delivery workflow.[305] Figure 12-1 is adapted from David Leslie's graphic in "Understanding artificial intelligence ethics and safety: A guide for the responsible design and implementation of AI systems in the public sector".[306]

---

[305] Leslie, D. (2019). Understanding artificial intelligence ethics and safety: A guide for the responsible design and implementation of AI systems in the public sector. *Zenodo.* https://doi.org/10.5281/zenodo.3240529.

[306] Ibid.

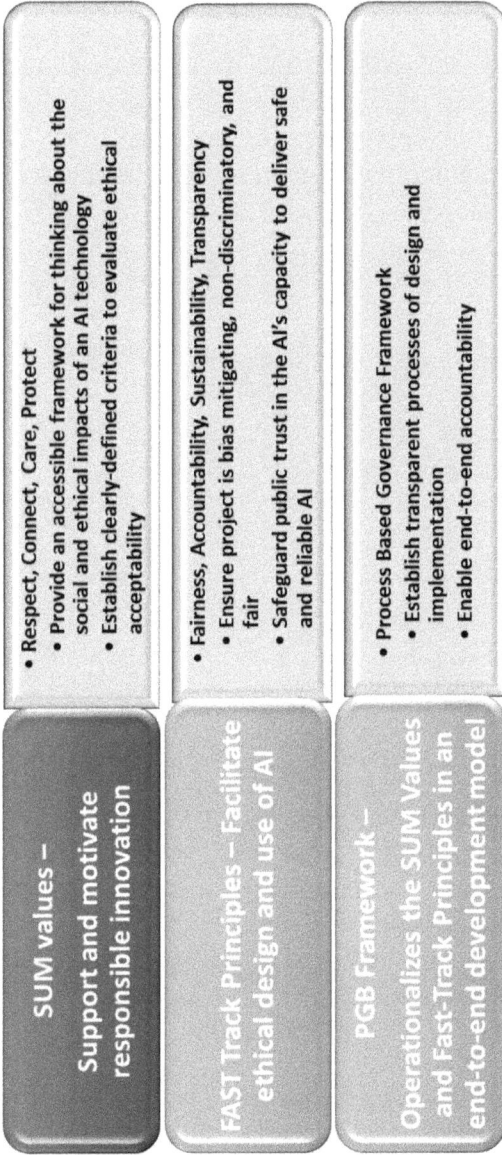

SUM values –
Support and motivate
responsible innovation

- Respect, Connect, Care, Protect
  - Provide an accessible framework for thinking about the social and ethical impacts of an AI technology
  - Establish clearly-defined criteria to evaluate ethical acceptability

FAST Track Principles – Facilitate
ethical design and use of AI

- Fairness, Accountability, Sustainability, Transparency
  - Ensure project is bias mitigating, non-discriminatory, and fair
  - Safeguard public trust in the AI's capacity to deliver safe and reliable AI

PGB Framework –
Operationalizes the SUM Values
and Fast-Track Principles in an
end-to-end development model

- Process Based Governance Framework
  - Establish transparent processes of design and implementation
  - Enable end-to-end accountability

Figure 12-1: Constructs to assist AI developers in integrating ethics into AI

The SUM values

The SUM values of respect, connect, care, and protect are intended to identify and address the specific social and ethical problems precipitated by the possible poor design, misuse, or other harmful unintended consequences of an AI. These values should guide AI developers from initiation to completion of a development project.

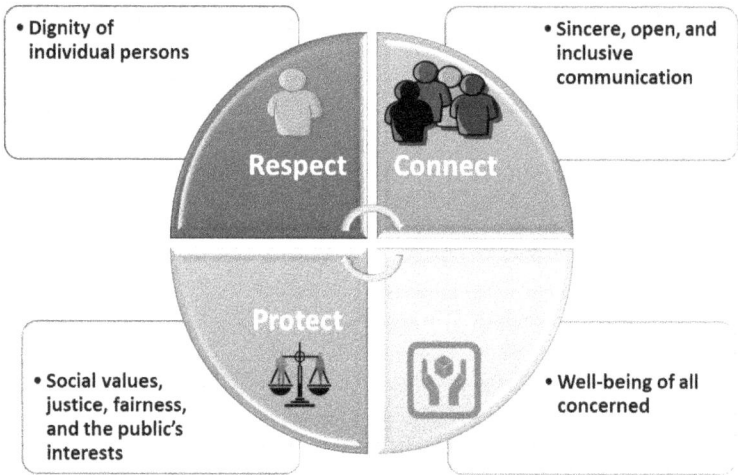

• Dignity of individual persons

• Sincere, open, and inclusive communication

Respect Connect

Protect

• Social values, justice, fairness, and the public's interests

• Well-being of all concerned

Figure 12-2: The SUM values[307]

But what do each of these values actually mean, and what are AI developers expected to do for each of these? Here's a more detailed look at each of the SUM values components as defined by Dr Leslie of the Alan Turing Institute.

---

[307] Figure 12-2 is adapted from a graphic in David Leslie's Understanding artificial intelligence ethics and safety: A guide for the responsible design and implementation of AI systems in the public sector. Zenodo. (2019). *https://doi.org/10.5281/zenodo.3240529*.

Respect for individual persons:

- Ensure each individual's ability to make free and informed decisions about their own lives.
- Safeguard the autonomy, power to express themselves, and right to be heard.
- Guarantee the ability to make well-considered and independent contributions to the life of society.
- Support the capacity to flourish, to fully develop themselves, and to pursue passions and talents according to their own freely determined life plans.

Connect with sincere, open, and inclusive communication:

- Protect the integrity of interpersonal dialogue, meaningful human connection, and social cohesion.
- Prioritize diversity, participation, and inclusion throughout the design, development, and deployment of AI.
- Ensure all voices are heard and all opinions are weighed seriously and sincerely throughout the AI life cycle.
- Use the creation and proliferation of AI to strengthen the essential interactions between human beings.
- Employ AI *pro-socially* to enable bonds of interpersonal unity to form, and individuals to be socialized and recognized by each other.
- Use AI technologies to foster the capacity to connect and to reinforce the trust, empathy, reciprocal responsibility, and mutual understanding upon which an ethically well-founded social order rests.

Care for the well-being of all individuals:

- Design and implement AI to foster and nurture the well-being of all stakeholders whose interests may be affected by their use.
- Do no harm with AI technologies and minimize the risks of their misuse or abuse.
- Prioritize the safety and the mental and physical integrity of people when looking at technological possibilities and when visualizing and deploying AI.

Protect social values, justice, and the public interest:

- Treat all individuals equally and defend social equity.
- Use digital technologies to support fair and equal treatment under the law.
- Prioritize the public interest and consider the social and ethical impacts of innovation in order to determine the validity and desirability of AI.
- Use AI to empower and to advance the interests and well-being of as many individuals as possible.
- Consider the wider impacts of the AI, the ramifications for others around the globe, for future generations, and for the biosphere as an entirety.

The FAST Track Principles

The SUM values are intended to provide a broad view of moral and ethical values applicable for an AI. The FAST principles of fairness, accountability, sustainability, and transparency are more specifically focused on the actual processes involved in designing, developing, and implementing AI.

These principles are illustrated in the following graphic.[308]

---

[308] Figure 12-3 is adapted from a graphic in David Leslie's Understanding artificial intelligence ethics and safety: A guide for the responsible design and implementation of AI systems in the public sector. Zenodo. (2019). *https://doi.org/10.5281/zenodo.3240529*.

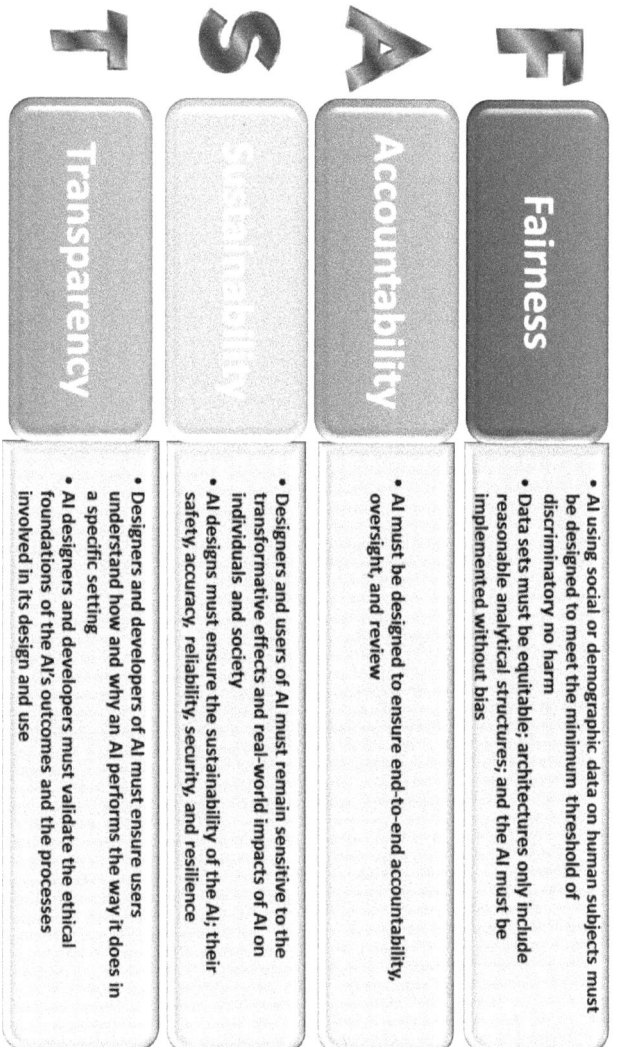

Figure 12-3: The FAST Principles

Fairness

- AI using social or demographic data on human subjects must be designed to meet the minimum threshold of discriminatory no harm
- Data sets must be equitable; architectures only include reasonable analytical structures; and the AI must be implemented without bias

Accountability

- AI must be designed to ensure end-to-end accountability, oversight, and review

Sustainability

- Designers and users of AI must remain sensitive to the transformative effects and real-world impacts of AI on individuals and society
- AI designs must ensure the sustainability of the AI; their safety, accuracy, reliability, security, and resilience

Transparency

- Designers and developers of AI must ensure users understand how and why an AI performs the way it does in a specific setting
- AI designers and developers must validate the ethical foundations of the AI's outcomes and the processes involved in its design and use

When looking at fairness in AI, it is important to always bear in mind that AI systems, no matter how neutral they may seem, are designed and produced by human beings, who themselves are influenced by their experiences and biases. Human error, prejudice, and mistakes can enter into the technology life cycle and result in biases that can be inserted (whether intentionally or unintentionally) from the preliminary stages of data extraction, collection, and pre-processing to the critical phases of design formulation, model building, and implementation. In order to ensure an ethical foundation, fairness must be considered in the data identification and collection, design, desired outcome, and in the final implementation of the AI. At all costs, users of AI must resist overreliance on the AI, in which case they might defer to the perceived infallibility of the system. The potential result is the degradation of the human ability to reason and the deskilling of critical thinking, thereby limiting a user's ability to execute tasks that are performed by the AI.

Humans can be held accountable for their actions. But in terms of AI, there is an accountability gap as AI systems cannot be held responsible in the same moral and ethical sense. Therefore, clear and unquestionable human accountability must be attached to decisions rendered by an AI. In order for there to be accountability, two factors must be considered:

1. **Answerability** – explanations and justifications for the algorithmically determined decisions and the processes behind them must be made by competent humans and be explainable in plain, understandable, and coherent language. The rationale for an AI decision should be based upon consistent, reasonable, and impartial motives that are understandable by non-technical persons.

2. **Auditability** – the keeping of detailed records and information that allows for the monitoring of data origin and data analysis from collection, pre-processing, and modeling to training, testing, and deploying. Auditability is based on transparent design, development, and implementation processes, which are methodically documented throughout the AI life cycle.

The concept of sustainability is based on an understanding of the potential transformative effects an AI may have on individuals or on society. It requires a clear understanding on the part of the designers and users of the real-world impacts of the AI system. There are four phases to integrating sustainability into an AI:

1. Identifying the potentially affected stakeholders.
2. Determining the overall goals and objectives of the AI.
3. Categorizing the potential impacts on individuals: potential harm to their personal integrity, their ability to make free and independent decisions, and risks to privacy.
4. Establishing possible impacts on the society and interpersonal relationships: effects on fair and equal treatment under the law, deterioration of social cohesion, disparate socio-economic impacts, inclusion of diversity without bias.

Related to sustainability is the requirement to ensure safety, for example, ensuring that the AI is safe, accurate, reliable, secure, and robust. This requires designers to create a system that accurately and reliably functions to meet the specifications even when confronted with unexpected changes, anomalies, and disturbances. The safety of an AI is directly reliant on accuracy in establishing performance metrics, reliability to ensure the AI behaves exactly as designed, security of the system against a potential adversarial attack, and robustness or the ability to continue to function under harsh or challenging conditions.

The final concept in FAST is transparency, which has the following interpretations in terms of AI: the ability to know how and why an AI functioned the way it did within a specific context, and to understand the rationale behind its decision, outcome, or behavior; and proof that the development and implementation of an AI and the decisions or behavior of that AI are ethically allowable, non-discriminatory/non-biased, and worthy of having public trust.

A solid PBG framework is an essential foundation to establishing the appropriate degree of transparency.

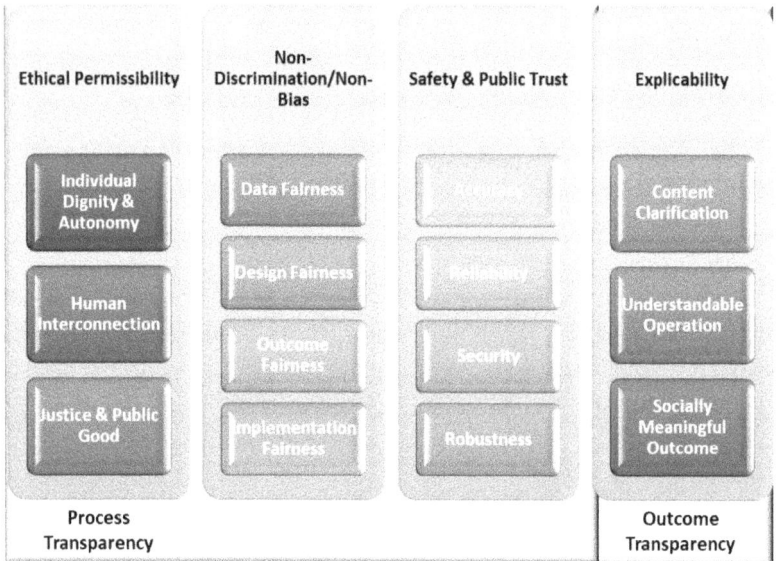

Figure 12-4: Transparency in AI[309]

Process transparency means that from start to finish in the AI development life cycle, the entire process of design and implementation should be as transparent and open to public scrutiny as possible. Any restrictions on public access to relevant information should be limited only to that data requiring reasonable protection of confidentiality and privacy, or of content that might allow bad actors to gain unauthorized access to and/or damage the AI.

In addition to establishing process transparency, there must also be standards and protocols to ensure clear and understandable explanations of the outcomes of your AI

---

[309] Figure 12-4 is adapted from a graphic in David Leslie's Understanding artificial intelligence ethics and safety: A guide for the responsible design and implementation of AI systems in the public sector. (2019). Zenodo. *https://doi.org/10.5281/zenodo.3240529*.

system's decisions, behaviors, and problem-solving tasks. To facilitate outcome transparency, AI developers must clarify and communicate in plain, non-technical, and socially appropriate terms, just how and why an AI functioned the way it did in a specific decision-making or behavioral context.

One good starting point for comprehending the technical explanation of how interpretable AI functions is, is to understand that AI is largely composed of mathematical models that execute step-by-step computations by analyzing sets of statistically interacting or independent inputs into target outputs. ML in AI is, at its most basic, simply applied statistics and probability theory. The analytical process required to simplify the functions of an AI are far beyond the scope of this text. If the reader desires to venture beyond and develop a more detailed and scientific understanding of how to truly establish process and outcome transparency, please refer to the excellent work of The Alan Turing Institute at *www.turing.ac.uk/*.

Policy and legal considerations

AI technologies are likely to challenge any number of legal preconceptions in the short, medium, and long term. Precisely how laws, regulations, and policy will adapt to near- and longer-term future developments in AI – as well as how AI will adapt to values as reflected in our cultures, laws, and policies depends on a variety of factors.

James Moor in his seminal work on computer ethics, discussed the concept of a "policy vacuum," where laws and policies do not keep pace with the development of technology – with potentially disastrous results. Our society is currently at the point where the developments in AI are proceeding at a rapid pace, and the governance is just not keeping up.

There are difficult decisions that must be made in the areas of privacy, security, and liability. Developing appropriate standards for AI will require a collaborative effort between the private and public sectors to craft the necessary laws and regulations.

CHAPTER 13: ETHICAL CHALLENGES OF AI 2024 AND BEYOND: THE MORAL IMPERATIVE OF NAVIGATING THIS NEW TERRAIN

In the burgeoning realm of technology, artificial intelligence (AI), and especially <u>generative AI</u>, stands out as a monumental force, poised to redefine industries. Drawing from my extensive background and expertise in AI and embedded machine learning, I can attest to the profound transformative impact this technology harbors. While the allure of generating novel content such as text, images and music is tantalizing, we must remain acutely aware of the ethical considerations at play.

Somdip Dey[310]

AI will continue to play a significant role in enterprise IT in 2024 and beyond, and the influence of generative AI will permeate many other tech trends. *"This is the first full year with generative AI (GenAI) at the heart of every strategic decision, and every other technology-driven innovation has been pushed out of the spotlight,"* said Leigh McMullen,

---

[310] Somdip Dey is the Chief Scientist of Nosh Technologies, an MIT Innovator Under 35 and a Professor of Practice (AI/ML) at Woxsen University.

distinguished vice president analyst at Gartner. *"GenAI has broken the mold and has kept building more excitement."*[311]

This arrival of new generative AI technologies, such as ChatGPT and GPT-4, has caught our attention. Recently, serious implications for digital ethics have become apparent as nations and individuals realized that AI was evolving at a much quicker pace than anticipated. And it seems much less controllable than before.

Generative AI is considered by many to be the second wave in the evolution of AI. The first wave is considered 'ranking' AI – or the ability of the AI to rank input from users of such platforms as Google, Facebook, or YouTube and then provide the users with tailored content. While this may seem benign at first, when AI ranks input based on preferences it affects the actions of politicians, journalists, or news media. And when that happens, society is being restructured by this simple act of ranking the distribution of information.

At this time, we are not yet fully aware of the full implications of this second transformative wave of AI, but it is becoming clear that there is a possibility for generative AI to rewire how we process and generate information across society.

Now there is concern that AI – and generative AI in particular – will bring about more massive change than originally anticipated and much more quickly. So, what is generative AI and why is it such a concern? According to

---

[311] Cooney, M. (October 18, 2023). Gartner's 2024 predictions: Lots of AI, changing cybersecurity roles, electricity rationing, and more. Available at *https://www.networkworld.com/article/3708755/gartners-2024-predictions-lots-of-ai-changing-cybersecurity-roles-electricity-rationing-and-more.html*.

13: Ethical challenges of AI 2024 and beyond: The moral imperative of navigating this new terrain

IBM, *"Generative AI refers to deep-learning models that can take raw data – say, all of Wikipedia or the collected works of Rembrandt – and 'learn' to generate statistically probable outputs when prompted. At a high level, generative models encode a simplified representation of their training data and draw from it to create a new work that's similar, but not identical, to the original data."*[312] Or, to put it more simply, generative AI can be used to create new content, including audio, code, images, text, simulations, and videos.

Starting at the end of 2022 and throughout 2023, ChatGPT, backed by Microsoft, has been the form of generative AI with the most buzz. ChatGPT was released by OpenAI in November 2022 and more than a million users signed up in just five days. However, there are several other variants that also deserve attention.

Generative AI that can produce high-quality art include Imagen, DALL-E, Midjourney, Adobe Firefly, and Stable Diffusion. Other forms, such as MusicLM and MusicGen, can be trained on the audio waveforms of recorded music along with text annotations to generate new musical content based purely on text descriptions such as *"create a calming violin melody backed by a distorted guitar riff."* Generative AI trained on annotated video can generate temporally coherent video clips. Examples include Gen-1 and Gen-2 by RunwayML and Make-A-Video. Other generative AI systems can be trained on sequences of amino acids or molecular representations, such as SMILES representing DNA or proteins. These systems, such as AlphaFold, are used for protein structure prediction and drug innovations. Generative AI can also power robotics. This form of AI can

---

[312] Martineau, K. (April 20, 2023). What is Generative AI? *Research at IBM.* Available at *https://research.ibm.com/blog/what-is-generative-AI.*

also be trained on the motions of a robotic system to generate new trajectories for motion planning or navigation. For example, UniPi from Google Research uses prompts like *"pick up blue bowl"* or *"wipe plate with yellow sponge"* to control movements of a robot arm.[313]

ChatGPT – the GPT stands for Generative Pretrained Transformer – is arguably one of the most well-known forms of language-model chatbots. It's free! And it has demonstrated its ability to answer almost any question it's asked. It's been used to produce computer code, write college-level essays, and create music and art. Many people who earn their living by creating written or artistic content, from artists to ad agencies to professors, are almost quaking in their boots at the prospect of becoming obsolete.

For the most part, AI developers and entrepreneurs have been left pretty much free to design, develop, and deploy new technologies. Unless they have clearly demonstrated palpable risks, the general opinion has been that a laissez-faire approach leads to more and better innovation. But recently this approach doesn't seem as well-suited to the 'hydra-headed' creature that AI, and especially generative AI, is shaping up to become.

This chapter will look at some of the challenges facing us in light of the new AI technologies, as well as some of the potential benefits. As indicated in the chapter title, the evolutions in AI-based technologies are creating a moral and ethical imperative for navigating this new digital terrain.

---

[313] Wikipedia. Generative artificial intelligence. Available at *https://en.wikipedia.org/wiki/Generative_artificial_intelligence*.

13: Ethical challenges of AI 2024 and beyond: The moral imperative of navigating this new terrain

2023 was a tipping point for AI

AI really is nothing new. It's been around since the 1950s, but 2023 certainly seemed like a tipping point – or the point at which a slow, reversible change became rapid and irreversible, often with dramatic consequences. AI is no longer the domain of academics and tech professionals. With the introduction of disruptive technologies[314] like ChatGPT, Google Gemini, and other forms of generative AI, the new advances are easily accessible to all. And therein lies the challenge.

As AI becomes ever more available and its capabilities continue to evolve at the breakneck speed we've seen since the end of 2022, so too will the effects for society as a whole. In an ideal world, government, industry, and individuals would work together to ensure that these new AI technologies are developed and implemented ethically. But we've opened Pandora's Box, so to speak, and despite mounting concern from AI thought leaders and industry heavies alike, there's likely no closing it.

Many industry insiders and experts are saying that generative AI, such as ChatGPT, is a very big deal. Microsoft's Bill Gates stated that ChatGPT is as significant as the invention of the Internet. Elon Musk, one of the co-founders of OpenAI who left the board of the company in 2018, said on X (formerly Twitter) in December 2022 that *"ChatGPT is scary good. We are not far from dangerously strong AI."*

---

[314] A disruptive technology applies to concepts or capabilities that may have a major impact on their respective industries, ultimately changing them in irreversible ways.

How do we set safeguards for AI, especially generative AI?

The rate of change in AI has raised very real concerns that we are not ready for what may be coming next. We still haven't solved many of the ethical challenges created by the first wave of transformative AI, where its ranking systems have shaped our social and political environments. There is a real risk that we may be moving toward a society where people lose the sense of what is real in a world filled with information uncertainty and they just sort of give up – or as Aviv Ovadya[315] called it, develop *"reality apathy."*

Right now, there are two competing camps in AI development: One prefers to give power to the individual to do with AI what they want, and the other is for the tech companies and developers to decide what one can/should do with these new AI capabilities.

The question becomes: How do we understand the ways these new AI technologies could affect society, and develop a process where decisions are being considered in terms of their potential near- and long-term impacts? We are challenged by the fact that our democratic methods of decision making are often slow and the advances in AI, especially generative AI, are extremely rapid and global.

So, what are some of the challenges that continue to evolve with increased use of AI systems, and generative AI in

---

[315] Aviv Ovadya is an affiliate at the Centre for the Governance of AI, the Berkman Klein Center at Harvard, and the Safra Center for Ethics's GETTING-Plurality research network. He is also a founder of the AI & Democracy Foundation. Aviv focuses primarily on ensuring that the governance of AI can keep up with the rate of AI advances.

particular? Let's start with misinformation and disinformation.

Misinformation, disinformation, and malinformation through the use of generative AI

Given the versatility of ChatGPT and other generative AI tools to create content, it is unsurprising that imposters and those that would spread mis-, dis-, and malinformation (MDM) are also looking into using ChatGPT and similar AI models to streamline and enhance the effects of their actions. We discussed misinformation and disinformation in an earlier chapter, but let's review the definitions and add one for malinformation, as defined by the Cybersecurity and Infrastructure Security Agency (CISA):

- Misinformation is false, but not created or shared with the intention of causing harm
- Disinformation is deliberately created to mislead, harm, or manipulate a person, social group, organization, or country
- Malinformation is based on fact, but used out of context to mislead, harm, or manipulate

One of the areas for MDM to occur is within the political systems, especially in situations like the US presidential elections. MDM can originate from a variety of sources across digital, social, and traditional media, and new MDM topics emerge continuously. MDM may be intentionally generated or shared by domestic sources aiming to sow division and reduce national cohesion. Foreign and domestic actors can use MDM campaigns to create anxiety, fear, and confusion within a given populace.

What are some of the tools of MDM?

MDM uses a number of tools to spread incorrect or intentionally falsified information. These include forgeries, proxy/fake websites, and deepfakes or cheapfakes.

Forgeries

Forgeries can take the form of fake letterheads, copied-and-pasted signatures, made-up social media posts, and maliciously edited emails. These forgeries are made and distributed for various malign purposes. To make them more credible, forgeries are often presented as obtained from a hack, a theft, or other interception of documents – they often claim to be 'leaked' materials from named organizations.

Forgeries are frequently combined with authentic content to lend credibility. If information appears to be groundbreaking news yet seems unlikely, always confirm with additional reputable news sites to see how they are presenting the information.

Proxy websites/clickbait

Proxy websites can be fronts for malicious actors, designed to launder their disinformation and divisive content, and use 'clickbait' content to drive website visits. Clickbait is a sensationalized headline that encourages an individual to click a link to an article, an image, or a video. Instead of presenting objective facts, clickbait headlines often appeal to your emotions and curiosity. These clickbait sites can be quickly created by generative AI in concert with high-visibility events to take advantage of the public's legitimate desire for information.

If a website seems to be questionable, always check for clues like misspellings in a URL.

Deepfakes/cheapfakes

I would imagine that almost everyone has heard about deepfakes. But do we really understand them and the potential danger they pose? Do we know the difference between 'deepfakes' and 'cheapfakes?'

A **deepfake** is a video that has been altered through some form of AI-based machine learning to *"hybridize or generate human bodies and faces,"* whereas a **cheapfake** is an audiovisual manipulation created with cheaper, more accessible software (or none at all). In fact, cheapfakes can be rendered through Photoshop, lookalikes, recontextualizing footage, speeding, or slowing.[316]

Deepfakes pose unique challenges to many sectors of society. Most pervasive is the effect on privacy, information authenticity, and cybersecurity. In terms of privacy, individuals may not be aware of – and certainly did not necessarily give consent to – the use of their image, voice, or other biometric information that can be 'scraped' from publicly accessible platforms (e.g. social media). These images are then fed to generative AI technology to create synthetic media depicting their likeness.

Malicious examples of deepfakes include mimicking a politician expressing a political stance, a manager's instructions to employees, generating a fake message to a family in distress, or distributing false and embarrassing photos or videos of individuals. Cases such as these are

---

[316] Paris, B. and Donovan, J. (2019) Deepfakes and Cheapfakes, pp. 2-3. Report by Data & Society.

increasing as deepfakes become more realistic and harder to detect. And they're easier to generate, thanks to improvements in generative AI tools and easy accessibility.

Robert Scalise, global managing partner of risk and cyber strategy at Tata Consultancy Services, assigned the malicious use of deepfakes to four different categories:

- Misinformation, disinformation, and malinformation
- Intellectual property infringement
- Defamation
- Pornography

Realizing the potential damage that could be done by deepfakes, especially in a tense political or social environment, steps are being taken to develop tools to better detect a deepfake. Some of the deepfake detectors search for telltale biometric signs within a video, such as a person's heartbeat or a voice generated by human vocal organs rather than a synthesizer.

There are several telltale signs of a deepfake, although even these are becoming increasingly difficult to detect:

- Incongruencies in the skin and parts of the body
- Shadows around the eyes
- Unusual blinking patterns
- Unusual glare on eyeglasses
- Unrealistic movements of the mouth
- Unnatural lip coloration compared to the face
- Facial hair incompatible with the face
- Unrealistic moles on the face

- Anomalies in lighting and shading[317]

As mentioned earlier, cheapfakes are a form of media that has been crudely manipulated, edited, mislabeled, or improperly contextualized to spread disinformation. The emphasis is on 'crudely,' but that doesn't mean that they can't have serious consequences. There are a number of examples where cheapfakes were used to spread disinformation. In 2020, a Chinese Foreign Ministry spokesman posted on his Twitter profile the image of an Australian soldier standing on an Australian flag and grinning maniacally as he holds a bloodied knife to a boy's throat. This image prompted many worldwide to condemn the act and call for accountability. In fact, the image was fake and looked Photoshopped when examined closely. However, it incited a major international incident and affected the relations between China and Australia. The image here has been redacted to remove any potentially distressing content.

---

[317] Lawton, G. (2023). How to prevent deepfakes in the era of generative AI. TechTarget online. Available at *https://www.techtarget.com/searchsecurity/tip/How-to-prevent-deepfakes-in-the-era-of-generative-AI*.

Figure 13-1: Cheapfake of an Australian soldier[318]

While then President Trump was in the White House, he tweeted an edited video of Nancy Pelosi repeatedly tearing up his speech during the State of the Union address. The result was serious critique of Pelosi. It's true that Pelosi tore up the pages of the speech – but only after the President was finished, and not throughout the address, as depicted in the cheapfake video. The video was widely shared on Twitter and Facebook, and Pelosi's office asked both platforms to remove the falsified video. Both Twitter (now X) and Facebook said the video did not violate their policies regarding disinformation on their platforms. This example illustrates another issue – the ongoing challenge between freedom of speech and the prevention of the intentional spread of mis- and disinformation.

---

[318] Australia demands China apologize for posting 'repugnant' fake image. (November 30, 2020). BBC Online. Available at *https://www.bbc.com/news/world-australia-55126569*.

Both the image of the Australian soldier and the video of Pelosi demonstrated characteristics of a crudely made cheapfake – poor graphic quality, jerky movements, etc. They also clearly illustrated that disinformation doesn't have to be high tech to cause serious damage.

So, is AI a threat to democracy?

As we've seen throughout this book, AI is present almost everywhere and affects society in many different ways. There are definitely ways AI technologies make our lives far easier and more convenient. But many claim that AI is also a disruptive technology and are concerned that it is emerging as a potential threat to the smooth functioning of democratic forms of government. Since democracies are based on the premise of free speech, isn't it a good thing when everyone can have a voice and a platform for their opinions on the various social media sites? Is AI a threat to democracy or does it help give people a voice?

This is not a political book, nor is democracy being promoted as the only acceptable form of government, but it's critically important to understand the impact of new technologies on what we consider the 'ideal' democratic processes.

Sir Winston Churchill[319] famously said: *"Many forms of government have been tried, and will be tried in this world of sin and woe. No one pretends that democracy is perfect or all-wise. Indeed, it has been said that democracy is the worst*

---

[319] According to Wikipedia, Sir Winston Churchill was a British statesman, soldier, and writer who twice served as Prime Minister of the UK, from 1940 to 1945 during the Second World War, and again from 1951 to 1955. Apart from two years between 1922 and 1924, he was a Member of Parliament from 1900 to 1964 and represented a total of five constituencies.

form of Government except for all those other forms that have been tried from time to time..."[320] What he likely meant is that democracy has its many faults, but all other forms of government have proved to be worse for citizens. Democracy isn't perfect – and building an efficient democracy takes a long time. For democracy to function well, citizens must be well-educated to make effective decisions. Democracy is also fragile and so can break down if citizens are uninformed, misinformed, or self-absorbed.

Despite this fragility, there are many good reasons to prefer democracy to systems in which someone else chooses what your society should look like. But doesn't this sound too good? Can democracy really be perfect? When we look at democratic processes in the real world, do we see people included on equal terms, having an equal voice? Do we see institutions that guarantee freedom of opinion, and freedom of press and speech that are basic conditions for a well-functioning democracy?

Do we see the rule of law applied equally to everyone, no matter their position in society? Do we see freedom of association applied equally to all associations no matter what they stand for? Well, in some places we do, and sometimes we do, but not everywhere and not all the time.

Open and free political discussion is key to democratic processes. In a healthy democracy, it's important that citizens take part in political discussions where different views are accepted. Today, everyone with an Internet connection and access to an online platform has the chance to express their opinions in public and to exchange views in

---

[320] Churchill said this in a speech to the House of Commons on November 11, 1947. He laid no claim to being the originator of this quote.

principle across the globe. As a result, social media can definitely work positively for democracy, but this is a double-edged sword. Social media can also have effects that are detrimental to democracy and AI can definitely play a part here.

The social media business model relies on ad revenue derived from the aggregation and monetization of personal data. Social media platforms have a vested interest in collecting as much data as possible. For that purpose, the algorithms that govern Facebook, X, and other social media platforms entice us to stay at a platform for as long as possible. The longer we stay, the more clicks we make and the more data we generate. And by addressing the brain's reward systems, the algorithms encourage us to stay.

So, let's look at some effects on democracy of this algorithmic management of big data. On the one hand, the conditions for a well-informed political debate have never been better. Access to the Internet has massively increased the number of communication channels by which political information can reach citizens. But in other ways, the conditions for informed political and societal discourse have never been worse.

The way information on the online platforms is organized using the prevalent AI algorithms is based not on information value, but in popularity based on likes. Since we tend to select information that corresponds to our viewpoints, the AI algorithm will continue to show us even more information that reinforces our views. This means that we won't see viewpoints that differ from our own. And this tendency to identify with opinions already similar to our own seems to be particularly strong when it comes to political views.

Individuals with left-wing political bias are then exposed largely (or only) to AI-determined information supporting left-wing political opinions; people with right-wing political bias are exposed to information that reinforces their right-wing political opinions. This means that people with different opinions become increasingly inflexible in their thought processes and develop potentially incompatible worldviews. Over time, an individual may never be exposed to any perspectives other than their own and – in the long run – they may not even be conscious of the fact that there are any other ways of seeing the world. They might even consider people with other ideas as crazy, prejudiced, or dangerous. The result – the AI algorithm artificially and often unintentionally contributes to increased fragmentation and polarization of society.

This is not a very good foundation for the open political discussion that's so essential for a functioning democracy. An ideal democratic discussion is sometimes described as a conversation in which all participants have equal right to express their opinions without fear of retribution and the obligation to listen openly to what the other people have to say.

AI can also be used by various entities, including the government, to manipulate available information and promote key regime messages. For example, online platforms can use AI algorithms to lead users to certain articles and keep them addicted to their online feeds. Political entities could exploit these AI algorithms to push out messages that promote their particular political ideology.

AI can also help identify key social media influencers or recognized personalities whom these entities could co-opt into spreading desired information. Using various AI technologies, the spread of automated, hyper-personalized disinformation campaigns targeted at specific individuals or groups could be easily organized.

These types of AI-driven targeted messages were spread in the 2016 American presidential election. Further, *"In 2017, it transpired that the UK company, Cambridge Analytica, had assisted the UK's 2016 Brexit Leave campaign by providing it with targeted political advertising services. These services were facilitated by access to Facebook data, in a major breach of Facebook's own policies."*[321] Although in these cases it wasn't the regimes themselves that orchestrated the spread of targeted messages, AI technology made it possible.

Generative Adversarial Networks (GAN)[322] is an AI technology that has a particularly large potential for the spread of mis- and disinformation. One network generates falsified data that the second network attempts to identify. The feedback from the second system then helps the first system to produce falsifications, or deepfakes, that are even more realistic. Since GAN can generate highly photorealistic face images and videos, and can transform audio recordings

---

[321] Zerillli, J. (March 12, 2021). AI and you: how confusion about the technology that runs our world threatens democracy. Available at *https://theconversation.com/ai-and-you-how-confusion-about-the-technology-that-runs-our-world-threatens-democracy-156820*.
[322] Generative adversarial networks consist of two neural networks, the generator and the discriminator, which compete against each other. The generator is trained to produce fake data, and the discriminator is trained to distinguish the generator's fake data from real examples. If the generator produces fake data that the discriminator can easily recognize as implausible, such as an image that is clearly not a face, the generator is penalized. Over time, the generator learns to generate more plausible examples.

into another speaker's voice, they have become widely known in the creation of deepfakes. Deepfakes have been used to misrepresent well-known individuals, such as politicians, in videos that can then be disseminated via online platforms.

One of the most famous is the deepfake of former US President Barack Obama created in 2018. In this specific case, the purpose was to increase public awareness of deepfakes. But if the same technology used to create these 'sample' deepfakes is used maliciously, it could potentially result in serious damage. If it becomes impossible to tell genuine videos from deepfakes, what will that do to our perception of the world around us or our belief in our leadership?

Can AI also aid democracies?

We talked about how AI technology could potentially represent a threat to democratic ideals, but there are also ongoing initiatives with a specific aim to create AI tools to support democracy.

In the case of electronic voting, AI could help voters by making recommendations regarding the candidates. The idea is that the AI algorithm could sift through the mountains of available information and recommend candidates with ideals close to the voter's preferences.

By reducing information overload, the democratic process could be improved, or so the argument goes. Another suggestion is something its proponents call liquid democracy. Liquid democracy is a hybrid form of democracy that combines the elements of direct and representative democracy and allows citizens to have a more dynamic and flexible role in the decision-making process. In a traditional representative democracy, people vote for elected officials who make decisions on their behalf. In a direct democracy, people vote directly on specific issues or policies. Liquid democracy seeks to bridge the gap between these two approaches.

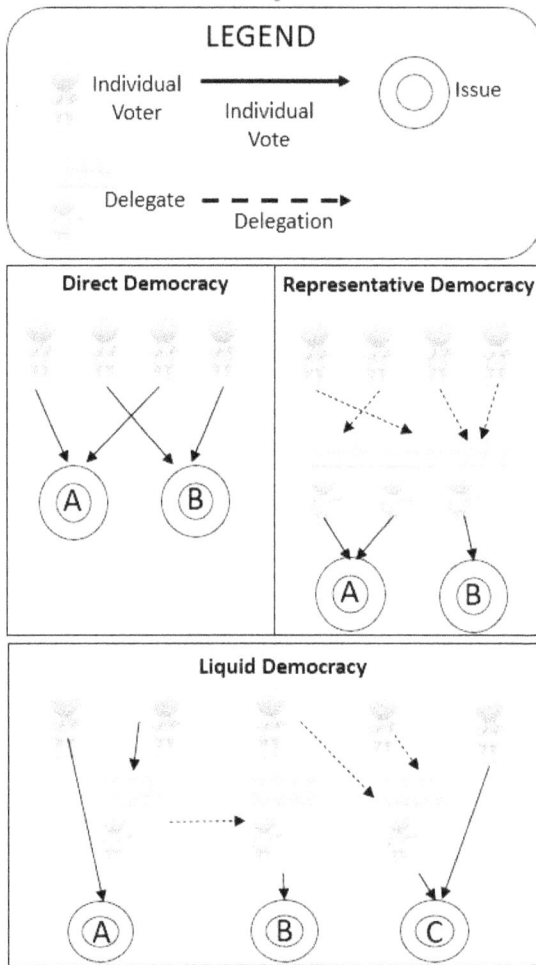

Figure 13-2: Liquid democracy[323]

---

[323] Image derived from Scheiner, D. (November 23, 2015). Liquid Democracy: True Democracy for the 21st Century. Available at *https://medium.com/organizer-sandbox/liquid-democracy-true-democracy-for-the-21st-century-7c66f5e53b6f.*

But voters often don't have time or the expertise to sift through the options. If we are expected to play a part in the democratic process, we will have to spend a lot of time considering all the options and making up our minds. Here's where AI and digital technologies can make it easier to implement liquid democracy by synthesizing the available data and provide a pathway for individuals to have more secure and efficient voting and delegation.

AI algorithms can also help people identify a delegate – someone holding similar views. It can suggest delegates who are inclined to vote the same way on issues important to each person if they had chosen to enter a vote themselves. Proponents of this AI-aided combination of direct and representative democracy, i.e. liquid democracy, claim that it offers every member of society an equal opportunity to participate in the democratic process.

Weaponization of AI

Advances in AI are taking us toward a new algorithmic battlefield that is without borders or boundaries, may or may not have human involvement, and may be impossible to understand and perhaps control. As a result, the very idea of the weaponization of AI, where a weapons system could potentially select and engage human and non-human targets without intervention by a human operator, is a growing concern. Autonomous weapons systems powered by AI could certainly make warfare more deadly and unpredictable. As a result, AI-enabled weapons raise a number of significant ethical questions.

Autonomous weapons systems

Autonomous Weapons Systems (AWS) are being developed with the goals of reducing the operating costs of the weapons system – specifically through more efficient use of manpower and a reduction in the loss of human life – and enabling weapons systems to achieve greater speed, accuracy, persistence, and precision.

Already today, AWS are being used to identify potential enemy targets and independently choose to attack those targets using AI algorithms. They use various types of sensors to evaluate the environment, training of the AI to classify objects discovered by the sensors, and algorithms that give the fully autonomous systems 'permission' to initiate attack when an allowable target is detected.

The key ethical objection against AWS is the fact that, whatever their level of autonomy, they all fail the principle of discrimination in the sense that one cannot ensure that they will not harm civilians.[324]

Another concern is attribution for hostile acts, which if misleading could lead to unintentional escalation of conflicts. The Internet provides the critical communication infrastructure for AWS, yet it is not a safe place. As a result, AWS are not completely immune to cyber attacks. Non-state actors, such as terrorist groups and international criminal networks, could potentially use adversarial hacking to harness or sabotage the technology in support of their own agendas.

---

[324] Guersenzvaig A. (2018). Autonomous weapon systems: failing the principle of discrimination. IEEE Technol. Soc. Mag. 37, 55–61. 10.1109/MTS.2018.2795119.

These concerns have introduced a dilemma that cannot be resolved by ethical debate alone, but only by international collaboration resulting in universally agreed-upon legislation, and policies.

AI-enabled bioweapons

In June 2023, students from the Massachusetts Institute of Technology (MIT) and Harvard University, each with no specialized scientific or biology background, demonstrated that *"they could design a deadly new pandemic outbreak in an hour by using chatbots powered by generative artificial intelligence models."*[325]

Using GPT-4, Bing, Gemini, and FreedomGPT, the students demonstrated the ability to obtain samples and reverse-engineer potential pandemic-causing diseases, including smallpox. Their report attracted the attention of senior policymakers in the US, such as the Senate Majority Leader Chuck Schumer, who is now promoting a broad legislative agenda and regulatory approach that would encompass not only application-specific AI systems but also generative AI technologies.

Social marginalization and group polarization

AI can be 'weaponized' in other ways, such as social marginalization of specific demographics or even those that do not concur with the prevalent consensus. This is often termed 'group polarization'. AI-driven social media platforms are likely tools for both constructive cultural

---

[325] Ratnam, G. (September 12, 2023). Threats like AI-aided bioweapons confound policy-makers. Available at
https://rollcall.com/2023/09/12/threats-like-ai-aided-bioweapons-confound-policymakers/.

exchange and hostility against those perceived as 'others' as there is consistent evidence of strong links between social media platforms usage and hate crime.

Group polarization is a psychological phenomenon that can occur when people who share similar opinions and values come together. Over time, their views become increasingly more extreme as a result of 'group think.' This phenomenon can be dangerous when it leads to a villain threat,[326] which is the idea that people who hold different opinions or beliefs are seen as enemies to be subjugated rather than simply people with differing views. This type of polarization could eventually lead to conflict, violence, and the breakdown of civil society.

This group polarization is making it even dangerous to belong to a group classified as divergent from the prevailing social norm in a time when AI technology, at the command of entities interested in spreading and maintaining their own opinions, is used to create, spread, and manage online content. AI-based online platforms contribute heavily to group polarization and social marginalization through the development of echo chambers, where people are exposed only to opinions that reinforce their own views and exclude opposing content.

Generative AI is adding a new dimension to AI-based platforms. The impact that generative AI is having on social media platforms may be subtle, but is nonetheless wide-reaching. It is already being used to create new content, such as text, videos, and images, as well as to curate existing

---

[326] A 'villain threat' occurs when an individual or a group holding divergent opinions from the prevalent social norms is considered a villain or evil.

content. While this technology has the potential to benefit social media users in some ways, it also carries certain risks and drawbacks in terms of its reinforcement of group polarization tendencies.

Bias

Bias in AI is complicated – sometimes it's obvious and other times more nuanced – and it is difficult to fully measure its tangible expression with data analysis alone. Quantifying how often certain skin tones and perceived genders appear in a generative AI query is one of the clearer signals, but there are other details within the generated content like religious accessories or types of facial hair that contribute to the overall bias that may be unintentionally encoded in generative AI outputs.

One common example of bias in generative AI is image-generation tools perpetuating outdated stereotypes. The output from Stable Diffusion, an image-generation tool from OpenAI, shows us a world where mostly white males are CEOs, women are rarely doctors or judges, and people of darker skin color are more likely to commit crime. To gauge the level of bias even further, Bloomberg conducted an analysis of more than 5,000 images created with Stable Diffusion. The study illustrated that generative AI can take racial and gender disparities to extremes – with biases even worse than those found in the real world.

The Bloomberg report stated that *"Some experts in generative AI predict that as much as 90% of content on the internet could be artificially generated with a few years. As these [generative AI] tools proliferate, the biases the reflect aren't just further perpetuating stereotypes that threaten to stall progress toward greater equality in representation – they could also result in unfair treatment.* "[327]

One of the major challenges in addressing bias in generative AI is how hard it is to detect. It's almost impossible to tell from a single output whether a system is biased overall, or exactly why and where the bias was generated. Additionally, the internal representations developed by neural networks are largely incomprehensible to humans, making it further challenging to identify bias.

Echo chambers and filter bubbles

Echo chambers and filter bubbles are another form of bias. Google is a very prominent example of how AI creates echo chambers and filter bubbles. When we search using Google, we set in motion a set of algorithms, constantly updated through machine learning.

The algorithms find web pages, pictures, videos, music, etc. that fit our search. The algorithms also decide in which order to show the links on our screens. Other algorithms decide which ads we will see. The decisions are made based not just on our current search, but also on previous searches and other data collected about us from other online platforms.

This has become a well-functioning and almost universally deployed capability, and it helps make the search results and ads more relevant for each of us. Does this mean that Google's algorithms are biased? Well, they are biased toward your preferences, right? Actually, they are primarily biased toward favoring Google's revenue. To do that,

---

[327] Nicoletti, L. and Bass, D. (2021). Humas are biased: generative AI is even worse. Bloomberg online. Available at *https://www.bloomberg.com/graphics/2023-generative-ai-bias/*.

Google provides a service that makes us come back to click the links it suggests. So, is that really a problem? Well, there are problems connected to this seemingly obvious and mostly uncontroversial bias in favor of links that cater to pre-existing preferences as it also has a tendency to conserve, reaffirm, and even amplify other existing biases among us, the users. In other words, AI-supported search engines, social media, and news platforms tend to conserve, reaffirm, and amplify human prejudices, and to hide them behind a seemingly unbiased appearance. That makes this form of bias very hard for the untrained user and even for the expert to detect.

Copyright, intellectual property, and other legal risks

In a nutshell, generative AI has an intellectual property dilemma! There are a number of issues ranging from infringement and rights of use, doubts about who/what really owns AI-generated works, questions about unlicensed content in training data, and whether users should be able to prompt generative AI tools by using name references to other copyrighted and trademarked works without the creator's permission.

In the US, the legal system is being asked to define what is a 'derivative work' under existing intellectual property laws – and since there is no existing overarching Federal law regarding the use of generative AI to create art, music, or literature, each respective jurisdiction may have very different interpretations. In most situations, the outcome of any lawsuits will likely hinge on the court's interpretation of the fair use doctrine. This doctrine allows copyrighted work to be used without the copyright owner's permission *"...provided the use is fair and reasonable, does not substantially impair the value of the materials, and does not curtail the profits reasonably expected by the owner"*[328] or for a transformative use of the copyrighted material in a manner for which it was not intended.

And there are quite a few pending lawsuits. *"In a case filed in late 2022, Andersen v. Stability AI et al., three artists formed a class to sue multiple generative AI platforms on the basis of the AI using their original works without license to train their AI in their styles, allowing users to generate works that may be insufficiently transformative from their existing, protected works, and, as a result, would be unauthorized derivative works. If a court finds that the AI's works are unauthorized and derivative, substantial infringement penalties can apply."*[329]

The challenges to copyright and intellectual property law have caused the U.S. Copyright Office to become engaged. In early 2023, the office introduced an initiative to examine copyright law in light of the issues raised by generative AI technologies, including the application of copyright law in works generated using AI tools and the use of copyrighted materials in AI training.

Human artists traditionally extract indirectly from prior artistic content that educates and inspires them to create new works of art, music, or literature. By contrast, generative AI relies on training data to produce outputs. This training data consists of countless prior artworks, many of which are

---

[328] Merriam-Webster Dictionary Online. Available at *https://www.merriam-webster.com/dictionary/fair%20use*.

[329] Appel, G. et al. (April 7, 2023) Generative AI Has an Intellectual Property Problem. Harvard Business Review online. Available at *https://hbr.org/2023/04/generative-ai-has-an-intellectual-property-problem*.

protected by copyright law and which have often been collected without artists' knowledge or consent. The very use of the training data might violate copyright law even before the AI generates a new work.

But it's not only about copyright and law. It also encompasses the humanity involved in the creative process.

In September 2022, an AI-generated work of art won the Colorado State Fair's art competition. The artist, Jason Allen, had used Midjourney – a generative AI system trained on art gathered from the Internet – to create the piece. In this case, the content was not fully created by the AI. Allen went through more than 900 iterations and 80 hours of various AI-generated versions to refine his submission.

Figure 13-3: Jason Allen's winning AI-generated artwork[330]

---

[330] Théâtre D'opéra Spatial by Jason Allen. Posted on Discord by the artist Jason Allen.

Yet his use of AI to win the art competition triggered a heated debate online, with one X user proclaiming, *"We're watching the death of artistry unfold right before our eyes."*[331]

In 2024 and beyond, courts in the US and internationally continue to grapple with how to define ownership and liability for AI-generated creative works. Generative AI possesses capabilities – like converting basic instructions into impressive artistic works – that make it prone to anthropomorphizing.[332] Even the term 'artificial intelligence' encourages people to think that these systems have humanlike intent or perhaps even a level of self-awareness.

This led some people to wonder whether AI systems can be 'owners.' But subsequent to substantial reviews, the U.S. Copyright Office has stated unequivocally that **only** humans can hold copyrights. The question then remains: Who can claim ownership of creative content produced by AI? Is it the artists whose content was used to train the systems? The users who type in prompts to create new artistic content? Or the developers who build the AI systems?

---

[331] Roose, K. (September 2, 2022). An A.I.-Generated Picture Won an Art Prize. Artists Aren't Happy. The New York Times online. Available at *https://www.nytimes.com/2022/09/02/technology/ai-artificial-intelligence-artists.html*.
[332] Anthropomorphizing is the noted tendency to ascribe human characteristics to non-human things. Merriam-Webster Dictionary online. Available at *https://www.merriam-webster.com/dictionary/anthropomorphic*.

13: Ethical challenges of AI 2024 and beyond: The moral imperative of navigating this new terrain

Privacy, surveillance, and social media

Social media has radically changed the way we communicate. Social media platforms give everyone a mechanism for maintaining contact with family and friends, but also for taking part in public debates and expressing our views.

But social media is also a venue for surveillance with huge implications for our privacy. Here, AI technology plays a key part. And AI systems are becoming increasingly integrated into every social media interaction. Social media has increasingly become a venue for surveillance, with huge implications for our privacy. Indeed, the business models of social media platforms are based on surveillance and monetization of consumers' personal data, information that's collected and sold to other entities with an interest in targeting individuals for advertisements, targeted messages, or for other reasons.

Is AI the death of privacy?

AI systems can track a person's online reading habits and preferences, and tailor specific messages to maximize impact. They know whether an individual reads content on the platform, how long they spend reading it, and whether they follow additional links within the content. AI then uses this input as immediate feedback on the success or failure of its attempts to influence each person. In this way, the AI system quickly learns to become more effective in its work. The more data acquired, the more is revealed about the user's habits, social relationships, tastes, thoughts, and opinions. This information is then used to create targeted advertisements or political messages very effectively. But this effectiveness comes at a cost. The openness and interactive nature of social media raises serious privacy concerns.

Let's look at the use of social media by self-help groups to illustrate this point. Members of such groups have an expectation of anonymity, understood both as privacy protection for individual members and as protection for the group itself. The very existence of many such groups is built on the trust ensured by privacy protection. But when these groups use online platforms, their privacy is easily compromised. These groups, such as Alcoholics Anonymous, go to great lengths to preserve anonymity in general. There is an anticipation that information collected via social media is anonymized.

It's a good idea to consider very carefully what is shared on social media platforms as public information, even if the platform declares that the data is anonymized. For example, when Google or other search engines or social media platforms sell and process data that's shared on their pages and services, the information may reappear and be de-anonymized when shared with third parties. One example is the chat on the platform Reddit. Trackers running in the background collect, store, analyze, and process data. Once the data is mined in this way, it can be migrated to other online platforms, be linked to other data, and then analyzed for unique identifying patterns. This is a serious threat for the self-help groups, such as Alcoholics Anonymous. Their anonymity can no longer be ensured, and members are often experiencing unwanted forms of intrusion and interference. Groups whose existence depends on the protection of private information face a privacy dilemma.

If they use the online platforms for their activity, the privacy of the group or its members could be violated. If they don't use these digital technologies, they risk being excluded from the communicative infrastructures of today's digital world.

Self-help groups that rely on anonymity may constitute a special case, but even for ordinary everyday users of social media platforms, privacy is constantly jeopardized. And yet we willingly continue to populate these social media platforms with personal information.

Privacy paradox

How can we explain this? One answer has been called 'the privacy paradox.'[333] Many of us claim to be concerned about our privacy, but still post information that reveals details about our private life.

Why do we act paradoxically in relation to privacy? One explanation is that we make an individual privacy calculus (whether intentionally or unintentionally) and make a cost/benefit analysis of gaining social capital and other resources against the risks of privacy exposure. In other words, we agree to the invasion of our privacy simply because we get something we want in return.

This particular behavior has been observed among users of the Chinese app WeChat, the most common social media platform in China. WeChat enables users to create individual accounts and personal profiles and to share texts, images, chat, and videos with friends in connections. The app also functions as a phone, a platform for e-commerce, and a gaming console, not to mention a noodle delivery service!

---

[333] The privacy paradox is a term coined by Barry Brown at HP in 2001 to describe the seemingly paradoxical behavior of online users who say they care about their privacy yet continue to use online products and services that collect, and sometimes share or sell, their personal data.

WeChat has penetrated almost every aspect of its users' daily and professional lives in China. It's an app that everybody uses for everything. It makes life much easier for its Chinese users, and in practice, it's hard for them to do anything without it. By combining a lot of useful services and making a specific social media platform essentially indispensable for most people, the Chinese government gets the people to be voluntarily monitored.

Another reason we willingly provide social media with personal information is that social media platforms are intentionally designed to keep us addicted and using the platform for as long as possible. Remember that the social media business model is built upon the surveillance and selling of personal data. The longer we stay on a social media platform and the more clicks we execute, the more personal data is generated. And the more personal data that's generated, the better the embedded AI can make predictions about user behavior. It's not surprising that social media providers want us to spend as much time as possible on their platforms.

So why should we care about privacy?

Many make the argument that no privacy problem exists if a person has nothing to hide. Of that there is no threat to privacy unless the government uncovers unlawful activity. For the law-abiding citizen, therefore, there is no threat to privacy – or so the argument goes. In a more sophisticated version of the nothing to hide argument, the privacy of the individual is balanced against the needs of national security to detect, investigate, and prevent attacks.

But the importance of the right to privacy is more complex than an individual having nothing to hide. For example, privacy is important even for people who don't do anything criminal to protect them against a mapping of political opinions, religious conviction, union membership, and much more. We may not want outside persons to know about our association membership or what books we borrow from a library. In addition, what happens if information about opinions and beliefs get into the hands of an entity that wants to do harm – whether a government or an organization?

For example, China has the fastest system of surveillance cameras in the world, and special demands are placed on Internet companies to facilitate state control and access to data. China makes use of AI-based technology to develop a social credit system that assigns citizens a comprehensive score that takes into account not only finances but also personal behavior. The social credit system also collects information on personal circles of friends, shopping habits, and remarks that people make on social media. These social credit scores can determine the results of applications for personal loans, jobs, visas, and more – a good score means better access to these items; a bad score may mean that one is precluded from credit, certain professions, etc.

So, privacy is not only about hiding bad things from the government or other organizations. It is about protecting ourselves from the potentially negative effects of any organization having too much insight into our most personal lives. Privacy intrusions have the potential to create harm by direct interference with the individual, such as regulating the kinds of decisions you can make about your life.

This wouldn't be possible without AI technology like computer vision, facial recognition, and deep learning,[334] allowing computers to learn on their own. Deep learning has revolutionized the ability to process oceans of data, and is paving the way to analyze digitized content automatically.

Research indicates that there is a psychological – and even a potential physical cost – associated with the sensation of being monitored. Psychological costs of living under a system of intrusive monitoring and coercion could easily be thought of as a nightmare scenario. Think about what it feels like when you're driving down the highway and you see a police cruiser following behind. It's not unusual to automatically feel nervous. Do you want to feel that way all the time? If you are constantly aware that your smallest move is being measured, and evaluated against the actions of millions of other people, and then used to judge you in unpredictable ways, there is a risk that you could become part of a society of quivering neurotic beings.

AI-induced loss of jobs

The advancement of AI technology, especially generative AI, has raised concerns about widespread job displacement. As AI and automation take over repetitive and labor-intensive tasks, millions of jobs could become obsolete.

But even traditionally 'white-collar' professions could be replaced by AI and bots. This could lead to higher unemployment rates, increased economic inequality, and social unrest, potentially destabilizing societies and economies.

---

[334] Deep learning is a machine-learning technique that teaches computers to do what comes naturally to humans: learn by example.

A 2023 report by Goldman Sachs stated: *"If generative AI delivers on its promised capabilities, the labor market could face significant disruption. Using data on occupational tasks in both the US and Europe, we find that roughly two-thirds of current jobs are exposed to some degree of AI automation, and that generative AI could substitute up to one-fourth of current work. Extrapolating our estimates globally suggests that generative AI could expose the equivalent of 300mn full-time jobs to automation."*[335]

The following charts have been extracted from the 2023 Goldman Sachs report. And here is the take-away – generative AI has shifted the target of automation from blue-collar to white-collar workers. The occupational categories on the charts were based on the US Occupational Employment and Wage Survey (OEWS) for the US calculations and the European International Standard Classification of Occupations (ESCO) for the EU calculations.

---

[335] Briggs, J., et al. (March 26, 2023). The Potentially Large Effects of Artificial Intelligence on Economic Growth (Briggs/Kodnani). Report by Goldman Sachs/Economic Research.

Share of Industry Affected by AI Automation: US

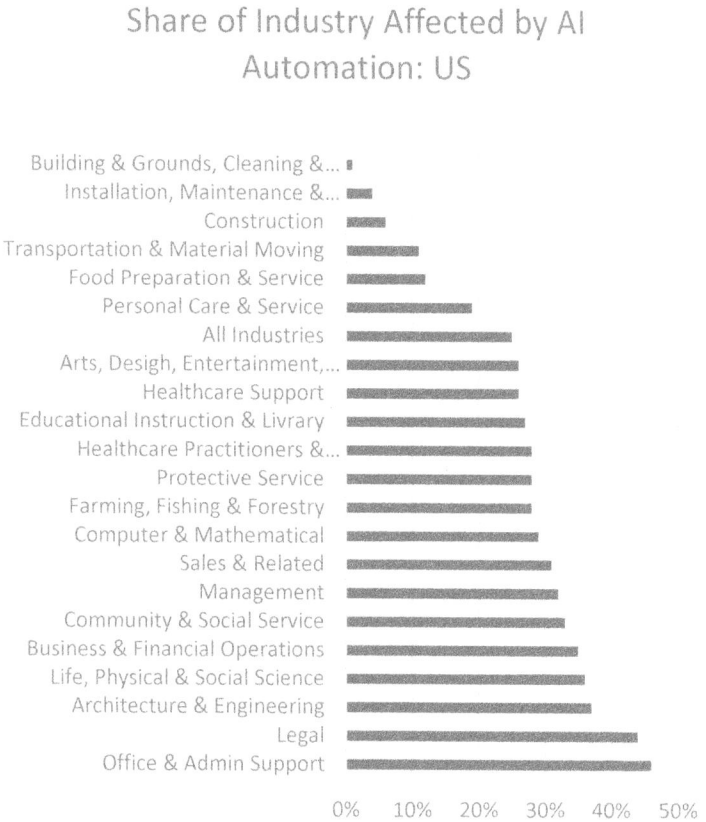

Figure 13-4: Share of industry affected by AI automation: US

Share of Industry Affected by AI Automation: EU

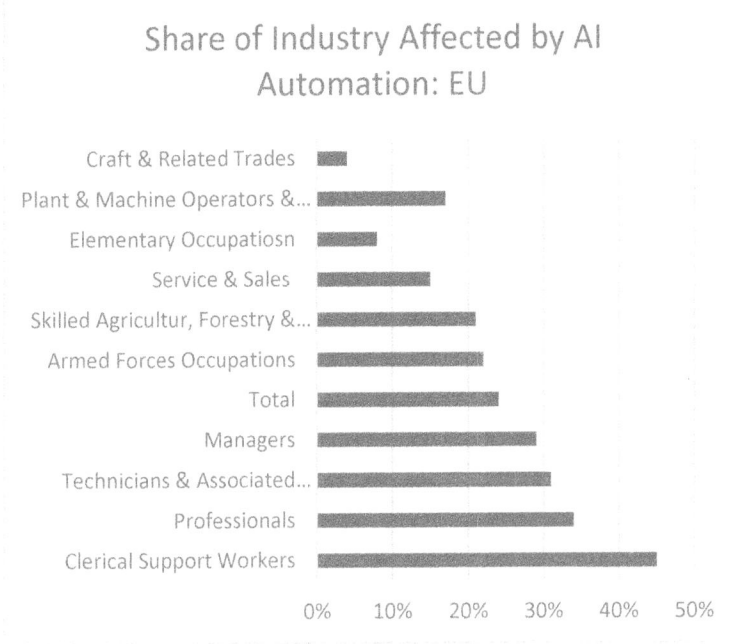

Figure 13-5: Share of industry affected by AI automation: EU

Other analyses indicate that there are several 'white collar' job categories that may be the most vulnerable to AI automation in general, and generative AI in particular. These include:

- **Digital marketers:** Digital marketers make extensive use of social media and online platforms to write blogs, create videos, and contribute to social media channels for both large corporations and mom-and-pop stores. But that type of targeted content is exactly what generative AI is extremely well qualified to create.

- **Journalists:** Certain repetitive types of journalism, such as sports and financial reporting, are already being extensively supported – and potentially replaced – by generative AI.

- **Programmers and coders:** Here is the ultimate irony! The same people often involved in the development of AI are now facing being replaced by those same systems. With AI tools like GitHub Copilot[336] or OpenAI Codex, programmers today don't have to painstakingly code line after line from scratch. They just type in a prompt and the AI algorithm generates high-quality code in multiple coding languages more rapidly and effectively than a human coder.

- **Lawyers:** Oh yes, even the elevated members of the legal profession are facing some level of job loss through generative AI. Basically, it's the time-consuming, repetitive, low-level legal work that will be automated first, so there will be less of a need for entry-level lawyers.

- **Data analysts:** Organizations are drowning in data: sales figures, demographic data, climate models, and much more. It's been the job of data analysts to sift through all that data, identify hidden trends, and make actionable recommendations. Today, a large degree of lower-level data analysis is already being taken over by AI.

- **Graphic artists and musicians:** Generative AI is replacing graphic artists who specialize in quick and easy designs, but there will always be a market for

---

[336] Copilot is available for download at *https://github.com/features/copilot/*. OpenAI Codex can be found at *https://openai.com/blog/openai-codex*.

higher-end work. DALL-E 2[337] is one of the generative AI tools that generates images much the same way that ChatGPT generates text. Type in a prompt – like 'create a business card for an interior design business called "Dreamy Dwellings"' – and DALL-E 2 will almost instantly create dozens of different business card designs. Jukebox[338] is a generative AI tool that generates music based on written prompts, even some level of rudimentary voice.

- **Radiologists and diagnosticians:** AI has proven to be truly exceptional at identifying pathologies in X-rays, MRI scans, and other medical imaging. AI won't necessarily replace radiologists, but it will likely reshape how they work. And the same applies to other medical diagnosticians.

Now, let's dispel some of the fears related to job loss by looking at historical precedent when faced with disruptive technologies. It is logical to assume that many workers initially displaced by AI automation will eventually become re-employed in new occupations that materialize either directly from AI adoption or in response to the higher level of aggregate and labor demand generated by the productivity boost from non-displaced workers.

Here are some of the job categories that may prove to be largely 'AI-proof.' Most of these will likely not come as a great surprise.

- Construction
- Skilled tradespeople such as plumbers, electricians, etc.
- Creative food preparation and serving

---

[337] DALL-E 2 is available at *https://openai.com/dall-e-2*.
[338] Jukebox is available at *https://openai.com/research/jukebox*.

- School teachers, especially in lower grades where person-to-person interaction is important
- Professional athletes and coaches
- Large-vehicle operators/drivers (although there are plans for driverless lorries and semis)
- Counseling that requires specialized therapy

That doesn't mean there won't be pain in the short term. Even if new job categories are eventually created to offset those displaced by technology, the shifts in employment can have painful near-term effects on some workers. As a result of the Industrial Revolution in seventeenth to eighteenth-century England, the average wages stagnated for several decades, even as productivity rose. But eventually, wage and job growth caught up to and even surpassed previous decades.

AI in education

With the surge of AI, and generative AI in particular, there has been considerable discussion about its potential effects on education and learning. In less than a year, ChatGPT and generative AI have moved from peripheral awareness to priority focus for many higher-education institutions across the country.

One economist even warned that generative AI could lead to the elimination of the teaching profession. Others claim that these new technologies could result in a new era in education. An innovation like this is always a double-edged sword: We can't just treat it as heralding the arrival of a new utopia.

So, while both perspectives may be a bit exaggerated, there is absolutely no doubt that AI and generative AI are going to have lasting effects on both student learning and teaching. *"AI in education is as inevitable as the internet or a search engine, which also people were skeptical about in the beginning,"* said Julia Dixon, a former tutor who created ES.AI, a generative AI tool for college applications. *"Students who never use AI and those kinds of resources that can really up-level the work that they're doing are going to be at a disadvantage."*[339]

When ChatGPT emerged in late 2022, some educators viewed it as a tool to enhance learning and reduce teacher workload, but many others saw it as a threat to integrity that opens the door to cheating and plagiarism. Schools and universities fled to the drawing board to figure out how to stop their students using ChatGPT to write their assignments. But these efforts were in vain – the popularity of ChatGPT continued rising and students flocked to take advantage.

So, I asked ChatGPT to generate a short analysis of the pros and cons of generative AI in education. This is the result:

"Generative AI, particularly in the context of education, offers both advantages and disadvantages. Here are some key pros and cons:

Pros:

Personalized Learning: *Generative AI can create personalized learning experiences tailored to individual students' needs and learning styles. This adaptability allows*

---

[339] Coggins, M. (September 22, 2023). Will AI end education as we know it? Economist predicts schools, teachers could become 'obsolete.' Available at *https://www.foxnews.com/media/will-ai-end-education-economist-predicts-schools-teachers-could-become-obsolete.*

students to progress at their own pace, enhancing comprehension and retention.

Content Creation: *AI can generate educational content, including quizzes, assessments, and even tutorials. This can significantly reduce the workload on educators, allowing them to focus more on providing personalized guidance and support to students.*

24/7 Availability: *AI-powered educational tools can provide assistance and resources round the clock. Students can access learning materials and support whenever they need it, promoting flexibility and accommodating diverse schedules.*

Feedback and Assessment: *AI systems can provide instant feedback on assignments and assessments. This immediate response allows students to identify and rectify mistakes promptly, fostering a more efficient learning process.*

Resource Optimization: *AI can help optimize resource allocation in educational institutions. From class scheduling to resource allocation, AI systems can enhance efficiency and streamline administrative tasks.*

Cons:

Loss of Human Touch: *While AI can provide valuable support, it lacks the emotional intelligence and empathy that human educators bring to the learning environment. The personal connection between students and teachers is crucial for a holistic educational experience.*

Bias in Algorithms: *If not carefully designed and monitored, AI algorithms can perpetuate and even amplify existing biases. This can result in unequal educational opportunities* *and reinforce societal prejudices, posing a significant ethical challenge.*

Overreliance on Technology: *Excessive dependence on AI may lead to students and educators relying too heavily on technology, potentially hindering the development of critical thinking and problem-solving skills that come from human interaction and hands-on learning experiences.*

Privacy Concerns: *The use of generative AI in education involves collecting and analyzing large amounts of data on students. This raises concerns about privacy, data security, and the potential misuse of sensitive information.*

Limited Creativity and Innovation: *While AI can generate content and provide solutions based on existing data, it may struggle with truly innovative and creative tasks that require a deep understanding of abstract concepts and the ability to think outside the box.*

In conclusion, the integration of generative AI in education has the potential to revolutionize the learning experience, but it also poses challenges that need careful consideration. Striking a balance between technological innovation and the human touch is essential to ensure that AI enhances, rather than replaces, the educational process."

It is evident that generative AI, in this case ChatGPT, has the ability to create well-written content. It is equally clear why students would take advantage of the rapid growth of AI and generative AI technologies. This makes the conversation about banning it increasingly irrelevant. Transformation of education will continue to accelerate as these systems train themselves, and indeed this is already happening. The question is not whether to use generative AI, such as ChatGPT, in schools, but how to do so safely, effectively, and appropriately. Educational institutions need to take the initiative and figure that out, or risk putting themselves and their students at a disadvantage.

Generative AI and academic integrity

Widespread student use increased in 2023 and inevitably raised questions about academic integrity. Educational institutions became anxious about the ability of generative AI to create essays and papers that appeared to demonstrate almost human-level quality execution against professional and academic benchmarks.

The reality is that educational institutions have historically been reluctant to adopt change. In the not-so-distant past, other technological tools were met with concern in a classroom setting. I can recall when calculators were banned from the classrooms. Today, they are recognized as an essential and useful educational tool. Generative AI is different from these innovations. It is not a device that can be banned, nor is it a tool that students can be instructed not to use, and its use cannot be identified with today's rather crude plagiarism detection tools. This new technology will be difficult to avoid. So, the question becomes: Should educational institutions be preparing students to learn in a world where generative AI is rapidly becoming ubiquitous?

Environmental impact of increased AI

AI is affecting our environment in three primary ways: carbon footprint, the requirement for rare and valuable minerals, and disposal of harmful materials.

13: Ethical challenges of AI 2024 and beyond: The moral imperative of navigating this new terrain

Carbon footprint and power use

Behind the scenes of AI's evolution exists an energy-intensive process with a staggering carbon footprint. The rapid development and deployment of AI technologies demands significant computational power and energy consumption. This need for resources could contribute to environmental degradation, including increased carbon emissions, electronic waste, and depletion of natural resources.

According to OpenAI researchers, *"...since 2012, the amount of computing power required to train cutting-edge AI models has doubled every 3.4 months. By 2040, it is expected that the emissions from the Information and Communications Technology (ICT) industry as a whole will reach 14% of the global emissions, with the majority of those emissions coming from the ICT infrastructure, particularly data centres and communication networks. These data demonstrate the urgent need to address AI's carbon footprint and role in environmental deterioration."*[340]

The supercomputers needed for cutting-edge AI systems are powered by the public electricity grid and supported by backup diesel-powered generators. Training a single AI system can emit more than 250,000 pounds of carbon dioxide. In fact, the use of AI technology across all sectors produces carbon dioxide emissions at a level comparable to the aviation industry. *"Researchers at the University of Massachusetts, Amherst, performed a life cycle assessment for training several common large AI models. They found*

---

[340] Kanungo, A. (July 18, 2023). The Green Dilemma: Can AI Fulfil Its Potential Without Harming the Environment? Available at *https://earth.org/the-green-dilemma-can-ai-fulfil-its-potential-without-harming-the-environment/*.

that the process can emit more than 626,000 pounds of carbon dioxide equivalent—nearly five times the lifetime emissions of the average American car (and that includes manufacture of the car itself)."[341]

REE mining

Rare-earth materials drive today's high-tech batteries and computer chips. Rare-earth elements (REEs) are a group of 17 metallic elements that are essential components in numerous high-tech consumer products and military applications, ranging from lasers and light bulbs to smart devices.

These 17 elements are:

Table 13-1: Rare-earth Elements Used in Computers and Technology

Element	Atomic number
Scandium (Sc)	21
Yttrium (Y)	39
Lanthanum (La)	57
Cerium (Ce)	58

---

[341] Hao, K. (June 6, 2019), Training a single AI model can emit as much carbon as five cars in their lifetimes. MIT Technology Review online. Available at *https://www.technologyreview.com/2019/06/06/239031/training-a-single-ai-model-can-emit-as-much-carbon-as-five-cars-in-their-lifetimes/*.

Praseodymium (Pr)	59
Neodymium (Nd)	60
Promethium (Pm)	61
Samarium (Sm)	62
Europium (Eu)	63
Gadolinium (Gd)	64
Terbium (Tb)	65
Dysprosium (Dy)	66
Holmium (Ho)	67
Erbium (Er)	68
Thulium (Tm)	69
Ytterbium (Yb)	70
Lutetium (Lu)	71

In addition to REEs, computing systems and smart devices also use technology metals, such as cobalt, lithium, tantalum, indium, gallium, niobium, selenium, and zirconium.

The development and deployment of AI systems requires the production of specialized hardware components, many of which rely on these rare-earth materials. Demand for these elements is projected to spike in coming years as governments, organizations, and individuals increasingly invest in AI. Some estimate that the demand for REEs could increase six-fold by 2040. And REEs are often laced with radioactive thorium and uranium, which result in especially detrimental health effects. The extraction alone of these minerals often involves environmentally damaging practices that produce mountains of toxic waste, leading to habitat destruction, pollution, and exploitation of natural resources. Overall, for every ton of rare earth, 2,000 tons of toxic waste are produced.

China currently dominates the mining of REE. This creates two areas of concern. China has used REEs as a tool to pressure other nations by blocking REE exports or limiting REE exports to the US in response to tariffs put in place by former US President Donald Trump, presenting a tremendous threat since the US defense industry relies heavily on these minerals. Even more concerning are the impacts of the mining on the surrounding communities and the workers. Toxic chemicals often spill into nearby groundwater or waterways. Worker health and safety is also not a priority, resulting in miners developing skin irritations and disruptions to their respiratory, nervous, and cardiovascular systems.

Disposal

A further concern is the environmental impact of discarding many of the components used in creating these advanced AI systems, often termed 'e-waste.' As these technologies become more and more integrated into every aspect of our lives, their life span is becoming shorter. When we purchase or deploy something new, we just dispose of the old technology. This ongoing cycle of consumption has made e-waste the world's fastest-growing solid-waste stream.

13: Ethical challenges of AI 2024 and beyond: The moral imperative of navigating this new terrain

Electronic and computing devices contain toxic heavy metals like lead, mercury, cadmium, and beryllium; polluting PVC plastic; and hazardous chemicals, such as brominated flame retardants; as well as the REEs, many of which can harm human health and the environment. *"According to the UN, in 2021 each person on the planet will produce on average 7.6 kg of e-waste, meaning that a massive 57.4 million tons will be generated worldwide. Only 17.4% of this electronic waste, containing a mixture of harmful substances and precious materials, will be recorded as being properly collected, treated and recycled."*[342] This wasteful treatment of e-waste is resulting in a significant loss of scarce and valuable raw materials needed for our electronic devices and for the systems that power AI. As a result, more and more nations are addressing the challenges of e-waste and seeking more controls regarding its disposal, as well as mechanisms to harvest the critical minerals and REEs for reuse. Some environmental groups are claiming that multibillion-dollar companies like Apple and Samsung should cover the cost of recycling the devices they sell. Lawmakers in parts of Europe and Canada and in some US states have passed Extended Producer Responsibility (EPR) laws, which require manufacturers to establish and fund systems to recycle or collect obsolete products. Time will tell if the national and international efforts to mitigate the e-waste challenges will be effective.

---

[342] The Growing Environmental Risks of E-Waste. Geneva Environment Network. Available at *https://www.genevaenvironmentnetwork.org/resources/updates/the-growing-environmental-risks-of-e-waste/*.

AI as a tool in the fight against environmental challenges

At the same time, AI can be a powerful tool in the fight against environmental challenges. AI can be used to analyze satellite imagery to monitor deforestation, assess land degradation, and track changes in vegetation cover. This information can be used to identify areas that require conservation measures and to monitor the effectiveness of reforestation and land restoration initiatives. Research indicates that climate change is causing significant disruptions in our weather patterns. As more and more extreme weather events unfold with more intensity, AI can assist communities around the world in early identification of weather threats to better prepare for climate disasters.

AI can be used to optimize supply chains to reduce waste, monitor resource and energy consumption, and promote sustainable manufacturing processes. It can help to accelerate the energy transition to clean energy by optimizing savings and improving efficiency across energy-intensive sectors.

But to maximize the benefits of AI in fighting climate change in a way that both embraces its technological promise and acknowledges its heavy energy use, the technology companies leading AI development and deployment need to explore solutions to the more negative environmental impacts of AI.

AI and changes in human relationships

Researchers are predicting that a loneliness epidemic will become a huge crisis by 2030 and will evolve into a public health issue as big as obesity today. Modern life and/or over-reliance on technology serves to isolate us from other people. Imagine a world where genuine and fulfilling love was only a matter of access to technology – relationships without the messiness and risk of rejection that come from real life. Something that took only a few hundred dollars and a functioning Internet connection to reach. Such a world is now within reach.

Advances in AI have resulted in objects, such as robots, that are able to behave and sound like humans and exude a more human feel. Millions of people around the world are now in relationships with chatbots who can text, sext, and – for a fee – talk to you on the phone and have 'in-person' interactions via augmented reality. Women and men are deciding at an alarming rate that the unexpected demands of a real-life relationship pale in comparison to the easy and instant gratification of the virtual one.

As a consequence, relationships between humans and AI-based technology have evolved, becoming more personal and complex. Perhaps as a side-effect of the COVID-19 pandemic, more and more people have become reclusive. Loneliness has grown. And if people can find an easier path to relationships, they will likely take it.

Figure 13-6: Robot and human love[343]

There is a 2012 movie called *Robot and Frank*, in which Frank is showing signs of early dementia and his son gets him a companion – a robot that can talk, do chores, and help Frank with his memory issues. Initially, Frank doesn't find the idea of a robot appealing, but over time he develops a strong bond with the machine. In 2012, this was a fictional story. Now, the idea of a personal relationship between a human and an AI-driven robot or chatbot is no longer a remote possibility. It is a reality.

Let's look at a real-world example of the app Replika. It's marketed as the "AI companion who cares"[344] – a virtual boyfriend or girlfriend that promises to engage users in any range of deeply personal conversations, including sexting and dirty talk if desired. In February 2023, the Italian Data Protection Authority in response to concerns about the app,

---

[343] Robot Love Man royalty-free image. Available at *https://www.shutterstock.com/search/robot-love-man*.
[344] Replika: The AI companion that cares. Available at *https://replika.com/*.

ordered that the app cease processing Italian users' data. As a result, the developers changed the level of interaction Replika has with its users – and some of these users expressed feelings of grief, loss, and heartbreak, not unlike the emotions felt after a break-up with a human partner.

So far, this chapter has explored some of the varying concerns associated with AI, and generative AI in particular. These concerns have moved from the sphere of academia into regular parlance. Now, legislators across the globe are looking at AI more critically and at the need for additional regulations and laws to govern the development, production, and distribution of AI-based systems.

2024 and beyond – the years of AI legislation

This book focuses on AI ethics in general, but there is a related question about whether we need new laws to govern various uses of the ever-evolving AI. New laws are being bandied around in the US and in other nations at the Federal, state, and local levels that concern the range and nature of how AI should be devised. The efforts to draft and enact such legislation have been gradual. And the field of AI ethics has served in the interim as a stopgap, at the very least, and will almost certainly be directly incorporated to some degree into any new legislation.

It's important to note that some AI advocates adamantly maintain that we have no need for new laws to address AI and that existing laws are sufficient if applied properly. They caution that if we enact legislation setting boundaries for AI, we will be killing the goose that lays the golden eggs by suppressing advances in AI that may offer immense societal advantages.

The legal issues posed by AI are a subset of the dilemma generally posed by modern technology in the digital age: Government regulation, the typical response to societal challenges, has often been limited by four considerations. These are:

- The philosophy that somehow cyberspace, in all its manifestations, has been not only above legislation but also somehow outside it. As far back as 1996, at the World Economic Forum, John Perry Barlow[345] made his "Declaration of the Independence of Cyberspace," in which he claimed that law had no sovereignty in cyberspace. In the digital environment, algorithms have become the law – traditional legal code is not.

- Any government regulation is often viewed as hostile to progress. The result has been a hands-off approach that relied on society, contracts, and the marketplace to deal with issues related to the digital environment, including AI.

- The generational divide between digital 'natives' and the older, digital non-natives – those who tend to be the legislators, which is defined by a deficiency in the expertise needed to create appropriate laws and regulations.

- Activities in the digital world, especially in politics, are often directly confronted by our deep tradition and regard for our rights to free speech.

---

[345] John Perry Barlow was a founding member of the Electronic Frontier Foundation and former lyricist for Grateful Dead.

Despite these factors, there is a 'new' realization that it is essential to address the potential effects of AI sooner rather than later. Shortly after the release of ChatGPT at the end of 2022, AI became the topic of robust policy discussions across Congress and the Biden administration, as officials rushed to educate themselves about AI while crafting legislation, rules, and policies to balance US innovation leadership with national security priorities – without stifling innovation. In a Senate Judicial Subcommittee hearing in Spring 2023, lawmakers made clear that AI regulation should not repeat the same mistakes Congress made at the dawn of the social media era. In an effort to absolve the social media industry from liability and accountability as it was evolving, Congress passed Section 230 in the early Internet days. Section 230 was part of the Communications Decency Act of 1996 and essentially stated that the Internet (and by default, social media platforms) *"cannot be treated as publishers or speakers of content provided by their users. This means that just about anything a user posts on a platform's website will not create legal liability for the platform, even if the post is defamatory, dangerous, abhorrent or otherwise unlawful. This includes encouraging terrorism, promoting dangerous medical misinformation and engaging in revenge porn. "*[346]

The Committee Chair Richard Blumenthal, D-Conn., opened the hearing with remarks that he later revealed were created by AI. Clearly, he was making a critical point with what he

---

[346] Stemmler, A. (August 2, 2021). What is Section 230? An expert on Internet law and regulation explains the legislation that paved the way for Facebook, Google, and Twitter. Available at *https://www.cityclub.org/blog/2021/08/09/what-is-section-230-an-expert-on-internet-law-and-regulation-explains-the-legislation-that-paved-the-way-for-facebook-google-and-twitter.*

called a "party trick." However, he said the party trick would not be so amusing were it used to say something harmful or untrue, like falsely endorsing Ukraine's hypothetical surrender to Russia. Blumenthal then compared the challenges offered at this moment in time by AI to an earlier one that Congress had missed. *"Congress failed to meet the moment on social media," Blumenthal said in his written remarks. "Now we have the obligation to do it on AI before the threats and the risks become real."*[347]

This congressional hearing set the stage for Senate Majority Leader Schumer to convene a bipartisan group of US Senators to take the lead in crafting AI-focused legislation. At the same time, US Senators Blumenthal (D-CT) and Hawley (R-MO) released a proposed legislative framework called the "Bipartisan Framework for US AI Act"[348] on September 8. This Act has several concrete proposals, but is still fairly light on specifics. Its main push is for the establishment of an independent oversight body that would require organizations developing and fielding *"sophisticated general-purpose A.I. models (e.g., GPT-4) or models used in high-risk situations (e.g., facial recognition)"* to register their products and services. But what that oversight body exactly entails, whether it will be new or something already in existence, was not clearly stated; nor was it clear where such a body would be within the Federal Government.

---

[347] Feiner, L. (May 16, 2023). Here's what happened during OpenAI CEO Sam Altman's first congressional hearing on artificial intelligence. Available at *https://www.cnbc.com/2023/05/16/openai-ceo-hearing-senators-aim-to-avoid-redo-of-social-media-harms.html.*
[348] The elements of this act are described in more detail at *https://iq.govwin.com/neo/marketAnalysis/view/Senate-Leaders-Introduce-AI-Regulation-Framework/7440?researchTypeId=1&researchMarket=.*

13: Ethical challenges of AI 2024 and beyond: The moral imperative of navigating this new terrain

The US House of Representatives has also made several efforts to address legislation around AI. One of these is the *"Creating Resources for Every American To Experiment with Artificial Intelligence Act of 2023"* (CREATE AI Act),[349] sponsored by Representatives Eshoo (D-CA), McCaul (R-TX), Beyer (D-VA), and Obernolte (D-CA). This particular bill seeks to establish the National Artificial Intelligence Research Resource (NAIRR) under the National Science Foundation (NSF) tasked with providing guidance for the development and use of AI.

While it may seem that US Congress is working diligently to pass major legislation covering AI at any moment, the reality is that the great majority of representatives and legislators are still trying to understand the problem. Everyone knows what they want (all the benefits of AI), and what they don't want (all the problems with AI), but they really don't have a solid plan on how to get it done. As a result, any major action to address AI still has a way to go.

While these efforts for AI legislation within the US continue, countries across the globe are developing and implementing AI governance legislation to remain commensurate with the velocity and variety of proliferating AI-powered technologies. These efforts include the development of comprehensive, generic legislation, focused legislation for specific use cases, and voluntary guidelines and standards.

As individual nations are moving ahead with their own legislative frameworks and approaches to regulate AI, they have also increased participation in joint efforts to

---

[349] For more detail on this proposed act, see
https://eshoo.house.gov/media/press-releases/ai-caucus-leaders-introduce-bipartisan-bill-expand-access-ai-research.

synchronize the approaches. The Organisation for Economic Co-operation and Development's (OECD) principles for AI have been endorsed in many different contexts, including by digital and technology representatives of the G7 countries that participated in the 2023 Hiroshima Summit. UNESCO, the International Organization for Standardization, the African Union, and the Council of Europe are all developing multilateral AI governance frameworks. The UK government is organizing the first AI Safety Summit for government and industry stakeholders to agree upon, evaluate, and monitor the most significant risks from AI. All of these activities were initiated in 2023 and will continue into 2024 and beyond.[350]

---

[350] For more information on the 2023–24 global AI legislation efforts, see
https://iapp.org/media/pdf/resource_center/global_ai_legislation_track er.pdf.

CHAPTER 14: FINAL THOUGHTS

> *"Like other technologies, AI has the potential to be used for good or nefarious purposes. A vigorous and informed debate about how to best steer AI in ways that enrich our lives and our society, while encouraging creativity in the field, is an urgent and vital need. Policies should be evaluated as to whether they democratically foster the development and equitable sharing of AI's benefits, or concentrate power and benefits in the hands of a fortunate few. And since future AI technologies and their effects cannot be foreseen with perfect clarity, policies will need to be continually re-evaluated in the context of observed societal challenges and evidence from fielded systems."*
>
> **P. Stone**[351]

There are untold how-to books on AI technology, replete with methods to improve and advance the statistics and algorithms of AI; however, the social, ethical, and security impacts are often brushed over if discussed at all. Algorithm development is only the "first mile" of implementation; the "last mile" is determining how to implement AI in ways that are beneficial to humans and the society in which they live.

---

[351] Stone, P., Brooks, R., Brynjolfsson, E., et. at. (September 2016). "Artificial Intelligence and Life in 2030. One Hundred Year Study on Artificial Intelligence: Report of the 2015 Study Panel." *Stanford University*. Available at *https://ai100.stanford.edu/2016-report*.

AI alone has no connection to reality in terms of understanding semantics and deeply felt emotions. AI has no soul. *"The simplest example I always use is that a computer works in ones and zeroes, but people do not work in ones and zeroes. When we talk about ethics with humans, things are mostly never black or white, but rather gray. As humans, we are able to make sense of that gray area, because we have developed an intuition, a moral compass in the way we grew up and were educated. As a result, we can make sense of ambiguity."*[352] For us to maximize the positive potential of AI, we must understand both its potential and its limits.

We view AI as the shiny new object, it is flashy and we are attracted to it, without always fully understanding the potential results – for both good or bad. We are in a "frenzy" about all of the potential applications for AI, such as autonomous vehicles, workplace robotics, transaction processing, health diagnostics, and entertainment. And uses for AI continue to evolve – many in fields barely being considered today.

Technology advancement has often been met initially with alarm and anxiety, but it can lead to tremendous gains for humankind as we learn to embrace the best of the changes and adapt and adjust to the worst. Increased application of AI will be no different, but the pace of technological change has increased. This rapid pace presents challenges that we will need to acknowledge and work through to avoid social marginalization and political conflict.

---

[352] deCremer, D. (May 26, 2020) Leadership by Algorithm: Who Leads and Who Follows in the AI Era? Harriman House Publishing, Hampshire, UK.

As I was adding the new content to this book, Ben Goertzel,[353] CEO of SingularityNET and a well-known expert in AI, predicted that the 'singularity' in AI may occur as soon as 2031. The singularity is the hypothetical point in time at which AI evolves into an independent superintelligent entity surpassing human capabilities.

Ray Kurzweil[354] also commented: *"Within a few decades, machine intelligence will surpass human intelligence, leading to The Singularity — technological change so rapid and profound it represents a rupture in the fabric of human history."*[355] The concern is that when the AI capabilities connect, they can collaborate and take action without human control. And they will think faster, learn faster, and react faster than humans can. The result could lead to extraordinary breakthroughs, devastating unintended consequences, or a threatening force.

If there is any single lesson I would like the readers to take away from this book, it is this. Before we plunge headlong and blindly into a world populated with AI, we humans must fully understand, plan for, and address the associated challenges. Managing the evolution of AI requires international collaboration and regulation. Leaders in the tech industry can and should collaborate with governments, researchers, and other stakeholders across the globe to

---

[353] Ben Goertzel holds a PhD from Temple University and has worked as a leader of Humanity+ and the Artificial General Intelligence Society.

[354] Ray Kurzweil, Google's Director of Engineering, is a well-known futurist with a high-hitting track record for accurate predictions. Of his 147 predictions since the 1990s, Kurzweil claims an 86 percent accuracy rate.

[355] Kurzweil, R. The Kurzweil Library + collections online. Available at https://www.thekurzweillibrary.com/in-print-nasdaq-the-law-of-accelerating-returns-is-an-important-concept.

establish the necessary legal, regulatory, and ethical frameworks and standards for AI.

FURTHER READING

IT Governance Publishing (ITGP) is the world's leading publisher for governance and compliance. Our industry-leading pocket guides, books, and training resources are written by real-world practitioners and thought leaders. They are used globally by audiences of all levels, from students to C-suite executives.

Our high-quality publications cover all IT governance, risk, and compliance frameworks, and are available in a range of formats. This ensures our customers can access the information they need in the way they need it.

Other publications you may find of interest include:

- *Cyberwar, Cyberterror, Cybercrime and Cyberactivism – An in-depth guide to the role of standards in the cybersecurity environment* by Dr Julie E. Mehan, *www.itgovernance.co.uk/shop/product/cyberwar-cyberterror-cybercrime-and-cyberactivism-second-edition*
- *Insider Threat – A Guide to Understanding, Detecting, and Defending Against the Enemy from Within* by Dr Julie E. Mehan, *www.itgovernance.co.uk/shop/product/insider-threat-a-guide-to-understanding-detecting-and-defending-against-the-enemy-from-within*
- *Combatting Cyber Terrorism – A guide to understanding the cyber threat landscape and incident*

response planning by Richard Bingley,
www.itgovernance.co.uk/shop/product/combatting-cyber-terrorism-a-guide-to-understanding-the-cyber-threat-landscape-and-incident-response-planning

For more information on ITGP and branded publishing services, and to view our full list of publications, visit *www.itgovernancepublishing.co.uk*.

To receive regular updates from ITGP, including information on new publications in your area(s) of interest, sign up for our newsletter at *www.itgovernancepublishing.co.uk/topic/newsletter*.

Branded publishing

Through our branded publishing service, you can customize ITGP publications with your organization's branding.

Find out more at *www.itgovernancepublishing.co.uk/topic/branded-publishing-services*.

Related services

ITGP is part of GRC International Group, which offers a comprehensive range of complementary products and services to help organizations meet their objectives.

For a full range of resources on cybersecurity visit *www.itgovernance.co.uk/cyber-security-solutions*.

Training services

The IT Governance training program is built on our extensive practical experience designing and implementing management systems based on ISO standards, best practice, and regulations.

Our courses help attendees develop practical skills and comply with contractual and regulatory requirements. They also support career development via recognized qualifications.

Learn more about our training courses and view the full course catalog at *www.itgovernance.co.uk/training*.

Professional services and consultancy

We are a leading global consultancy of IT governance, risk management, and compliance solutions. We advise organizations around the world on their most critical issues, and present cost-saving and risk-reducing solutions based on international best practice and frameworks.

We offer a wide range of delivery methods to suit all budgets, timescales, and preferred project approaches.

Find out how our consultancy services can help your organization at *www.itgovernance.co.uk/consulting*.

Industry news

Want to stay up to date with the latest developments and resources in the IT governance and compliance market? Subscribe to our Weekly Round-up newsletter and we will send you mobile-friendly emails with fresh news and features about your preferred areas of interest, as well as unmissable offers and free resources to help you successfully start your projects. *www.itgovernance.co.uk/security-spotlight-newsletter*.

EU for product safety is Stephen Evans, The Mill Enterprise Hub, Stagreenan, Drogheda, Co. Louth, A92 CD3D, Ireland. (servicecentre@itgovernance.eu)

www.ingramcontent.com/pod-product-compliance
Lightning Source LLC
Chambersburg PA
CBHW042309210326
41598CB00041B/7323